ET   32427

At the Grass Roots in the Garden State:
Reform and Regular Democrats in New Jersey

Vicki Granet Semel

Rutherford • Madison • Teaneck
Fairleigh Dickinson University Press
London: Associated University Presses

© 1978 by Associated University Presses, Inc.

Associated University Presses, Inc.
Cranbury, New Jersey 08512

Associated University Presses
Magdalen House
136-148 Tooley Street
London SE1 2TT, England

Library of Congress Cataloging in Publication Data

Semel, Vicki Granet.
    At the grass roots in the Garden State.

    Bibliography: p.
    Includes index.
    1. Democratic Party. New Jersey. 2. New Jersey —
Politics and government — 1951-   I. Title.
JK2318.N5   329.3'09749   75-5246
ISBN 0-8386-1737-9

To Bill

Contents

List of Tables

Preface

The reform politician has suddenly had a resurgence through the Eugene McCarthy movement of 1968 and the George McGovern campaign of 1972. The problem this study explored was how the new reformer differed from past amateurs. In attempting to characterize the modern reformer, I examined the historical roots of amateur politics. I then analyzed in detail one recent group, the New Democratic Coalition of New Jersey (N.D.C.). A survey mailed throughout New Jersey in the spring of 1970 to the N.D.C., as well as to a comparative group of regular Democratic committeemen and committeewomen, provided support for four main series of hypotheses, grouped as demographic, motivational, issue-oriented liberal, and ideological. The statistical analysis was mainly gamma correlation and multiple regression.

The demographic variation between regulars and reformers according to occupation, religion, and cosmopolitanism was confirmed with the N.D.C. clearly more cosmopolitan in orientation, more professional in occupation, and less likely to be Catholic in religious identification.

After reanalyzing certain views of volunteer incentive systems, purposive motivations were examined as initial and continuing sources of political activism. I claimed that divisible benefits were unlikely to sustain the political involvement of any activist, since patronage was both dwindling and less attractive in its available forms. Purposive motives were expected to predominate as a source of continuing activism for the N.D.C., while both insurgents and regulars were likely to claim initial purposive motives. Support for these hypotheses existed, but not with any great strength. It was when the liberal hypotheses were analyzed that the strongest distinctions appeared.

After exploring the philosophical roots of liberalism, that

11

concept was operationalized as a permissive attitude toward social change, as well as through procedural- and substantive-issue positions. Reformers were expected to be more liberal than regulars on procedural rather than substantive issues, such as government involvement in the economy or law and order. Instead, reformers were strongly liberal on procedural and all substantive issues. This finding carried into the ideological hypotheses.

Ideology was defined as constrained issue interrelationships between distinct policy areas, as well as ideological interpretations of the proper role of parties. The constrained ideology hypotheses like those on direction and intensity of liberalism were strongly confirmed, while those on ideological parties were only weakly supported.

While liberalism and demographics illustrated clear and present dichotomies between regulars and reformers, these characteristics were not reflected in role perceptions or tasks performed for the party, nor in patronage nor party positions held. Both sets of activists were involved in campaigns and were as likely to perceive their roles in electoral terms. The pragmatic liberalism of the reformer suggests a growing political wisdom visible in the trends of increasing citizen participation and the loosening of traditional party loyalties. The reformer's overwhelming liberalism — a multiple regression did not indicate that any other variable came near the strength of liberalism in predicting N.D.C. membership — now seems tied to political effectiveness, for the new insurgent manipulates his skills to secure electoral victories.

Acknowledgments

My involvement with the reform Democrat has been a long and intimate relationship. Over the many years of contact, I have learned much and become wiser in my own political activism. My work became truly a learning experience — beyond the formal and academic meaning of that term — for in studying the New Democratic Coalition and the Democratic Party, I gained a respect for both reformers and regulars alike that precipitated a continuing participation in politics. The state Democratic Party, through two executive directors — Joe Gannon and John T. Connor, Jr. — was always helpful. But it is to the New Democratic Coaliation that I owe a personal debt of gratitude. The split that developed and destroyed that group before I even began my study was one of those pathetic occurrences that continues to injure the course of reform politics.

As I spent time with the many participants in that organization, I felt a growing desire to gather the opposing forces together and "explain" them to each other. The respect I felt for them and the sadness over their misunderstandings made it difficult to remain an objective, noncommittal researcher. If this study in any way permits the various members to see their experience in a different light, then I am especially pleased to have undertaken such a project.

While many N.D.C. members spoke with me at length and do receive my sincere thanks, I owe a special debt to Daniel Gaby, chairman of the N.D.C., who gave his detailed files to me and also spent long hours trying to reconstruct the events of that period.

To thank the subjects of my study in such detail is only to underscore the academic obligations I have accrued during a rather long graduate career. To thank all the people one really should after a superb graduate education would be impossible, but I do believe that my experience at Rutgers provided me with a unique environment where faculty showed concern and willingness to give individual attention to students.

Perhaps it is more my experience with a rather unusual adviser that has made my studies at Rutgers so unique. In any case, no one ever had a more perfect blend of intellectual guidance and psychological proddings than found in Professor Gerald Pomper, Livingston College. Professor Pomper is responsible not only for this completed effort, but also for all the thought-provoking and useful ideas that this study may contribute. In fact, Professor Pomper encouraged and admonished me with somewhat the following advice of Jonathan Swift:

> Blot out, correct, insert, refine,
> Enlarge, diminish, interline;
> Be mindful, when Invention fails,
> To scratch your Head, and bite your Nails.

Other academic obligations are legion. I would like to offer a belated thank you to Professor Neil McDonald, who kindly listened to and supported me during several early stages. Let me especially single out Professor Steve Salmore, Douglass College, whose suggestion originally set me looking for the holy grail — or at least, the New Democratic Coalition. If it sometimes seemed like the former quest, I am sure his motives were pure — or should I say purposive? Steve deserves further thanks for the attempts he made to teach me what a dummy variable was and how it differed from an interval scale. Besides this statistical guidance, he undertook the mammoth task of introducing me to computers and explaining *SPSS* to a rather unskilled political scientist. As a good friend he gave more of his time than I should have permitted.

Where Steve Salmore left off, Steve Koffler of the Computer Science Center of Rutgers took over, interpreting errors and alleviating the gloom that one's 200th error message sometimes produces. Besides his kindnesses in explaining my mistakes, he provided many suggestions for possible statistical analysis.

For early suggestions on sampling and reliability of responses, I would also like to thank Professor John Blydenburgh of Eagleton Institute of Rutgers University.

Michael Rappeport and Opinion Research Corporation of Princeton did the best they could to help code and keypunch my massive data. And to the National Science Foundation, I also extend my gratitude for a year in which I could work undisturbed on this project. Interviewing people all over the state was made possible through this grant, which gave me a block of time to talk with people and then to analyze my data.

For bibliographic help, Allan Cohen saved me many tedious hours cross-checking references.

A rather distinct kind of guidance also came from Dr. John Simmons, whose subtle suggestions never permitted me to say, "I quit," without ever requiring that I continue.

Besides my academic and political obligations, there are some very special people who also deserve apologies as well as thanks. For all the hours of remoteness and isolation from my family I can only express my regrets. No one understands this more completely than my husband, Bill. He urged me to work even when the effort was likely to inconvenience him and ruin his evenings, weekends, and vacations. There is no way to thank him enough for his years of kindness and support for my endless thesis. But since he is a rather unique person, telling him this should be enough. For our girls, Debra and Robin, there has been no other life, except computer printout on the dining-room table and books piled on the kitchen counters. I can not even promise that this will change, but for their forbearance and acceptance of a disorganized life I do say thank you.

In conclusion I also have sincere apologies to two typists: Dot West, who struggled through my scribble for years; and Sandy Arslan, who made the final copy look infinitely better. A friend once described my rough drafts as "words pasted together." With such conditions in mind, Dot and Sandy deserve sympathy as well as gratitude.

I wish to thank the following publishers for permission to quote from published works:

Harvard University Press and Schocken Books, for permission to quote from Mancur Olson, Jr., *The Logic of Collective Action: Public Goods and the Theory of Groups.* © 1965 by the President and Fellows of Harvard College.

Alfred A Knopf, Inc., for permission to quote from Richard Hofstadter, *The Age of Reform: From Bryan to F.D.R.* (1955).

Oxford University Press, for permission to quote from Max

Weber, *Politics as a Vocation. Max Weber: Essays in Sociology.* Translated, edited, and with an Introduction by H. H. Gerth and C. Wright Mills.

Introduction

In the history of American politics there runs a thread — or perhaps a tangled skein — between idealistic expectations that politicians should be standards of moral rectitude, and more pragmatic evaluations of these "dissolute thieves." The reaction to the Watergate scandals of 1972 illustrates the two strands in this pattern. On the one hand an enraged public sought to "throw the rascals out," while on the other hand this same electorate assumed that "they all do it."

The two variations in expectation — one idealistic, the other cynical — can also be related to contrasting descriptions of the politician as either reformer or party professional. The reform politician has always been the model activist, eager and willing to "throw the rascals out" and find a "better class" of men to operate government. Thus the amateur epitomizes the idealistic stereotype of political participation. The party regular, however, exemplifies the more realistic idea that most people are active in politics for self-interested reasons. Rather than expecting highly ethical behavior from politicians, this view assumes that public officials are much like any other group of people: motivated by egocentric concerns.

While ideals would have one praise the reformer above the regular, his record and reputation in American politics is without distinction. In fact, it is quite the contrary, since the reformer's contribution is often viewed as the inconsequential effort of a rather unsubstantial activist. Not only is the seriousness of his involvement questioned, but the quality of his substantive effort is also denigrated.

It is this capriciousness to which the regular politician responds in most deprecating fashion, labeling the amateur a "morning glory"[1] who passes from the scene so quickly that his impact is minimal. Yet from the civil service associations at the turn of the

17

century to the McCarthy reformers of the late 1960s and the Mc-
Govern activists of 1972, these amateurs have a long, if intermit-
tent history.

While these episodes of political reform are rather diverse, there
are many characteristics that the civil service associations share
with later reform movements. Thus the newer developments, evident since the 1950s, present certain similarities with past efforts
at reform. The resurgence of amateur politicians echoes and devi-
ates from prior reform history in very distinct ways.

Perhaps the most questionable description of these most recent
reformers has become their epithet "morning glories," applied so
comfortably by that machine politician, Plunkitt, to his enemies in
the early part of this century.

For activists whose longevity ranked as one of their least outstanding traits, it seems rather amazing that a subfield of political
science could now be nourished by such alleged dilettantes.[2]
Yet this is exactly what has happened. From the club movement,
spawned by Adlai Stevenson's presidential campaigns of 1952 and
1956 to the 1972 McGovern candidacy, an acceleration in the pace
of reform movements confronts any observer.

In fact, the amateur in politics has become such a perennial on
the American scene that I wonder if a new breed of reformer has
not sprouted under more favorable conditions than his predecessors
found. Environmental changes may create a more fertile soil for
a new species of amateur. One of the main goals of this study,
therefore, is to understand why the amateur became and why he
continues to be involved in party politics.

In order to pursue this goal, it is important to review historical
patterns of amateurs in conflict with professional politicians. Highlighting these reorientations in the battles between reformers and
regulars is, then, a prelude to delineating the characteristics of the
amateur, alias reformer, alias insurgent, in a systematic and comparative fashion.

This approach and the issues it raises is complemented by a further direction. Besides an examination of the variations that have
influenced the shape of reform, there will also be a focus upon the
relevant aspects of one specific reform movement. The analysis of
one recent reform organization enables one to test these alleged revisions. To this latter purpose, I concentrated on the 1968 New
Democratic Coalition of New Jersey (N.D.C.). This group represented a new species of amateurs. In characterizing these differences, one can answer queries of how it varied from the earlier

movements, as well as the more recent Stevenson Clubs. Comparing just these two modern episodes, it seems clear that for both these political reform movements major national events led to their germination.

The first, through the unsuccessful presidential campaigns of Adlai E. Stevenson in 1952 and 1956, fertilized a new type of insurgent politics, especially evident in the amateur club movements of Chicago, Los Angeles, and New York City.

The second revival of these fairly static reform organizations came through the impact of the war in Vietnam. Reactivated by this intensely important issue, amateurs could implement their antiwar interests through the presidential aspirations of Senators Eugene J. McCarthy, Robert F. Kennedy, and George S. McGovern.

While the reformers of the 1950s flowered only after Adlai E. Stevenson became the Democratic Presidential nominee, the 1968-type massed and organized for preconvention primaries.[3] Following the 1968 primaries, many of these activists attempted to transform their basically antiwar movement into a genuine and continuing reform organization. The National New Democratic Coalition adopted a more far-reaching goal "to eliminate poverty and racism and [restore] order based on justice."[4] With varying degrees of effectiveness the New Democratic Coalition attempted to influence national and state politics.

In the party and electoral arena, the various state branches of the N.D.C. attacked many old-time regulars, from a successful challenge to the King County (Seattle, Washington) Democratic chairman to upsets on a precinct level of county committees. By May 1969, thirty-five states could be counted with at least some semblance of N.D.C. organization.

Both of these recent reform movements were galvanized by national Democratic politics; yet a valid difference between the two was the centrality of a single issue — the war in Vietnam — for the later activists. This focus even predated the location of a presidential candidate in 1968. The peace movement was becoming a visible force well before Senator Eugene McCarthy sought his party's nomination, and probably influenced his decision to a large degree. Once the antiwar groups were defeated at the Democratic Convention in Chicago, they met to propose a continuing organization, which eventually became the New Democratic Coalition, devoted "to restucturing the Democratic Party [by means of] a genuine voter interest in a more activist brand of issue-oriented politics. In effect, the broader concerns for political change were a natural outgrowth of McCarthy's, Kennedy's, and McGovern's peace-oriented campaigns of 1968.

Quite differently from the 1950s, by 1968 urban race riots and civil rights groups had increased the salience of domestic problems revolving around poverty and urban decay. The clarity of the dilemma was a product of both increasing crisis and growing media coverage that carried these new stresses into every living room.[5]

For these reasons, among others, the magnetism of presidential politics was translated into local postelection tasks in such diverse states as California, Colorado, Florida, Kansas, Maine, Maryland, Michigan, Missouri, New Jersey, New Mexico, New York, Pennsylvania, South Dakota, Texas, and Washington.

National problems, besides Vietnam, induced local organizations to form and attempt to deal with broader questions of governmental priorities. Thus, to understand these basically local structures of the N.D.C., I selected one of these states, New Jersey, where the organization had a substantial following.

My limited purpose (to study the N.D.C. of New Jersey) has possible significance beyond this case study of aberrant political activists. The increasing recurrence of reform movements since the 1950s permits one to note the regular appearance of amateur activists in most political parties.

From this visibility of the reformer, another question arises: "What can understanding the importance of the reformer teach one about the direction that the professional politician and his party may be taking?" For while this research is specifically concerned with the party amateur, potentially there are important implications for the more general areas of political organization.

Party organization, or perhaps just organization of some continuous nature, is essential for meaningful election choices.[6] In the boss-machine-dominated party, this organization was possible through patronage and other material rewards. There existed an exchange in which the desires of party workers to receive jobs or minor appointment powers meshed with the routine activities necessary for the machine to survive. If the precinct worker wanted the rewards of public jobs, he had to produce the votes on demand. Sanctions were available to the boss: no votes, no jobs.[7]

For a multiplicity of reasons (civil service laws, the technical complexity of bureaucratic jobs, government welfare programs, rising income and education levels, and decrease in unacculturated immigrant groups, to suggest several), patronage is no longer available in massive quantities, nor attractive in its traditional forms.[8]

The new-style party worker must be motivated by other than concrete or material rewards. Parties still require grass roots electioneering, and workers must still be motivated to produce the efforts necessary to win elections. For this reason the study of the amateur is actually the study of most party activists in the interrelationship of certain motivations and goals that permit a party to reward the faithful and keep them active.

The increasingly debilitated regular organization makes one suspicious about the supposed strength of the professional's motivation, compared with the amateur's. After all, the decrease in material rewards, mentioned above, should undercut any logical explanation of the regular politician's continuous commitment. Mancur Olson emphasizes this very point — the essentiality of such divisible material rewards in energizing volunteer workers for a cause.[9] This analysis of motivations will be explored more thoroughly in a later chapter. Yet all these political, social, and economic transformations make a raison d'être for a study of the amateur much broader than the utility of understanding a bizarre political occurrence, for instance, "amateurism." In addition, this study may raise alternate queries about the meanings of "professionalism" and the direction of all party politics in future years.

Thus, rather than the atypical activist, the reformer may reflect the style of motivations most likely to support continuous involvement, where the traditional foundations of political parties have been hopelessly weakened.

It is important to reiterate that this analysis of the new reformer also traces the modifications in the regular politician's motivations and style. In this continual comparison, the study has wider allusions for the analysis of party organization, since the N.D.C. insurgent may reflect general trends in American politics.

Brfore proceeding further, let me briefly outline the path that the pursuit of this *homo politicus* will take. The first task will be to review the history of the amateur or reformer in American politics, dealing generally with more distant movements and more specifically with the recent New Democratic Coalition. The findings of political science literature in analyzing these reform and/or regular grass roots activists follows. From this glimpse at the past and at the literature, one can define the reformer and propose specific hypotheses to be tested about his attitudes and behavior. Next I shall describe the operational procedures and statistical techniques employed in the study. The main body of the study will deal with findings evoked from my research.

The analysis throughout is comparative. I shall contrast amateurs with professional politicians in regard to a series of variables, which will be delineated in the next two chapters. The following chapter sets the stage for understanding the political reformer in his historical context, an essential step before more recent generalizations can be presented.

Notes to Introduction

1. William L. Riordon, *Plunkitt of Tammany Hall* (New York: E. P. Dutton & Co., 1963), pp. 17-20.

2. The Stevenson reformers were examined through the club movement by: James Q. Wilson, *The Amateur Democrat: Club Politics in Three Cities* (Chicago: University of Chicago Press, 1966); Robert S. Hirschfield, Bert E. Swanson, and Blanche D. Blank, "A Profile of Political Activists in Manhattan," *Western Political Quarterly* 15 (September 1962): 489-506; Francis Carney, *The Rise of the Democratic Clubs in California* (New York: Henry Holt & Co., Inc., 1958); Donald C. Blaisdell, *The Riverside Democrats*, Cases in Practical Politics, No. 18 (New Brunswick, N. J.: Eagleton Institute, 1960); Stephen A. Mitchell, *Elm Street Politics* (New York: Oceana Publications, Inc., 1959).

The later McCarthy and Kennedy and McGovern followers of the 1968 campaign were compared with the professional politician: John W. Soule and James W. Clarke, "Amateurs and Professionals: A Study of Delegates to the 1968 Democratic National Convention," *Americal Political Science Review* 64 (September 1970): 888-98; C. Richard Hofstetter, "Organizational Activists: The Bases of Participation in Amateur and Professional Groups." *American Politics Quarterly* 1 (April 1973): 244-76.

3. Andrew Hacker, "The McCarthy Candidacy," *Commentary,* February 1968, pp. 34-39; Arthur Herzog, *McCarthy for President* (New York: Viking Press, 1969); Eugene J. McCarthy, *The Year of the People* (Garden City, N.Y.: Doubleday & Company, Inc., 1969).

4. N.D.C., "Call to Action," n.p., n.d., mimeographed; these citations from N.D.C. material come from files collected by Daniel Gaby, former Chairman of the New Democratic Coalition of New Jersey.

5. Much has already been written on the data that indicates that blacks have increased their standards of living compared to twenty years ago. It becomes more evident, however, that perception plays as important a role as objective reality, so that this sense of crisis can easily be explained. *See* Lester W. Milbrath, *Political Participation: How and Why Do People Get Involved in Politics?* (Chicago: Rand McNally & Co., 1965), pp. 33-38, 115-16; Leon Festinger, *A Theory of Cognitive Dissonance* (Stanford, Calif.: Stanford University Press, 1957); Robert E. Lane, *Political Thinking and Consciousness: The Private Life of the Political Mind* (Chicago: Markham Publishing Company, 1968).

6. Removing parties from local politics simply leads to their replacement with a variety of other recruiting mechanisms, mainly derived from civic associations. *See* Jean L. Stinchcombe, *Reform and Reaction: City Politics in Toledo* (Belmont, Calif.: Wadsworth Publishing Co., Inc., 1968), pp. 75-81; Charles R. Adrian, "Some General Characteristics of Nonpartisan Elections," *American Political Science Review* 46 (September 1952): 466-76; Charles R. Adrian, "A Typology of Nonpartisan Elections," *Western Political Quarterly* 12 (June 1959): 449-58.

7. Sonya Forthal, *Cogwheels of Democracy: A Study of the Precinct Captain* (New York: The William-Frederick Press, 1946); Harold F. Gosnell, *Machine Politics: Chicago Model*, 2nd. ed., with a Foreword by Theodore J. Lowi (Chicago: University of Chicago Press, 1968); David H. Kurtzman, "Methods of Controlling Votes in Philadelphia" (unpublished Ph.D. dissertation, University of Pennsylvania, 1935).

8. Edward C. Banfield and James Q. Wilson, *City Politics* (New York: Vintage Books, Random House, 1963), pp. 121-25; Fred I. Greenstein, "The Changing Pattern of Urban Party Politics," in *Annals of the American Academy of Political and Social Sciences* 53 (May 1964): 7-8.

9. Mancur Olson, Jr., *The Logic of Collective Action: Public Goods and the Theory of Groups* (©1965 by the President and Fellows of Harvard College; New York: Schocken Books, 1965), pp. 132-67.

At the Grass Roots in the Garden State

1
History of
Reform Movements

The continuing conflict between the reformers and the regulars, the idealists and the pragmatists, the "upright" and the "corrupt" reads like a collection of short stories in which good confronts evil, battles assiduously, and loses "with honor." This seems to be the historical theme of political reform in the United States, although the details compose many diverse and heterogeneous chapters. At first glance one would conclude that the Populists, civil service associations, the National Progressives, municipal reformers, Democratic-reform club movement of the 1950s, and — my particular concern — the New Democratic Coalition share few common features. Closer inspection, however, illustrates the links between these groups. While developing in distinct historical periods and emphasizing varied aspects of political reform, the traits these movements share are as important as the differences they exhibit.

This chapter, in tracing the forebears of the New Democratic Coalition, proposes a developmental relationship between many of the past efforts at reform and the contemporary N.D.C. Rather than sharp breaks with the past, the N.D.C. represents a continuity of reform trends. In order to see this more clearly, certain salient concepts will be employed in the analysis of each movement. I will examine the demographic, motivational, and programmatic characteristics of each reform attempt. Before this review, however, a short detour is necessary to describe in a bit more detail what I mean by *demographic, motivational,* and *programmatic* analyses.

The social characteristics of reformers provide important demographic information. The early activists are so often described in class and ethnic terms that one should carefully consider such explanations. Yet an even more fruitful frame work relates these "objective" traits to the subjective orientation of an individual. Does he focus his attention as well as interpretations of political problems on the national/international scene or on the local arena? These differences are described by Robert K. Merton as either a cosmopolitan or a local orientation. Merton freely adapts his terms from Ferdinand Toennies's *gemeinschaft* and *gesellschaft* categories of social relationships.[1] This distinction, to be more carefully delineated later in the book, will be an important aspect of the demographic analysis of the N.D.C. The activist who describes his concerns in personal, face-to-face, community-based terms might develop quite distinct motivations from the individual whose world is shaped by impersonal, distant, national, or society-wide forces.

The analytic categories that derive from Toennies are implicit in a recent brand of historical interpretation that emphasizes culture conflict as an influence in United States politics. Lee Benson's multivariate analysis of Jacksonian Democracy and Paul Kleppner's similar methodology applied to Midwestern politics from 1850 to 1900,[2] explain political participation in terms of more salient "ethnocultural and religious" factors, rather than only economic backgrounds. The schism between the pietists and the ritualists might, at its very heart, be the religious dimension of this "local" versus "cosmopolitan" orientation. In any case, these studies direct the book to a broader range of demographic concerns than class variables alone would suggest.

My second concept, motivation, is not unrelated to the cosmo-politan-local dichotomy. While the details of motivational theory will be explored in the chapters on motivation, it is important to mention the approach. In studying interest groups, Mancur Olson claims that activists donate their energies only when the benefits they receive are divisible. By divisible, Olson conceives of scarce goods (such as material rewards) of which some people, the partici-pants, can get more than others, the nonparticipants. The very inequities in distribution convince certain people to join and actively support an organization. In effect, Olson asks: "Why should an individual become active in a voluntary cause? " His answer implies an immediate personal benefit. Thus Olson assumes self-interest and personal rewards impel people toward participa-tion, not their higher vision or concern for the national interest.

While distinct from the interpretation of Merton, there is a

similarity between motives of personal rewards and local orientations as well as the possible relationship between motives of
impersonal rewards and cosmopolitan orientations. This will be
illustrated later.

Another way to describe these impersonal or personal rewards is
presented by Peter B. Clark and James Q. Wilson in their discussion of material, solidary, or purposive rewards. Clark and
Wilson's material rewards translate freely into Olson's divisible
ones. Solidary incentives imply both socializing and status as
motivating forces for activists, while purposive incentives require
that policy formulation and enactment be rewards in themselves.
Clark and Wilson and Olson contribute theoretical implications for
any study of a reform movement.[3]

The concern with motivation also permits one to focus upon
the programmatic character of past reformers. In fact, another
way to look at individuals activated by issues is to describe in detail
their purposive incentives. In asking what direction this policy
orientation takes, I will deal with its liberal or conservative components. Besides content of individual issues, I will explore the
coherence and interrelatedness of different opinions.

Employing these categories for the purpose of understanding
the roots of the N.D.C., a brief and historical background of
reform will present this type of activist as a cosmopolitan, purposive, and liberal politician. Some of these categories will fit the
varied historical shapes of the reformer far better than others.
Continuing to be aware of possible discrepancies as well as accurate
portraits, however, one can explore reform movements in a comparative framework to clarify more recent patterns evident in the
N.D.C.

After this historical overview, the following chapter will detail
the social science findings about reformers, compared with regular
activists. Combining historical analysis and contemporary research,
I will then indicate hypotheses tested in this study of the N.D.C.
The remainder of the book will present these findings in the context briefly delineated above.

After this short digression into some of the concepts and
approaches used in this study, I can return to my present interest:
the historical ancestors of the N.D.C.

To examine the political reformer is to trace a recurrent historical
theme. One might suggest that the Puritan tradition with its deep
concern for private as well as public morals provides the foundation
for these sporadic drives to purify government and punish the evil-

doer.[4] When leaders were chosen by the advantaged groups of society, the need for political reform was seen as relatively unimportant. New York's Tammany Hall began as a middle-class organization of bankers and merchants in 1805.[5] Reformist sentiments blossomed only after the massive influx of immigrants during the nineteenth and early twentieth centuries.

Widespread suffrage, coupled with a multiplicity of elective offices and an almost infinite appointment power, gave scope to the development of machine politics. Only then did Tammany Hall become a synonym for corruption and bossism. The urban party that grew from these conditions was more than a different form of political organization, compared to the old patrician and middle-class structures that had preceded it.

Richard Hofstadter has suggested that these styles were reflections of the deeper conflict in cultural ethics and class background that supported the early reform movements:

> Out of the clash between the needs of the immigrants and the sentiments of the natives there emerged two thoroughly different systems of political ethics. . . . One, founded upon the indigenous Yankee protestant political traditions, and upon middle-class life, assumed and demanded the constant, disinterested activity of the citizen in public affairs, argued that political life ought to be run, to a greater degree than it was, in accordance with general principles and abstract laws apart from and superior to personal needs, and expressed a common feeling that government should be in good part an effort to moralize the lives of individuals while economic life should be intimately related to the stimulation and development of individual character. The other system, founded upon the European background of the immigrants, upon their unfamiliarity with independent political action, their familiarity with hierarchy and authority, and upon the urgent needs that so often grew out of their migration, took for granted that the political life of the individual would arise out of family needs, interpreted political and civic relations chiefly in terms of personal obligations, and placed strong personal loyalties above allegiance to abstract codes of law or morals.[6]

Thus Hofstadter finds a variation in whether one is motivated by general versus particularistic interest. This certainly seems similar to Merton's expression of this dichotomy as that of the cosmopolitan versus the local. Samuel P. Hays described these differences through an emphasis upon the geographically more inclusive "society" versus small-scale "community" interests.[7] Both Merton and Hays interpret this ethical orientation as a conflict between those with a small-community identification and those who perceive the needs of a particular system in terms of the larger society. Thus, for them the difference is not essentially one of cultural ethics, but rather of perception and definition of one's "level-of-analysis".

A. Populists and Civil Service Reformers

Since reform waited upon the development of urbanization and industrialization, I will begin with the first reactions to these phenomena. The nineteenth century culminated in two quite varied efforts at reform, which set the tone for all future attempts. While both the Populists and the civil service reform movement sought a world of face-to-face relations, the former displayed a more particularistic ethos, while the latter conformed to the stereotype of a man motivated by concern for the general good.

In this respect both were focusing upon the small unit of analysis, or the community, as Hays describes it. Their concern for a pre-industrial system, either of the country or the town, sets both groups aside from twentieth-century reformers. Emphasizing *gemeinschaft* as a valued life-style, both the Populists and the patricians turned against urbanism and the impersonal, large-scale *gesellschaft* relationships that usually result from such industrial structuring of society.

Related to this cultural orientation was the fact that the two movements could not have been more distinct in their adherents' demographic backgrounds. The Populists were strongly tied to agrarian, noncommercial farming of the South and West,[8] while the civil service reformers were clearly Northeastern professionals, with town dwellers predominating.[9] One represented the tenuous position of the yeoman farmer, the other the delicate situation of the old governing classes.[10]

These two movements from the opposite ends of the class spectrum shared one trait in common: they each represented an obsolete way of life, which was rapidly being threatened by industrialization, urbanization, and the transportation revolution.[11] The lot of the farmer was clearly worsening. Populism sprouted from this economic discontent, but the patrician, who had a fairly secure income, was threatened as insidiously as the yeoman with loss of status. Both groups were motivated by a fear of the industrial life-style, yet each focused upon different programs to reform, or rather regain, their past utopias.

The Populists waged a much broader attack upon the evils of industrialization. William Jennings Bryan, the Populist standard-bearer, not only fought large-scale enterprises in general, but also specifically those that centralized economic and political power.

> Government was to be democratized in order to make it more amenable to reform. Reform meant primarily the ending of governmental interventions that benefited large-scale capital and a rapid increase in the interventions that favored men of little or no capital.[12]

It is important to distinguish Bryan from his followers. While his appeals were essentially to inhabitants of rural areas, it was more his pietistic moral fervor that lured his adherents. Kleppner points out the very select attraction of Bryan's 1896 "Democracy": "The usual picture of this organization as a vehicle of rural economic protest ignores the fact that it drew negligible support from Catholic and German Lutheran farmers."[13] Rather the basis for Bryan's support can be discovered in the pietistic Protestant sects for whom the battle over "free silver" was representative of other moral conflicts about prohibition and evangelical Protestantism.

While Bryan's converts to the "Democracy" were magnetized by religious issues, Bryan did provide specific programs to accompany his rhetoric of return to community-based interests. Among these proposals were the referendum, initiative, and direct election of United States Senators to produce truly popular government. These reforms would decentralize monopoly power of capitalists and other urban conglomerates. Since at its foundation the cry for popular democracy was a plea to return to rural and pietistic styles, the verbal attachment to direct government by the people was accompanied by an overt hostility toward the recent urban immigrant.

This reform crusade against plutocrats through antitrust action was an attack upon the newer industrial wealth. Any association with those twin ogres, large-scale urbanism or industrialization, was enough to corrupt totally. This was corruption in a deeply moral sense.

The Populists proposed vehicles to return power to the people — or at least to some of the people. As wide as its rhetoric was in embracing participatory democracy for all, Populism collapsed because its narrow appeal in specific policies — Bryan's 1896 campaign was organized almost exclusively around the issue of free silver — attracted only groups who were clearly in eclipse. This failure to win the urban worker crippled the Populist effort to push forth its other programs aimed at destroying the monopoly power of private interests.

If the Populists faded because of their limited policies, the civil service reformers were predestined to fail for the same reason. Not only were these men attached to a single goal, for example, placing "good" men in administrative positions, but they were also exclusively attached to that goal.[14] As Faulkner has pointed out, these reformers were roused to act only rarely, and then for national issues.[15]

The philosophical pronouncements that favored civil service reform were strongly flavored with religious overtones of a moral crusade, much like the Populists. "The moral tone of the country is debased. The national character deteriorates," preached the *First Report* of the Civil Service Commission in 1871.[16]

The civil service reformers also spoke of democratic participation, but they were most concerned with placing the elite in political jobs. As outdated aristocrats, venting anger at their changing status through the civil service reform movement, they emphasized the importance of education and upper-class credentials in running uncorrupted and uncorruptible government.[17] With the passage of the *Pendleton Act* in 1883, instituting examination requirements for federal jobs, the fervor for reform diminished.

These early reformers differed considerably from the Progressives who followed them in their belief that any educated generalist could do the job of governing effectively. No special techniques were needed; simply the placement of "better classes" in administrative and political positions would produce the desired goal, an honorable government. It is no wonder that their battle for reform centered around outlawing the spoils.

While the patrician reformers thought their one issue was tantamount to complete social reform, the Populists could not have contradicted them more in this philosophical area. It is useful to note that Bryan's approach to patronage rivaled that of the city bosses of his time. Being concerned with the interests of farmers, he simply wanted his people to share the spoils.

In practice, the Populist belief in the common man's decision-making talent may only have been faith in the independent farmer. Yet this confidence in his brand of democracy explains well Bryan's attachment to patronage and his indifference to the one-issue obsession of civil service associations.

In terms of demographic characteristics, motivations for political activity, and even philosophy, the Populists and civil service reformers varied significantly. Yet each provided certain strands that were rewoven into later efforts at reform. With these differences, both shared the fight against centralized monopolies and struggled for a return to a more secure and parochial life. From the rural, pietistic, and lower-status demographic characteristics of the Populists to the Eastern upper-class, traditional, aristocratic backgrounds of the civil service reformers came a programmatic "conservatism." This conserving element in rather diverse philosophies was directed toward regaining the simple preindustrial life of the small town and the farm. Out of these parochial philosophies and heterogeneous backgrounds one could also detect variations in motivation, highlighted by their conflicting attitudes toward patronage. The Populist leadership strongly supported material rewards, while the civil service activists made abolition of patronage its purposive goal.

Yet to concentrate upon the lower-status backgrounds, material incentives of the Populists in contrast to the upper-status, purposive goals of the civil service reformers is to emphasize the less essential points. Diverse in demographic characteristics and even motivations, these two early movements display an important aspect of reform in its incipient development: fear of technological-bureaucratic society. Perhaps both these groups could better be described by the term *reactionary,* rather than either liberal or conservative. It is in their holding operation against preordained industrialization that their most outstanding characteristics become evident.

B. National Progressives and Municipal Reformers

If the Populists and civil service associations clearly turned their backs upon the glory of industrial progress, no such serious claim can be made for the next wave of reform. While some authors find in the Progressive movement a continuation of this dislocation and status deprivation of the nineteenth-century reformers,[18] more detailed descriptions reveal the fallacy of this contention. One might fairly describe the old Mugwump Republican in this more reactionary light, but surely not the Progessive movement as a whole. In fact, looking at the same series of variables — the demographic, motivational, and policy ones — in relation to the Progressives, one discovers that the Progressive movement was much more complex than a simple continuation and expansion of civil service reform.

On the whole, Progressivism (which gave direction to reform efforts from about 1900 through Franklin Delano Roosevelt's administration) echoed the new middle class in demographics, motivations, and issue orientation. While a good portion of the Progressives were professionals, they were not the traditional type, for example educators, lawyers, physicians, and clergymen, as were the civil service supporters.[19] Even when they came from traditional fields, they were the new technicians, working out "the inner dynamics of professionalism in modern society, these reformers derived from the new middle class, eager to "apply expertise to public affairs."[20] Furthermore, the businessmen who were involved in progressive reforms represented quite a divergent economic base from the civil service activists. The Progressives were likely to be manufacturers, while the civil service vanguard retained a strong tie to nonindustrial wealth, as merchants, brokers, and bankers.

Some, discovering the strong business involvement in the Progressive movement, have suggested that these economically specialized groups took part in reform in order to provide for their own economic control.[21] This ignores the fact, however, that the large body of Progressives were not the immensely wealthy industrialists, but rather the specialists who had learned how to rationalize businesses or systematize and apply professional knowledge.[22] This growing faith in science and the ability to regularize organization was especially evident in the social sciences, with the founding at the turn of the century of such journals as *Political Science Quarterly* and *Annals of the American Academy of Political and Social Sciences.*

Besides these journals, a major influence upon social thought during this period was Herbert Croly's *The Promise of American Life.* His book abounded in technocratic suggestions to fulfill America's national goal through organization, efficiency, and expertise.[23]

If these developments do not answer all questions about the industrial orientation of the Progressives, there is some other evidence. A glance at the socioeconomic status of these new groups indicates the fresh source of their positions. In fact, the motivation for reform seems directly related to the demographic backgrounds of these activists: urban as well as professional or business "scientists."[24] This orientation will be explored in greater detail in a later discussion of cosmopolitan styles. But it should be noted here that reformers during the Progressive era clearly exhibited this concern with applying general scientific principles to political organization.

Because these Progressives were urbanites in an occupational sense, much more than the upper-class civil service reformers and quite distinct from the Populists, the immorality of the immigrant-based machine was seen in its complex relationship with big business.[25] The tremendous waste of public funds through municipal venality was a major motivating factor behind the renewed efforts at reform. The goal of efficiently operated governments, similar in style to businesses, did not remove the stigma from the immigrant, but rather extended the stain to big industrialists.

For people who were technically oriented by training, it was a short step from the realization that "better classes" in administrative roles were as capable of corruption and waste as the party hack was, to a dedication to correct the machinery of government that made this inefficiency possible.

The Progressive reformers, while attacking the monopolies detested by the Populists, did so because of the irrationality, for instance, waste, of party-business collusion, not because of an immorality in large-scale urban enterprises.

In fact, Hays makes a very good case for the reformers' drive to streamline government, as actually an effort to centralize it from the municipal level to the state or national one. The municipality was fragmented by ward systems that gave the party boss his means to control a small particularistic community.[26] The goal in destroying the party was the same as destroying the monopolies: to pass decision making from community special interests to society general interests.

Political reform was touted as a means whereby political power would be shifted from the "interests" to the "people," and mass involvement in decision making would be restored. In reality, however, the movement for political reform was an attack upon entire party system as it had developed in the nineteenth century, a rejection of. community involvement in decision making, and a demand that public decisions be made through mechanisms other than the political party. It stemmed from fear of, rather than faith in, community political impulses.[27]

Motivated by the ethic of economic rationaltiy, the Progressive reformers adopted much of the Populist program (initiative, referendum, direct election of United States Senators, graduated income tax, trust busting) to weaken control of privately oriented party and business interests. Then with a flourish and almost an adoration for mechanical devices, the reformers attached themselves to further efforts to destroy the party: merit system, direct primary, recall, short ballot, to mention a few.

The desire a centralize decision making, quite the reverse of the Populist and civil service movement, made use of many of the same programs. While these reformers were optimistic about changing institutions, this was accompanied by a pessimism about human nature.[28] The rhetoric of democracy stood, but the fear of the voter was obvious. Although the Progressives provided a "transient movement," they spawned a continuing interest in urban change that was the hallmark of reform through the Second World War.[29]

What most characterized the National Progressives and their municipal successors was an optimistic desire to correct the evils of urban life, but not to destroy urbanism. As I have stressed, these were the new urban elite, whose training led them to a belief that one could improve the quality of city life by minor adjustments in formal structures. The ideals of tinkering were certainly begun by the Progressives, as were the specific goals of hamstringing the political party.

While one might have an impossible time characterizing the Populists and civil service reformers as liberals — the term *reactionary* has been suggested above — no such problem exists with the National Progressive movement and the municipal reformers who followed. Yet it is essential to note that this liberalism does not emphasize social welfare or redistribution of income. This is the liberalism of bureaucratic rearrangements, or tinkering.

The drive to create efficient organizations led these urban revisionists to embrace a wide range of governmental devices: commission and city manager or strong mayor, nonpartisan and off-year local elections, elimination of ward election districts in favor of proportional or at-large representation, short ballot, home rule, direct primary. This municipal reform movement reached its peak in the second and third decades of the twentieth century, proving its influence and philosophy by the number of businessmen elected to public office during the interwar years.

Just as the National Progressives continued to speak about returning power to the people, so did these municipal reformers.

All these forms would free the citizen from domination by selfish interest and provide a means for true participation, "untainted by self-interest."[30]

The fact that the Progressives and other municipal reformers spoke *ad infinitum* about democracy has misled many of their critics. Their detractors claim that these groups were frauds, since no lasting social reform or redistribution of wealth took place.[31] Quite the reverse was indicated as national income earned by the top ten percent of the nation's income recipients increased from thirty-four percent in 1910 to thirty-eight percent in 1921.[32]

This complaint confuses two rather distinct factors: structural reform and social reform.[33] The first reformers of the twentieth century were concerned with mechanistic devices to insulate government from special interests. The deprivation (economic as well as political) of lower-class groups was irrelevant. Eager to have the government participate in control of monopolies, they were not tainted by any socialist pretensions that might attack private property.

Post-World War I reformers continued this pattern. They were aroused by specific scandals or by muckraking literature. Their indignation burst forth and then subsided, in the typical pattern of the reform movement. A rare exception to this pattern of structural reform proves this point. Fiorello LaGuardia became reform mayor of New York City through a fusion party that combined the middle and wealthy classes of both parties to throw out the rascals.[34] Expansion beyond this limited coalition of "go-goo's" (a phase Theodore Roosevelt developed to characterize disparagingly those interested in moralistic "good government") was rare. When it did develop, as it did with Mayor LaGuardia, into some attempt at social reform, many of the original middle-class supporters were repelled.[35]

This middle-class reaction illustrates the limited goals of the municipal reformers. Except for LaGuardia and the settlement movement, with its desire to apply the "Social Gospel" to ameliorate poverty, such goals did not tinge these efforts.[36] True social reform was practically nonexistent except in a few large cities. Medium-sized places were the bastion for the mechanistic approach to urban change.

Prior to World War II the reform movement, centering upon urban defects, was motivated by specific issues of venality and reacted to threats of corruption by creating *ad hoc* organizations outside party politics. The fusion movements in New York could win one election, but rarely won two. Furthermore, the only choice offered was of "organization and non-organization government."[37] The Progressives attacked parties to centralize government, while these later municipal reformers seemed to focus on the party organization as an evil in itself.

Just as the spoils system was originally innovative, but solidified to defend the status quo, so did the reform orientation against party dominance in the early twentieth century rigidify reformist sentiments against all forms of governmental organization that were not purely administrative.

The Progressives were truly forward thinking in their attempts to come to terms with the inefficiency of urban structures. The reformers of the interwar years provide a very different picture, and yet these later municipal activists were demographically similar to the Progressives. One would describe them as high-status Republicans.[38] Their goals, correction of urban ills — also like the Progressives — were pursued outside the party structure. Furthermore, the Progressive view of direct democracy carried through this period. Yet the effect of applying these general principles became conservative.

As social perspective moved beyond the community focus to that of society in general, the stress on larger, more inclusive entities functionally required centralization of decision making.

Motivated by the same goal of efficiency as the Progressives, these reformers, however, were particularizing political decisions through the development of independent administrative authorities. In an era of positive government and increasing national direction of decision making, weak elected leaders, responsible to no party and impervious civil servants with tenure, hindered any fight for change, pressed by the federal government.[39] This conflict made a mockery of the view that one could separate values and administration, long touted by the reformers as the main benefit of their policies.

The "go-goo's" became as defensive as the nineteenth-century civil service reformers. Furthermore, the policies of the Depression, which culminated in alleviation of some social inequities, took place firmly within the Democratic Party structure, and had little to do with the reform movement of that period. Centering his steam on economic reform, Franklin Delano Roosevelt ignored both bossism and its resulting corruption as an issue.

The New Deal created for all lower-status groups an affinity for the party, which neither the Populists nor the Progressives, with all their rhetoric, had been able to do. Thus, by 1941 the reformers, supposedly the descendants of the Populist and Progressive heritage of direct democracy of the people, found themselves at opposite ends of the political spectrum from those whose good they allegedly sought. Reform seemed to have reached a dead end during F.D.R.'s time. In fact, the next period of reform did not begin until the 1950s.

To summarize briefly the characteristics of the National Progressives and the municipal reformers, before turning to more recent attempts, it is useful to note their demographic character-istics. Quite distinct from the Populists and civil service associations, these twentieth-century reformers illustrate a shift in backgrounds, which reflects their acceptance of industrialism and its implications. In the above discussion, one could find middle-class professionals and businessmen, concerned with applying "scientific techniques" to governmental operations. Focusing upon political efficiency for the wider society, their motivations could be described quite accurately as purposive. The attempt to tinker with political struc-tures, to change the legal arrangements and, hence, political behavior, makes their suggestions innovative and somewhat "liberal."

This liberalism, however, in its effort to move beyond the status quo, was in no way characterized by leanings toward social welfare programs. While the Progressives touted solutions that centralized government, in contrast to the municipal reformers, both had one goal: efficiency. Yet government, efficiently delivered, had little to offer the poverty-stricken municipal dweller whose interests these reformers believed they were representing.

With such irrelevant programs, it is no wonder that the New Deal overshadowed and made obsolete these reform appeals. Only after World War II did another episode of reform arise — and then under quite different circumstances.

C. The Democratic-Club Movement

Adlai Stevenson's presidential campaigns of 1952 and 1956 were the new catalyst. At first glance this movement might seem to be a continuation of past reform efforts in terms of demo-graphics, motivations, and issue orientation. I shall try to indicate how misleading this assumption would be. In the first place, it is true that the demographic characteristics of these reformers seem identical to the prewar types: middle-class suburban or urban professionals.[40] Yet these reformers, rejuvenating the movement for political change were young, compared to their immediate predecessors.[41]

While the reform movement in this country can always be defined by the professional man it attracts, the subtype of professional has varied over time. The civil service reformers were traditional professionals of clerical, academic, legal, or medical backgrounds; the Progressive era reformers were technical scientific professionals; and the post-Second World War reformers possessed legal or communications backgrounds.[42]

Although they were motivated by the same concern for efficiency, were as violently antimachine, antipatronage as their forerunners, a social conscience had been added. These young politicos were clearly liberal in a much broader sense.[43] In contrast to the older municipal reformer who could be found lodged in such associations as the municipal league, which was Republican even in the 1950s, these younger men and women were on the left side within the Democratic Party.

Liberalism can be stressed as a trademark of the reformer of the 1950s, yet this is not as essential as the fact that his issue orientation took ideological shape.[44] Interest in the great issues of the day was itself a motivating force behind political participation.[45]

Ideological interpretations become the essential core in arousing the club reformer to action. Past reformers were awakened by corruption. It took the New York City scandals of Mayor Jimmy Walker's administration in 1929-32 to produce the fusion ticket that elected LaGuardia. Scandals or corruption are rather different from the types of issues evident in the club movement of the fifties.

There does seem to be a clear shift in emphasis for the reformers of 1952, who expressed themselves through substantive national and international, rather than municipal, concerns. The insurgents eventually turned toward municipal reform, but even then defined it through national goals: "With Stevenson, we can find no rest while poor housing, poor schools, and discrimination exist in our midst. We will work together until we can all be proud of the community in which we live."[46]

Motivated by issues, these Democrats (as they were) illustrated another contrast with their predecessors: fascination with politics. While past municipal reformers had always been disgusted by politics and politicking, these newcomers gloried in the social interactions that derived from their issue involvement, creating their own clubs because of this social and political attraction.

Furthermore, this was participation on a seemingly uninfluential level of the political horizon. Past reformers had sought only the prestigious higher-echelon positions. But here were young men and women eager to do the local and often tedious work necessary to win elections.

Embracing the Populist rhetoric about participation and the middle-class reformers' ethos about the citizen's duty to fight for the general good, these reformers participated with a vengeance. The type of activity varied from previous movements, as did the focus.

From 1952 on, the reform club member worked zealously to improve party government through party machinery. Past movements, disgusted with politics, kept themselves untainted (but also ineffectual) by working outside all party structures. Leaving the party intact, these reformers were survived by the regular who would still control the recruitment process long after the reformer grew weary or bored.

The 1950's reformer, on the other hand, attacked the regular head on. Separate state-reform organizations fought pitched battles on regular organization territory in primary elections, mainly succeeding in New York City. The defeat of Carmine DeSapio, boss of Tammany Hall, was probably the most impressive coup of all the separate conflicts involving the reform-Democrat club movement.

Copying the regular organizations, these reformers developed around independent clubs. Each club articulated its own policies and recruited its own leadership. Any attempt to set up city-wide or state-wide organizations was fought as an attempt to thwart grass roots democracy.

Calling these historical efforts at government — and more specifically party reform — "movements" may be misleading. It would be incorrect to impute any coherence or central direction to these groups. Municipal leagues and civil service associations, however, were intensely disciplined and centralized compared to the fragmentation that existed in the reform club movement.

The understanding of politics that led these reformers to attack undemocratic procedures from within the Democratic Party indicated some new political astuteness. Furthermore, the participation in a fight for greater principles was satisfaction in itself. Such motivations are the model for purposive incentives.

Victory for the modern reformer, as it was for the traditional one, was in setting up the mechanics for greater democracy or the procedure for attracting "better people." Winning general elections was almost beside the point, once the initial victories that permitted the activist to implant these new structures was achieved. These liberals with social consciences were, in fact, more concerned about intraparty democracy than substantive policy. This finding comes as no surprise to anyone who has explored the history of party reform. Nowhere did one encounter any contact with the socialist or revolutionary left. All reformers have been establishment types — out to open government to a new class (or return it to an old one). Few within this tradition have done more than talk about the poor, the dispossessed. Real compassion and commitment to reallocate wealth is not apparent.

Thus by the late 1960s the reformer in politics once again was at ebbtide, having exhausted his appeals. The club movement had redirected the path of reform from certain of its previous trends, but had failed to sustain itself or to effect any long-term transformation of the political process. Similar to previous reformers in general demographics, when one examines the specifics, some deviations from previous patterns are revealed. Unlike the traditional lower-status Populists or old aristocracy of the civil service reformers, but also distinct from the technical and business middle-class professionals of the Progressive and municipal-reform period, the club movement was composed of professionals with legal or communications experience. Middle class, as its most recent predecessors, its intraclass character, however, reflected quite varied occupations. Furthermore, the purposive goals similar to all prior movements (except the Populist) differed in their programmatic interpretation.

In these policies the 1950s reformer was clearly liberal. This liberalism related not only to willingness to innovate or eagerness to embrace only structural reform, but also, and encompassing both of these, it opted for social welfare programs that could be described as liberal in multiple ways.

These liberal issue concerns, however, were outweighed by an overriding emphasis upon intraparty democracy. In this respect the 1950s and 1960s amateur reflected the "tinkering" attempts of his ancestors. All was not lost for the reform cause, since the regular Democrats were willing to provide an issue in keeping with the tastes of the reformer. The war in Vietnam had all the credentials for a reform catalyst: moral implications, international scope, intraparty authoritarian behavior that ignored pressure from the grass roots, and, above all, a national "boss," Lyndon Baines Johnson, whose style was repugnant to potential reformers. Once a candidate — first Senator Eugene McCarthy and later Senators Robert Kennedy and George McGovern — was found, the movement fused with single-minded purpose to provide a referendum on war through presidential politics. Here was issue-oriented politics in its purest state. Out of this cause evolved a rebirth of the reform movement that is the particular interest of this study.

D. The New Democratic Coalition Revives Reform

Having explored past reformers in their historical setting and through their demographic, motivational, and issue-oriented traits, I can now concentrate on the New Democratic Coalition (N.D.C.) in terms of these characteristics.

The New Democratic Coalition has deep roots in the middle-class peace movement, coalescing around the "Dump Johnson" forces. It formally organized in August 1967 as the "Conference of Concerned Democrats."[47] When McCarthy announced in November 1967 that he would challenge President Johnson, the issue had found a standard bearer.

During the months that followed, the nucleus of the pre-N.D.C. group expanded to bring youth from colleges and high schools into the anti-war campaign, ringing doorbells for either McCarthy or for Senator Robert Kennedy, who declared himself a candidate in mid-March 1967. President Johnson soon decided not to press for another term, but the war remained paramount with Vice-President Hubert H. Humphrey, another candidate and heir to Johnson's strength, refusing to disagree with the President on Vietnam.

It is important to set the tone of these organizational efforts, which preceded the N.D.C., and at the same time influenced its direction. The McCarthy campaign illustrated the reform political organization, operating on issues through primaries, as opposed to personalities.[48] Since issues were paramount, however, intense feelings about their ideals led the McCarthyites to villify those who did not agree with them. The "insistence on ideological purity [made] even the Kennedys somewhat suspect."[49]

Furthermore, this emphasis upon issues, colored by a stress on democracy and equality, led the campaigners to question the necessity of all forms of organization. The call for democracy was interpreted through an antileadership, antiauthority bias. As a result of this orientation, coherent direction was practically impossible to find within the McCarthy campaign.[50] With the death of Robert Kennedy, ironically, the McCarthy movement stopped functioning. McCarthy withdrew from active campaigning and awaited the Chicago convention.

Although the various campaigns had paused, there were motions to establish an ongoing national reform organization outside the McCarthy campaign and in coordination with Kennedy people. One tentative step took place as the "Coalition for an Open Convention," which drew these groups together in Chicago prior to the convention. This was mainly the McCarthy workers' attempt to draw the Kennedy group into their organization.

By the convention, however, there was a moratorium on most activity. In this atmosphere one can not underestimate the impact of the August convention. Both procedures inside the convention hall, which provided fuel to the reformers' claim that the entire party structure was closed to dissent, as well as the external confrontation between Mayor Richard Daley's police and antiwar youth rekindled the determination of campaigners to pursue their policies after Hubert Humphrey took the Democratic nomination for President.[51]

At the convention, in fact, Paul O'Dwyer, who had previously won a surprise primary victory as a Senatorial peace candidate in New York, called a meeting to urge that the reform forces remain together, return to their states, get others involved, and keep in touch.

The N.D.C., seeming to learn from the lack of central direction of the McCarthy campaign, set the stage for a nationwide organization to coordinate the grass roots energies of the municipalities and the states. A loose rein was proposed from the apex of the pyramid to the base, but a continuous structure was implied. The first national meeting of the N.D.C. was held in Minneapolis, 5-6 October 1968. This conference proposed expansion of the movement from the issue of Vietnam to the goal of reordering national priorities.

The main purpose was to keep 1968 campaign workers active. This could best be accomplished by "participatory democracy" and local organizations to prod the rank and file. Thus the national N.D.C., a paper organization, set forth on a crusade to disseminate the gospel of Democratic Party reform through a coalition of

McCarthy and Kennedy supporters, labor, blacks, and other minority groups.

In a period of black separatism, they sought integrated politics; in an era of intense lower-class white ethnic animosity, they proposed a bond between this group and blacks, as well as between the liberal middle class. This may not have been a very auspicious setting, but the N.D.C. optimists flowered.

Since my purpose is to describe the new reformer, I shall concentrate upon the geographic level where he is most visible, the state. The national organization became an information clearing house, as well as a public relations focus. Yet the essence of the movement could be found on a state level. New Jersey had a remarkably active reform movement called the *New Democratic Coalition of New Jersey,* to distinguish it from the Nation Democratic Coalition.

At that first national meeting, New Jersey was represented by Dorothy Eldridge, head of S.A.N.E. and McCarthy coordinator in Essex County; Daniel Gaby from Somerset County, cochairman of the New Jersey McCarthy delegation with Betty Wenk of Bergen, who also attended; Richard Samuel, McCarthy delegate from Union County; Nathaniel Johnson, unsuccessful black Essex County McCarthy challenger; Joel R. Jacobson, official of United Auto Workers as well as a Kennedy and McCarthy supporter. Back in their own state, these McCarthy workers, joined by others active for peace, set up a series of meetings to galvanize the reformers to create a permanent organization.

The spirit of Chicago was there, upon which to draw. An interview with two observers is indicative:

"After Chicago we are radicals . . . and we want people to know it. . . . Here we are . . . middle aged, respectable, established citizens of the community. And we are radicalized. . . . After the brutality we saw on the streets, and the undemocratic abuses we saw in the convention, we have pledged . . . to continue forever if necessary to fight the conditions which made them possible. We will join any demonstration, go where we can . . . . "

"Chicago has 'radicalized' us and I'm sure many like us. . . . Yes we are radicals in the sense that the young people use the word . . . according to its orginal meaning. It comes from the Latin 'radix,' the root, you know. In ninth place is the definition of 'leading or following extreme principles.' But it means going to extreme — not away but back to — essential principles."

A small first state meeting at the Robert Treat Hotel was called by Ned Parsekian, a maverick regular who had supported McCarthy in Chicago. State volunteers for McCarthy, Kennedy, various liberal groups, and regulars with reform interests were invited. At this meeting a decision was made to work within the Democratic Party to achieve greater impact on issues and candidate selection.[53] The main short-term purpose was to aim for a statewide convention based upon representatives from the counties.

Approximately ten people were involved in this first meeting. Thus an immediate goal was to expand the organizing group. The second gathering could boast of 150 interested people. Beyond the original, small liberal group were "activists from autonomous black political organizations, labor unions, students, and individual regular-organization Democrats.[54] Daniel Gaby and Richard Leone, state coordinator of Kennedy for President organization, were named temporary cochairmen as a show of solidarity between the McCarthy and Kennedy forces. (Since Kennedy had not entered the primary in New Jersey, the vast majority of antiwar campaigning was accomplished through McCarthy. Thus the selection of Leone was in fact a gesture.)

In any case, the meetings commenced, "interminably" as several have suggested privately,[55] with "extensive discussions,"[56] stated the minutes. There was divergent pressure from the beginning either to provide a forum for issues or to emphasize the gubernatorial election of 1969. These potential conflicts were shelved when the organization became intensely involved in its own creation, to be formalized at a convention in November 1968. This date was set back from November to January 18, 1968, and finally to March 22. The Temporary Steering Committee had underestimated the amount of grass roots work necessary to furnish delegates for the convention.

In December, most counties were still getting under way with their operations. Only Middlesex, Union, and Bergen claimed to be viable. Mercer and Essex said they were somewhat organized. Hudson, Monmouth, Passaic, and Warren were still in the formative stages.

The counties were essential to the strategy of the N.D.C., since the constitution stated that membership was to be through county coalitions. The structuring of the N.D.C. along county lines was an accurate reflection of New Jersey's political structure, which the N.D.C. was seeking to attack. Thus the county divisions were quite logical for their purposes. The Steering Committee, large in size, was mainly composed of county delegates, selected by the county organizations (plus eight at-large members, a sprinkling of students, and elected officers). The constitution clearly delineated the line of command from the local to the state level, emphasizing democratic procedures: open meetings, advertised in advance. While the Steering Committee was to be the governing body through required meetings at least six times a year, an Executive Committee was also established.

> The Executive Committee shall be empowered to act on behalf of the steering committee between meetings of the steering committee. The executive committee shall report for ratification at the next meeting of the steering committee all actions taken by it since the preceding meeting of the steering committee.[57]

Among the other committees created by the constitution were an Issues Committee and a Committee on Party Structure. This reform organization institutionalized its issue concerns quite specifically in the constitution and clearly committed itself to liberal objectives:

> The objectives of the State Coalition are to improve and strengthen the Democratic Party in the state of New Jersey by making the party more aware of the major issues that confront our people and more eager and willing to seek intelligent solutions; and by supporting candidates of integrity, ability, and devotion to the public welfare.[58]

The constitution emphatically had an electoral orientation. Article 15 gave details on the procedures for endorsing candidates and contesting primaries. State conventions and polling procedures were developed for selecting candidates. These rules eventually became the focal point over which a battle for the gubernatorial nomination centered.

Besides the time spent on the constitution and by-laws, a phenomenal effort went into a complex formula to allot county delegation size and voting weight at the state convention. Nominations to leadership positions were also paramount. The one area that was slighted was issue or policy formulation. This was evident even though the issues committee developed a long manifesto of priorities: taxation, education, fair and appropriate housing, welfare, water and air pollution, and ethics in government; with a secondary list including analysis of: abortion and divorce laws, mental health facilities, jetport, transportation, consumer protection, and antiballistic missile system. Yet after developing this list, it became noticeable that this issue-oriented group soon relegated issues to a subordinate position. Emergencies of an organizational nature replaced policy goals in the newly developing structure.

There was a concerted drive at this point to "involve different kinds of people," to get beyond their "homogeneous" beginnings.[59] Yet even the homogeneity of their inception was not enough to stop the growing dissension. Conflict surfaced around the role of the N.D.C. in the gubernatorial primary. Should candidates be invited to the convention? Since the purpose of the convention, besides formal organization, was to decide whether or not to take part in the primary, the leadership concluded it would be unwise to involve the N.D.C. with gubernatorial politics at that point.[60]

A short time after this decision, Ned Parsekian, a member of the Steering Committee and panel head of an N.D.C. workshop on organized crime, declared his candidacy. Embarrassed by Parsekian's announcement, the cochairmen "rebuked"[61] him in public to make it clear that the N.D.C. did not support Parsekian or anyone else for governor.

The press reports of Gaby and Leone's statement set off a furor. A rump meeting of the Steering Committee attended mainly, but not only, by Parsekian supporters produced the statement that the leaders could not speak for the N.D.C. as a group, only a majority of the Steering Committee could do so.[62] This episode was finally resolved by a last-minute invitation of all potential candidates to the Founding Convention.

The eve of the March convention gave glimpses of a group whose internal divisions over leadership responsibilities shadowed the bond of solidarity that might have grown from agreement over the importance of issue-oriented politics.

This founding convention brought together many activists who had known each other during the presidential primary and Democratic National Convention the previous year. Conflict between Parsekian and Gaby forces was based upon past as well as present contacts. Thus, with the gubernatorial election on everyone's mind, the rules and officers selected would not produce officers who were objective comrades in the common cause of reform. The individuals and by-laws endorsed would represent clearly differentiated interests.

With this background in mind, one can appreciate the intensity over many relatively minor decisions that characterized the organizing convention. In fact, one might describe this gathering not as an "organizing," but rather a "disorganizing" convention. The problem created by a lack of orderly procedures (after all, it was the N.D.C.'s first convention) was accented by a weak to non-functioning communications system. Add these physical problems to the underlying political realities of the approaching gubernatorial primary and one understands why the N.D.C. spent the entire day adopting rules and electing officers.[63] The decisions would influence who the N.D.C. endorsed for governor.

The selection of N.D.C. chairman illustrated this conflict. Gaby ran against Sam Zitter, a Parsekian supporter. The outcome, 472 to 194, produced a clear vote of confidence for Gaby's activities. Also elected were Richard Leone, John Bell, and Joel Jacobson as vice-presidents.

A black caucus spent much time together, as did a student caucus. Only their recommendations were accepted for constitutional revisions. All other motions for change were defeated. The black caucus pressed for mention of minority groups in the constitutional revisions. All other motions for change were defeated. The black caucus pressed for mention of minority groups in the constitution, while the students helped the coalition eliminate any age requirement for membership.

An interesting development at the convention, which led to much confusion later, involved a motion that passed easily. "A delegate moved that the convention endorse a graduated state income tax and support in the primary and general elections only those candidates who supported such a tax." This action is surely an ideal exhibit of how purposive and liberal reformers could create organizational rules to implement their policy concerns.

After a long day of adopting by-laws and selecting officers, the convention turned to the gubernatorial issue. Before the N.D.C. could go too deeply into it, the Parsekian forces moved to table the question of gubernatorial endorsements until April 12, because they knew they were going to lose if a vote were taken.[64] The black caucus joined them to enable their supporters to get to know the candidates. After much confusion, the convention was disbanded until April.

Between March 22 and April 12 the N.D.C. focused on gubernatorial questions. The only contest within the N.D.C. was between U.S. Representative Henry Helstoski, Jr., a liberal, antiwar Democrat, and Parsekian, both from Bergen County. Gaby did try to get the counties involved in primary fights on all levels and engaged in voter registration. All interest, however, converged on the gubernatorial nominee. The resumption of the convention, more organized than the first meeting, produced a victory for Henry Helstoski. The Helstoski win surprised no one. It might have been predicted from Sam Zitter's defeat in the selection of N.D.C. chairman. The lines between factions had been clearly drawn at that time.

The N.D.C. formally went to work for Helstoski. Since Parsekian continued to run, the liberal vote was split. Some contended that the organization splintered completely when Helstoski was endorsed.[65] Gaby denied this.[66] Each group worked for its own man, while ex-governor Robert Meyner easily swept the June primaries, but lost the general election. So small was the total reform vote that even if Parsekian had dropped out, Helstoski could not possibly have won.

Then began the complex question of whether the N.D.C. should endorse Meyner or not. This was confused by the requirement that any nominee of the N.D.C. be committed to a state income tax, which Meyner was not. Considering that Meyner had not received a single vote at the second convention, Gaby, in his open support of Meyner, had an uphill fight on his hands. To help the N.D.C. decide about any endorsement, Meyner answered a series of written questions and then met with the Steering Committee.

This conflict about Meyner reflected a much deeper division over the role of the insurgent in party politics. Violent disagreements broke out within the group over its relationship to the Democratic Party. Gaby claimed that the N.D.C. had a commitment to the party it sought to reform, and that Meyner's liberal response to N.D.C. questions were far more in accord with N.D.C. philosophy than the actions of U.S. Representative William Cahill, the Republican aspirant.[67] Helstoski himself urged the N.D.C. to endorse Meyner.[68]

The issue of endorsement centered on the convention motion about a state income tax. Those who were against Meyner fought not to rescind the income-tax requirement.[69] A mail poll of all delegates revoked the income-tax provision, 168.19 to 167.25, but rejected the Meyner endorsement 163.06 to 167.25. What this poll revealed, more than any substantive support for any particular candidate, was the apathy of most N.D.C. members: only 448 ballots were returned from a total of 938 ballots mailed.[70] The N.D.C. was obviously in trouble.

Gaby resigned to work for Meyner, and another episode in the history of reform movements came to a bizarre close. After all those weeks of hammering out a constitution, a Steering Committee contingent claimed there was no provision for succession and voted for someone other than the next vice-president, Joel Jacobson, in line for the office. Jacobson was not trusted by this segment of the N.D.C. because of his ties to the regular party organization.[71] Jacobson legally claimed the chairmanship and then left the meeting, never to call another. Thus the N.D.C. was left in limbo.

Organizations that continued to exist, such as Bergen and Union (probably the most antagonistic to the elected leadership) did so on a county level. The state N.D.C. was neither dead nor alive — not permanently disabled on the rocks of issue-oriented politics, but rather on the shoals of personal animosity.

What began as a blessing, the fact that many already knew each other from the presidential campaign, ended as the cause of incapacity. Each had a history to haunt him — perhaps a position taken that was considered morally wrong by some or personally aggrandizing by others.[72] In any case, the leadership was suspect. Within an organization created to be "responsible" to the rank and file, this permitted the crippling blow.

One should not carry this explanation of personal animosity too far. There were genuine divisions in philosophies and approaches of N.D.C. participants. If one can characterize the reformer as a middle-class professional, much as his precursors, there was still evident in the ranks of the N.D.C. a noticeable contingent of minorities, labor groups, and youth. Perhaps the growing heterogeneity of reform groups, as they attempt to broaden their bases to implement participatory democracy, introduces intense strains. The N.D.C. was mainly a middle-class organization, by any standards, but its ideology and commitment to political reform led it to identify with certain deprived groups long ignored by past reformers. In fact, this commitment led to a large overrepresentation of minorities on the Steering Committee.

Thus it seems that the potentially conflicting issues of "clean democratic party structure" versus "delivery of social welfare programs" was a constant source of division. The incapacitating division over the Meyner endorsement was predicted upon this split between the procedural reformers and the substantive issue-oriented reformers, a distinction Wilson drew.[73] Gaby could be placed in this latter group. His concern for liberal economic issues led him to be comfortable with Meyner.[74]

Gaby was joined in this orientation by the Middlesex and Essex contingent, who were also more likely to emphasize the outputs of politics: programs and policies. This pattern contrasted markedly with one in which the process or input side of political decision making was essential. Concentrated in Union and Bergen County, these N.D.C. reformers wanted to take over the Democratic Party to democratize its structures.[75] To these adherents Meyner was the bosses' choice and automatically disreputable because of the process of selection.

What grows out of these conflicts is a possible new shape to the reform movement of the future. Both groups could be described as purposive activists according to the past classifications. Yet this common commitment to cosmopolitan and issue concerns does not describe one homogeneous type of reformer.

As the reformer becomes more aware of the advantages of electoral politics, he must also make essential decisions to "compromise" his principles or remain firm. Should he settle for a candidate who supports many of his policies in weakened form, or should he continuously press for the ideal solutions he holds dear?

In answering this question, N.D.C. members represent both the traditional-procedural reformer and also the substantive newcomer. The administrative tinkering, the antiparty viewpoint — the whole story with traditional reformers — is only part of the tale of the N.D.C. Process and programmatic reformers are both visible in this new group. Furthermore, one should not exaggerate the distinctions between the two types. While the divergent orientations may have stymied the N.D.C., both factions are likely to emphasize process and program — merely in different degrees.

Wilson describes the Stevenson reformers as liberal, but minimizes this programmatic bent.[76] Process or democratic procedures are so much more important. In the N.D.C., I do not find only party reformers seeking democratic procedures. A large and dominant segment leans toward liberal issue formulation that involves social welfare programs. Much of the conflict in the N.D.C. revolved around emphasis. The factions both supported democratizing party structures and implementing liberal programs. Where they varied was in their priorities. These differences might have been resolved, if it had not been for the immediacy of the gubernatorial election and the pressure to take a position.

The schism created by Helstoski's and Parsekian's candidacies accentuated all the other conflicts. Most organizations have to deal with conflict during some periods. This probability, however, implies a continuing commitment to the organization as a framework for resolving the disagreements. When participants can and are willing to "take their marbles and go home," the possibility of continuing to meet and fight is endangered. The N.D.C. developed no institutionalized procedures and elicited little loyalty. Loyalty to it, above and through political divisions, could not be expected in a few short months.

The reasons for this inability can be found in more than these philosophical points of view. The structure of New Jersey politics was county based, as I have already mentioned. Each county had different problems and possibilities. For the N.D.C. member from boss-dominated Essex to concentrate on taking over and democratizing the party would have been a most defeating strategy for reform success. Better for these activists to direct their energies to moving the policies and nominations of the Democratic Party to the left. The reverse approach would be fruitful in Bergen, where a strong reform organization exists. Thus the organizational needs of distinct counties conflicted with the development of a homogeneous strategy. Furthermore, the imminence of a gubernatorial campaign drove the N.D.C. into premature electoral politics that rigidified the conflicts in a neonatal organization.

Certain facets of reform movements lead one to question the old stereotype of this activist as the cosmopolitan, purposive liberal. Historical descriptions of past reformers discover cosmopolitans and purposive participants, but hardly social welfare liberals. Yet in the N.D.C. member this programmatic liberalism may be an accurate description of his motivations and philosophy.

While the New Jersey N.D.C. did not survive as a formal institution, the reform activist has certainly continued in good health. The 1972 campaign, which garnered the Democratic presidential nomination for George McGovern, showed the growing strength of this new breed. The powerful showing McGovern made in New Jersey, carrying most of the state in the primary, can not be ignored. Whether the same activists were involved is not the point. What does seem to be essential to understanding the increasing salience of the reform style of politics is the incremental growth in strength of these supposed amateurs. The N.D.C. may have faded away, but its impact on New Jersey politics is still noticeable. Even the massive defeat McGovern suffered in the general election can not diminish the growing influence of reform appeals. The potentially new strength of the reformer is important and should be examined in depth. This is, of course, the purpose of this study.

The changing appeals of the reformer are marked by new orientations. The N.D.C. activist displays not only liberal-issue commitments, but also a certain degree of electoral professionalism. This concern with winning elections in order to implement policy was quite evident in the conflicts that destroyed the N.D.C. It is possible that the purposive reformer's concern with administrative reorganization has been superseded by this social welfare liberalism. If liberal philosophy opposed to mere procedural goals becomes more important in motivating the reformer, there may be a qualitative change in the kind of behavior an insurgent exhibits.

In tracing the historical roots of the reform movements through their demographic, motivational, and programmatic characteristics, I have tried to indicate the similarities as well as contrasts between the movements. Demographically, the reformer has been a middle-class professional. Yet the type of professional has varied over time. The implications of these shifts are evident in the programs and policies espoused. The civil service reformers and Populists sought a return to a simpler way of life. This contrasted remarkably with the Progressives and municipal reformers who sought ways to apply their newly developing technocratic skills to the "business" of urban government. Tinkerers, rather than programmatic liberals, these early twentieth-century reformers still appear rather remote from the civil service reformers. A similar distance has been noted between the Progressives or municipal reformers and the Democratic-club amateurs of the 1950s. These post-World War II insurgents, rather than destroying the political party, sought to take it over for liberal purposes. Much of their activities centered around procedural democracy *within* the political party. The newer N.D.C. reformer also exhibits strong variations in his approach to party politics. The procedural liberalism of the club movement may have been relinquished in favor of substantive liberalism — a relatively new theme in reform history. Thus the trends diverge and become refined in subsequent examples of the genre *reformer politicus*.

I turn from history to contemporary political science research. Having placed the reformer in his historical context, it is now necessary to locate him in the niche of party politics, comparing him with the regular Democratic politician he continues to oppose. While one might have described the municipal reformers or civil service activists without much allusion to political parties, an essential aspect of the post-World War II reformers involves the relationship with the Democratic Party. This party focus has become central to understanding all recent efforts at social reform.

In the next chapter I shall move from recent findings about regulars and reformers to hypotheses about the N.D.C. member and his demographic, motivational, and issue-oriented characteristics. These hypotheses will then be tested and the findings evaulated in the remainder of this study.

Notes to Chapter 1

1. Robert K. Merton, "Patterns of Influence: Local and Cosmopolitan Influentials," in *Social Theory and Social Structure*, in Merton, 1st revised and enlarged ed. (London: Free Press of Glencoe, 1957), pp. 387-420.

2. Lee Benson, *The Concept of Jacksonian Democracy: New York as a Test Case* (New York: Atheneum Press, 1961); Paul Kleppner, *The Cross of Culture: A Social Analysis of Midwestern Politics, 1850-1900* (New York: Free Press, 1970).

3. Olson, *Logic of Collective Action,* chap. 6; Peter B. Clark and James Q. Wilson, "Incentive Systems: A Theory of Organization," *Administrative Science Quarterly,* (September 1961): 129-66.

4. Richard Hofstadter, *The Age of Reform: From Bryan to F.D.R.* (New York: Alfred A. Knopf, 1955), pp. 181, 202; Arthur Mann, *Yankee Reformers in the Urban Age* (Cambridge, Mass.: The Belknap Press of Harvard University Press, 1954), p. 229; Theodore J. Lowi, *At the Pleasure of the Mayor: Patronage and Power in New York City, 1898-1958* (New York: Free Press of Glencoe, 1964), p. 229.

5. Charles Garrett, *The LaGuardia Years: Machine and Reform Politics in New York City* (New Brunswick, N. J.: Rutgers University Press, 1961), p. 11.

6. Hofstadter, *Age of Reform*, pp. 8-9.

7. Samuel P. Hays, "Political Parties and the Community-Society Continuum," in *The American Party Systems: Stages of Political Development*, ed. William Nisbet Chambers and Walter Dean Burnham (New York: Oxford University Press, 1967), pp. 153-55.

8. Walter Dean Burnham, *Presidential Ballots, 1836-1892* (Baltimore: Johns Hopkins Press, 1955), p. 147.

9. Walter Dean Burnham, "Party Systems and the Political Process," in *American Party Systems*, ed. Chambers and Burnham, p. 284; Ari Hoogenboom, *Outlawing the Spoils: A History of the Civil Service Reform Movement, 1865-1883* (Urbana, Illinois: University of Illinois Press, 1961), p. 10

10. Harold U. Faulkner, *Politics, Reform, and Expansion, 1890-1900,* The New American Nation Series, ed. Henry Steel Commager and Richard B. Morris (New York: Harper & Brothers, 1959), pp. 56, 26.

11. Hoogenboom, *Outlawing the Spoils,* p. 197; Hofstadter, *Age of Reform,* p. 93; Benson, *Jacksonian Democracy*, chap. 2.

12. Eric Goldman, *Rendezvous with Denstiny: A History of Modern American Reform* (New York: Alfred A. Knopf, 1952), p. 75.

13. Kleppner, *Cross of Culture*, p. 353.

14. Frederick C. Mosher, *Democracy and the Public Service*, Public Administration and Democracy Series, ed. Roscoe C. Martin (New York: Oxford University Press, 1968), pp. 64-65.

15. Faulkner, *Politics, Reform, and Expansion,* p. 26.

16. Paul P. Van Riper, *History of the United States Civil Service* (White Plains, N. Y.: Row, Peterson and Company, 1958), p. 82.

17. Melvin G. Holli, *Reform in Detroit: Hazen S. Pingree and Urban Politics* (New York: Oxford University Press, 1969), p. 163.

18. Hofstadter, *Age of Reform*, pp. 131-72, is one of the major proponents of this school; *see also* George E. Mowry, "The California Progressive and His Rationale," *Mississippi Valley Historical Review* 36 (September 1949): 239-50; George E. Mowry, *The California Progressives* (Chicago: Encounter Paperbacks, Quadrangle Books, 1963).

19. Hoogenboom, *Outlawing the Spoils*, p. 10; Dorothy Ganfield Fowler, *The Cabinet Politician: The Postmasters General, 1829-1909* (New York: Columbia University Press, 1943), pp. 148-49.

20. Samuel P. Hays, "The Politics of Reform in Municipal Government in the Progressive Era," *Pacific Northwest Quarterly* 55 (October 1964): 158, 160.

21. Gabriel Kolko, *The Triumph of Conservatism: A Reinterpretation of American History, 1900-1916* (New York: Free Press of Glencoe, 1963); Robert H. Wiebe, *Businessmen and Reform: A Study of the Progressive Movement* (Cambridge, Mass.: Harvard University Press, 1962).

22. Samuel P. Hays, *Conservation and the Gospel of Efficiency: The Progressive Conservation Movement, 1890-1920* (Cambridge, Mass.: Harvard University Press, 1959); Richard M. Abrams and Lawrence W. Levine, "Business Interests in the Progressive Movement," in *The Shaping of Twentieth-Century America: Interpretive Articles,* ed. Richard M. Abrams and Lawrence W. Levine (Boston: Little, Brown & Company, 1965), pp. 252-53.

23. Herbert Croly, *The Promise of American Life,* ed. by Arthur M. Schlesinger, Jr. (Cambridge, Mass.: The Belknap Press of Harvard University Press, 1965).

24. Richard C. Hofstadter, ed., *The Progressive Movement, 1900-1915* (Englewood Cliffs, N. J.: Prentice-Hall, Inc., 1963), p. 9.

25. Lincoln Steffens, *The Shame of the Cities* (New York: Hill and Wang, 1957), p. 40.

26. Hays, "Politics of Reform," pp. 161-63.

27. Hays, "Political Parties," in Chambers and Burnham, pp. 176-77.

28. Richard S. Childs, *Civic Victories: The Story of an Unfinished Revolution* (New York: Harper & Brothers Publishers, 1952), pp. 222-24.

29. Hofstadter, *The Progressive Movement*, p. 14.

30. Stinchcombe, *Reform and Reaction*, p. 35.

31. Hofstadter, *The Progressive Movement,* p. 14; Christopher Lasch, *The New Radicalism in America, 1889-1963: The Intellectual as a Social Type* (New York: Alfred A. Knopf, 1965).

32. Abrams and Levine, "Business Interests . . . ," in Abrams and Levine p. 252.

33. Holli, *Reform in Detroit,* pp. 162-71.

34. Arthur Mann, *LaGuardia Comes to Power: 1933* (New York: J. B. Lippincott Company, 1965), p. 153.

35. Holli, *Reform in Detoit*, pp. 9-10; Arthur Mann, *LaGuardia: A Fighter Against His Times, 1882-1933* (New York: J. B. Lippincott Company, 1959), pp. 147-62,

36. Allen F. Davis, *Spearheads for Reform: The Social Settlements and the Progressive Movement, 1890-1914* (New York: Oxford University Press, 1967).

37. Lowi, *At the Pleasure of the Mayor*, p. 179.

38. James Q. Wilson, "Politics and Reform in American Cities," in *American Government Annual, 1962-63,* ed. Ivan Hinderaker (New York: Holt, Rinehart & Winston, 1962), p. 52.

39. William Seal Carpenter, *The Unfinished Business of Civil Service Reform*

(Princeton, N. J.: Princeton University Press, 1952), pp. 28, 46.

40. Wilson, "Politics and Reform," in Hinderaker, pp. 44, 49.

41. Ibid.

42. Wilson, *Amateur Democrat,* p. 14.

43. Ibid., pp. 140-53.

44. Curran V. Shields, "A Note on Party Organization: The Democrats in California," *Western Political Quarterly* 7 (December 1954): 681; *see* Angus Campbell et al., *The American Voter: An Abridgement* (New York: John Wiley & Sons, Inc., 1964), pp. 111-13. The word *idealogy* is used throughout in its loosest sense, meaning a fairly consistent (liberal or conservative) orientation toward political and social issues. Further discussion of this concept will follow in later chapters.

45. Seyom Brown, "Fun Can be Politics," *Reporter,* 12 November 1959, pp. 27-28.

46. Quoted from the Riverside Democrats Club Newspaper, March 1957, in Blaisdell, *Riverside Democrats,* p. 8.

47. Herzog, *McCarthy for President*, pp. 21-23.

48. James Reichley, "The Last Stand of Accommodation Politics," *Fortune,* October 1968, p. 228.

49. Ibid.

50. McCarthy, *The Year of the People*, pp. 248-49, 256; Herzog, *McCarthy for President,* pp. 226-29; Jeremy Larner, "Nobody Knows . . . Reflections on the McCarthy Campaign-Part I," *Harper's Magazine,* April 1969, p. 69.

51. Robert Walters, "McCarthy, Kennedy Backers in New Coalition," *Newark Evening News,* 7 October 1968, p. 6.

52. Glendhill Cameron, "'After Chicago, We Are Radicals,'" *Trenton Evening Times,* 4 September 1968, p. 21.

53. N.D.C. "Coalition Agenda," Recap of Meeting at Robert Treat Hotel, Newark, N. J., n.d., (mimeographed.) The history of the N.D.C. comes from the private files of Daniel Gaby, when other sources are not cited.

54. N.D.C. "Coalition Report: A Newsletter of the New Democratic Coalition of New Jersey," November 1968.

55. Ned Parsekian, private interview, Hackensack, N. J., 15 January 1971; Joel Jacobson, private interview, South Orange, N. J., 11 January 1971.

56. N.D.C., Minutes of the Preliminary Meeting, United Auto Workers, Cranford, N. J., 14 October 1968.

57. N.D.C., "Constitution of the New Democratic Coalition of New Jersey," n.d., mimeographed.

58. N.D.C., "Constitution."

59. N.D.C., Minutes of Meeting of the Steering Committee.

60. Letter from Daniel M. Gaby and Richard C. Leone to members of N.D.C. Steering Committee, 21 January 1969.

61. Angelo Baglivo, "Democratic Coalitions' Primary Role Uncertain," *Newark Evening News,* 17 January 1969, p. 11.

62. John Plaut, private interview, Summit, N. J., 4 January 1971; Angelo Baglivo, "Parsekian Gets Support," *Newark Evening News,* 25 January 1969, p. 1.

63. The description of the convention, except where specifically noted, came from minutes of meeting of New Democratic Coalition of New Jersey, New Brunswick, N. J., 22 March 1969, typewritten.

64. Plaut interview.

65. Joseph Carragher, "Can Dem Coalition Survive a Decision? " *Newark Star*

Ledger, 6 April 1969, sec. 3, p. 4.

66. Ibid.

67. Gaby interview.

68. "Meyner Backed by 2 Liberals," *Newark Evening News*, 3 September 1969, p. 11.

69. "Coalition Group Stands Pat on Income Tax," *Newark Evening News*, 24 September 1969, p. 14.

70. Jack Mehl, "Meyner Backer Quits after Coalition Snub," *Newark Evening News*, 18 October 1969, p. 1.

71. Betty Wenk, private telephone interview, 13 January 1971.

72. Series of private interviews with N.D.C. members, December 1970 to January 1971.

73. Wilson, *Amateur Democrat*, pp. 132-33.

74. Gaby eventually made and lost a Democratic primary bid for U.S. Senator and it was on a platform of updated "populism," returning power to the people away from the control of large corporate interests. He also emphasized responsive social service programs much in keeping with his position in the Meyner controversy.

75. With some help from the corruption issue, the reformers did take over the Union County Democratic Party and had for quite a while been a major force in the Bergen Regular Organization.

76. Wilson, *Amateur Democrat*, pp. 127-53.

2
Previous Research and Pertinent Hypotheses

One of the most visible trends in reform politics has been the increasing relationship between party organization and the reform movement. The early amateurs, such as the municipal reformers, did not seek to reclaim the insidious political party, but rather to destroy it. Ever since the club movement, however, attempts at reform have been intrinsically tied to the regular organization. The party had become a vehicle — in purified form, of course — to implement issue-oriented concerns. This slow development provides the researcher with a very characteristic and fairly new shape to reform movements.

Some of these possible shifts in attitudes and priorities can be presented by distinguishing the "reformer" from the "amateur." I have been careful not to refer to the N.D.C. movement as amateur based. The reasons for this are not self-evident. In order to distinguish the reformer from the amateur as well as the professional politician, it is worth a bit of time to explore the meanings implicit in such terms. By this task I shall set out some implicit hypotheses of the historical discussion just completed. Making these hypotheses explicit, I shall then examine the social science literature for supports, refutations, and refinements of these reform and professional models of political behavior.

Comparatively analyzing reformers and professionals for the purpose of clarifying the characteristics of this new reformer, I shall then specify the kinds of demographic, motivational, and programmatic variables that would be essential for an understanding of the N.D.C. movement. These variables will be polished and presented through further hypotheses. Necessary operational procedures and methods will conclude this chapter.

Before delineating any hypotheses, it is useful to cull from the previous chapter certain accepted truths about the reformer, often called *amateur*, and the professional politician.

In everyday usage, the word *amateur* reflects the reality that an individual is not involved in his work for a living. Amateur, implying dilletantism, bears a stain for one who is not taken seriously by those who do the same job full time or "professionally."

"Professional" is itself a complex word, since it involves more than the assertion of full-time, paid positions. There are a series of professional occupations (medicine or law, for example) requiring specialized and unique training in a body of knowledge. Besides the specialized skill, inherent in the professions, there is also supposed to be a "deep and lifelong commitment" to the specified field.[1] Detachment from the end result of applying one's skill relates to a profession's lack of self-interest, which enforces a "primary orientation to community interest."[2]

Another characteristic of a profession is that the "system of rewards is a monetary and honorary set of symbols of work achievment and are ends in themselves, not means to some end of individual self-interest."[3] The last trait of professions is that they are self-regulatory, through internalized codes of ethics, which are inculcated during the training or socialization process.[4]

Although varied uses of the term *professional* are employed to describe the politician, it is important to note that there are rather distinct meanings. For one to relate politics to the usage of professionalism presented above, meaning a distinct set of ethics and knowledge, may seem absurd. While one may find an amateur politician, has anyone ever encountered an "amateur physician" Yet there is a body of know-how, if not knowledge, associated with politics.

In Great Britain this information is imparted to a technician, the party agent, through course work and examination. The salaried and trained agent is responsible for winning elections for his party. While American parties do not organize this knowledge formally, there certainly exists on-the-job training or apprenticeship.

The emphasis upon elections as the object of political professionalism is valuable in separating the amateur from the professional. Would the professional and the amateur agree that there was a body of knowledge to be transmitted and the specifics of

that knowledge? In most fields one would assume the answer to be
yes. In the case of politics, however, this is not certain. The essential purpose of politics for the regular or professional politician is
to win elections. Only to the successful party do the benefits of
patronage or public status accrue. Thus the skills — campaign techniques and strategies — are the bases of political knowledge.

According to the historical description of the amateur, however, his political goals revolve around his purposive motives. The
end of political activity is the adoption of policies and principles
that conform to his view of the public good. This is not simply
concern about issues, but issues as they are molded by the amateur's
selfless motivation. Thus in politics, the professional and the amateur could not even agree on the very subject matter of the discip-
line: one would develop schools for winning elections, the other
colleges for educating the public in "higher principles."

This selfless involvement leads back to the first distinction
usually associated with the regular and the professional, that is,
the relationship of occupation to politics. The amateur, by definition, is one whose income is not derived from politics. Both the
amateur and the regular chose a political life because of interest in
the subject matter, yet the sustaining motivation is quite different
for the professional. Fascination with politics might still be important, but for the regular it has become tied to the material necessity of supporting himself and his family. Max Weber has explained
this contrast well:

> There are two ways of making politics one's vocation: either
> one lives "for" politics or one lives "off" politics. By no means
> is this contrast an exclusive one. The rule is, rather that man does
> both, at least in thought, and certainly he also does both in
> practice. He who lives "for" politics makes politics his life, in an
> internal sense. Either he enjoys the naked possession of the
> power he exerts, or he nourishes his inner balance and self-feel-
> ing by the consciousness that his life has *meaning* in the service
> of a "cause." In this internal sense, every sincere man who lives
> for a cause also lives off this cause. The distinction hence refers
> to a much more substantial aspect of the matter, namely, to
> the economic. He who strives to make politics a permanent
> *source of income* lives "off" politics as a vocation, whereas he
> who does not do this lives "for" politics.[5]

Weber correlated the ability to live "for" politics with the posses-
sion of wealth or economic independence. Amateurs do work, but
their incomes may be enough to permit free time to devote to

politics. This is to be shown by research and can not be a foregone conclusion about the N.D.C. An economic independence may protect their pursuit of the public weal, since there may be little material advantage to self-serving orientations. This is a bit like saying they live "for" politics because — and only because — they can afford to do so. The role of economics is at the root of the variation between the two groups. All other differences flow from this, according to Weber's analysis.

The amateur who finds politics "intrinsically interesting[6] is supported mainly by his continuing fascination. The necessity of arousing his interest explains the most impressive fact of the movements traced above: the seasonal nature of all efforts. "Mornin' glories," contemptuously stated one machine "philosophe," referring to New York City reformers.[7] If the reformer's concern with issues coheres to his independence from politics as a living, this may mean that his conscience has to be aroused to precipitate his activity.

The regular politician parts company with the definition of a professional in the area of selfless involvement for community good. From my previous chapter, one can expect Anthony Downs's rational politician, who formulates policies to win elections so that he can advance his own self-interest.[8] The regular does not depend upon issues and ideology for his own satisfactions or incentives. The amateur is supposed to reverse the regular's pattern, if he contests elections only to formulate policy, and finds deep fulfillment in ideology and issue involvement.

Indignation seems to feed the amateur's interest. Usually, the attachment to a "cause" indicates the desire for some change in political organization or activities. Historically, then, amateurism has been associated with reform. But this reform has not been revolutionary in purpose. The movements explored sought revised arrangements between political entities: civil service reform, party reorganization. This transformation I call *procedural reform* or *tinkering*. The true programmatic liberal occurs only recently in reform movements.

Since a hallmark of the amateur is supposed to be his labor for the sake of principles, I do anticipate a strong refusal to compromise. Winning is not as important as making a fight for ideals to which he intensely clings. This is the moral approach to politics. The amateur remains intransigent in his positions because concessions are compromising — in more ways than one. The regular would bargain or move from a particular stand, if he thought it would attract votes. I expect the amateur to be a moral educator and the regular a pragmatic campaigner. These traits have other implications.

Individuals who operate according to philosophical inclinations are likely to be uncomfortable in American nonideological parties. This becomes quite obvious through election chronology. After the primary comes the general election in which all good regulars work for the candidate they disliked in the primary. The professional's loyalty to the party creates a frame of reference for him to judge all outsiders as considerably worse than one's own incompetent. This is not simply a question of economic self-interest, but also of psychological ties to an institution such as the Democratic Party. The reformer feels little underlying party loyalty and may be more willing to sit on his hands during the general election if his first choice does not win the primary. The conflict generated in the N.D.C. over Meyner's endorsement provides a recent example of this characteristic.

These definitions of the amateur, derived from the interpretations of amateurism and also from the historical overview, can be concisely expressed and tested as hypotheses. One can divide these components into the three areas that structured the previous historical analysis: demographic, motivational, and programmatic.

Demographic Definitions

1. The amateur politician does not earn his living through politics. The professional's occupation is tied to politics.
2. The amateur politician illustrates upper-class or high-status background. The professional politician derives from a lower-class or lower-status one.

Motivational Definitions

3. The amateur politician was *first* aroused politically for disinterested purposive reasons, such as issues or causes. The professional was impelled by selfish or materialistic reasons.
4. The amateur politician *continues* to be active because of his interest in issues. The professional continues because of material or nonmaterial solidary rewards, such as jobs or status.
5. The amateur politician is sporadically active. The professional is perpetually involved.
6. The amateur politician defines his role in issue-oriented terms. The regular does so in campaign-oriented ones.

7. The amateur politician is not willing to compromise on any issue. The regular is pragmatic and used to compromising.
8. The amateur politician is a procedural reformer. The regular defends the organizational status quo.
9. The amateur politician is an independent, not closely attached to one political party. The professional is intensely loyal to his party.

Now that I have listed these interrelated definitions of the amateur, a backward glance at the historical episodes of reform will illustrate which ones conform to the pattern. The civil service reformers, the Progressive-era reformers, and the interwar municipal reformers all fit into this mold: high-status, patronage-free independents, unwilling to compromise on the procedural issues that explain their reasons for sometime political activity.

It is ironic that the more one becomes involved in substantive issues (the rallying cry of the amateur), the less amateurism can be discovered. The municipal reformers, who espoused the "Social Gospel," while middle-class professionals, were continuously active on behalf of social welfare. These activists are less the stereotypic amateur.

Another glaring reversal of the pattern is the movement expanded by LaGuardia. One of the most pragmatic reformers, he was a professional politician in time spent as well as inclination. Identification with the immigrants, whose background he shared, gave him an objective picture of what substantive policies they required to escape from the burden of poverty. None of this dabbling or "do-goodism" for LaGuardia. Politics was his paid vocation.

A further question is raised by the Populist movement, which grew from the immediate self-interest of the yeoman farmer. While these farmers were not full-time politicians, neither can one comfortably call them amateurs. To verify this lack of amateurism, one has only to recall the total distaste of the civil service reformers for the Populists. The parochial nature of the Populist, and his low status, make it very difficult to consider Populism an example of the amateur dimension in politics.

There are certain discrepancies between the amateur ideal and the Democratic-club movement as well as the more recent N.D.C. While reflecting the amateur model in demographic and motivational character, these newer insurgents indicate a variation from the programmatic aspects presented above.

The growing electoral orientation of the N.D.C. reformer in his attempts to take over the Democratic Party, rather than incapacitate it, illustrate a certain development in the tradition of the amateur. Understanding the political process, using campaign strategies, the insurgent seems less an amateur than the previous definition might suggest.

The N.D.C. member takes the variation one step futher in his in-increasing concern with substantive — not only procedural — liberalism. For these reasons, the view of the N.D.C. activist as an "amateur" politician does not appear totally accurate. Thus I have chosen to consider the N.D.C. member a reformer and not an amateur in his political endeavors, avoiding the pejorative connotation of that epithet, as well as its possible inaccuracies.

Reform has been distinguished from amateurism. The amateurs of the past and present have been reform oriented, but their ways have been distinct. In fact, from historical research, one would claim that what characterizes the traditional reformer may not be his programmatic aspects, but rather the motivations that impel him toward political action. Looking at the N.D.C., as I have done quite briefly, I do not find motivational analysis the distinguishing trait of the present reformer.

In place of motivations, the programmatic variables have mushroomed in importance. In fact, this substantive liberalism of the N.D.C. might be an intrinsic part of his purposive motivation. So primary do the programmatic or policy variables appear that two related sets of variables may be more useful for studying the N.D.C. than simply grouping policy variables into one mass. By refining the policy analysis, I shall describe the actual programs supported according to their degree of liberalism. In addition, I shall then interrelate the various opinions to discover ideological constraint.

I have found the other categories useful, as they stand. The demographic or background attributes explored certain socialization, status, or geographic characteristics of the amateur. The motivational variables emphasized political incentives and rewards. These four main classes of variables, identified as demographic, motivational, liberal, and ideological, will be operationalized to differentiate the reformer from the professional politician.

Before any actual research is done, however, these sets of variables must be delineated more clearly through additional hypotheses. But this entails another component, reviewing the literature in political science that has dealt with the local activist. Since this survey places the reformer in a comparative framework, it is essential to analyze the professional politician, as well as the insurgent. Furthermore, since much of the literature in political science emphasizes the professional, this will help detail the regular's characteristics more thoroughly than I have.

Up to this point I have centered attention on the reformer. Now I shall turn to the regular grass roots politician, both in a historical and a current context. I have chosen the locally involved regular to study, since the N.D.C. illustrated a grassroots level of activity. This study would not, in fact, be comparative if I contrasted locally selected reformers with those professionals who served a statewide or national constituency. From this review, I shall evolve hypotheses to contrast the reform style with the regular one.

A. Demographic Characteristics

The demographic attributes, deriving from the definition of a reformer as a person of high status, who is not a full-time government or party employee, will be the first explored in relation to the professional. I have questioned some of the stereotypes of the amateur applied to the N.D.C. The same queries can be raised about how well the traditional view of the regular politician illustrates the present characteristics of the professional.

The status of American politicians is nothing about which a regular can be proud.[9] Much of the reputation of the politician is based upon the continuing myth of the lower-class, boss-dominated machine. To look at this myth from a demographic point of view highlights the visibility of certain assumed socioeconomic characteristics. The politician is alleged to: be poorly educated, if not totally illiterate; derive from immigrant parents; identify with Catholic or Jewish religions; live in an urban ghetto; work at lower-status occupations; achieve higher income than expected only because of chicanery. The attack upon the machine by the Progressives and later municipal reformers was, in fact, according to demographic findings, the war of one class upon a less fortunate one.

While many of the attributes mentioned above were true of the urban politician in the early twentieth century,[10] it is a tribute to the strength of antiparty feeling that such a view exists today for the reformer to evoke. In fact, most literature indicates the basically middle-class character of both Democratic and Republican regulars (with perhaps slightly higher socioeconomic status apparent for Republicans). My purpose now is to describe these findings.

Although this study compares only the Democratic Party's

reformers and regulars, the literature usually compares grassroots Democrats and Republicans. Since Republicans are expected to be wealthier, better educated, and so forth than Democrats, the fact that most reports indicate the middle-class character of *even* Democrats is interesting in relation to past steretyping. In California, Ohio, and Wisconsin precinct (grass roots) leaders from both parties can not be usefully differentiated on the basis of class.[11]

One can refine this contention with the realization that a greater class differential exists in the urban setting than in the rural ones. In a study of Detroit, Eldersveld locates middle-class executive boards in both parties, but not necessarily in the precinct leadership.[12]

While leadership might usually be middle class, the mass of party workers is likely to reflect the community from which it is drawn. Thus, in homogeneous districts, both parties are likely to recruit from similar groups, and so will any reform organization. Althoff and Patterson found both Democrats and Republicans to be Catholic Poles in one area of Illinois, and both to be Protestant Germans in another.[13] The precinct leaders of *both* parties in suburban Maryland differed significantly (and in the expected direction) from those in agricultural and industrial Illinois.[14]

These findings suggest that demographic differences may not be crucial in explaining political differences between reformers and regulars. This is clearly in keeping with a hypothesis that the demographic variables will not be as useful in segregating the insurgent from the professional as the other motivational, liberal, and ideological constructs will be.

The question of how demographically representative a precinct leader is of his district emphasizes the distance between the myth of the party activist and the actuality. It is interesting to note that in several grassroots studies, where Democrats represented slightly lower-status backgrounds than Republicans, these same Democrats were above the general public in most socioeconomic rankings. Both Democrats and Republicans seem to be better educated than the general state populations from whom they derive in Illinois and Michigan.[15]

Not only is this evident in the precinct leader of the second half of the twentieth century, but it was probably valid for the early machine politician as well. In Illinois, precinct leaders were more likely to illustrate professional occupations than the general population in 1938.[16] Forthal also found the precinct leader less illiterate and more educated than the voters he represented.[17]

Thus it appears that the lower-class, socioeconomic status of the regular Democratic politician has changed over the recent past. (And it was probably exaggerated grossly by the early reformers, who encountered machine politicians in their heyday.)

Basically, then, I no longer expect class variables to be significant in separating regulars from reformers, since both types of Democrats will be middle class. The rather elitist view of many amateurs, that the regular is poorly educated, is not expected to provide an important difference between the two groups. Although Wilson did speak of the reform movement as overrepresentative of the middle-and upper-middle class, women, professional occupations, young, and better educated, he did not identify these traits as important distinguishing characteristics of reformers.[18] Furthermore, other empirical studies do not illustrate any significant distinctions between the two groups, except in age.[19]

My orientation in this project takes on a slightly different focus. For while major class distinctions are not anticipated between the groups of activists, one can expect to uncover some hidden demographic distinctions *within* categories. Thus, while both activists may be middle class, the reformer will present a professional background compared with the regular, who is more likely to have a business occupation. The reformers, analyzed in the previous chapter, were all characterized as professionals. So, too, can one expect such occupations in the N.D.C.

Also emphasizing the middle-class status of both groups, I do anticipate finding a difference in upward mobility patterns for the amateur and the regular. Upward mobility and relative affluence from middle-to upper-middle class in relation to one's parents may introduce greater tensions for an individual in reacting to a material set of incentives, which appear philosophically tainted or unclean. I also expect the upward mobility of the regular to be firmly based in parental lower-class status, where ties to material rewards are more likely sources of political motivation.

An even more potent variable than parents' class might be their political activity and party identification. It has been suggested that the amateur, compared to the regular, comes from a home that was basically apolitical.[20] Thus the reformer becomes interested in politics at a later stage in development. These interesting parental variations can be discussed in terms of socialization experiences that could produce further distinctions between insurgents and professionals even when they come from the same class background.

It seems likely that if politics was not a natural part of one's early socialization, an individual would feel no primary loyalty to a particular party or a brand of pragmatic politics. The other socialization force, the schools, might direct one toward the amateur ideal of selfless, issue-oriented politics, abounding in American civics texts.[21]

Furthermore, the earlier decisions of the regular may involve less complex rationalizations. Children do not think in philosophical terms as readily as adults or even adolescents. If the amateur's political commitments appear at a time when ideological thought is developed, it seems more likely such thinking will be predicated upon issues than if one imbibes party attachment and political interest almost subconsciously in his early years.

In examining childhood socialization as well as later adult experiences of these activists, one should not ignore the geographical or areal traits associated with the life-styles of these participants. Several studies of county or city grass roots activists speak of an "amateur style" of politics within regular suburban organizations.[22] This research seeks to explain some political attitudes through the influence of community characteristics. The suburban existence is supposed to support a politics of purposive motivation, in its attraction for certain middle-class activists.

In such expectations is the implicit belief that class variables will explain one's leaning to reform or regular politics. Lower-class activists, since their economic need is greater, will be more likely to need material rewards for their political efforts. The middle-class and relatively affluent activist can be motivated by other rewards. I shall explore these implications in greater depth in the chapter on motivations, but it is also necessary to indicate the underlying reasons for certain expectations about the political effects of demographic variables.

Besides suburbanism, another areal trait associated with Democratic reform politics is its appearance in communities where the party is notoriously weak because of Republican dominance. Republican dominance might merely be another way of characterizing upper-status communities. If this is so, one is describing upper-status areas that illustrate a strong contingent unmoved by Republican politics. In effect, homogeneous middle-or upper-class districts that spawn reform Democratic politics would seem to be a description of areas that are contributing upper-middle-class activists to the political spectrum, who are not comfortable within the Republican Party. What one might ask is whether it is liberal issues that have activated these reformers, turning them toward the Democratic Party? If this is true, then not so much areal traits, but issues might be important as motivations.

Generalizing about suburbanism and Republican Party dominance is almost impossible on the basis of past research. These studies provide such varied geographic sites that drawing their examples into major hypotheses may be misleading at this point. Since most studies have concentrated mainly upon limited areas, such as counties or municipalities,[23] their conclusions about the effects of suburbanism can not provide strong proof of their case for areal attributes. Less circumscribed analyses, on the other hand, seem to concentrate upon a higher level of organizational membership than the grassroots.[24] I merely note this problem in passing and shall return to it later.

Whether employing demographics or areal attributes to this interpretation of the regular and the reformer, former inquiries do not lead one to emphasize these qualities in separating the two groups of activists. For while demographics might provide important variations to study, the classic work has located the heart of the insurgent in his unique of incentives and rewards.[25] This perception of the reformer is so intrinsically related to the myth of the regular that it is important to explore incentives for both groups.

B. Motivational Attributes

The machine-age regular was motivated by material incentives, which supplied him with tangible rewards such as patronage and jobs, according to the number of votes he produced for the ticket. The studies of grassroots leaders on the public payroll support this view: eighty percent of the ward committeemen and seventy percent of the Chicago precinct captains in 1927 were paid by the government.[26] This is true for sixty percent of the precinct committee in Philadelphia, 1938, and thirty-five percent of Democratic committeemen in Albany, New York, 1935.

The foundation of machine politics rested upon recruiting people to do unappealing election and party work on a local level. These workers required some payoff. Since those willing to act for the organization were likely to need economic help, a functional relationship was built between a party and its workers. The machine depended upon votes and the poorly trained precinct worker wanted income. The bond between these requisites and the poverty of the constituents in one's district helped to impose political coordination upon essentially decentralized systems.

No one can doubt the centrality of material rewards for the machine-style regular. Yet too much of the original source material speaks of the "great game of politics" for scholars to deny the importance of solidary incentives for the old-time professional.[28] Solidary incentives provide the participant with associational rewards through activity itself, that is, sociability or group loyalty, with minimal relation to the success of the organization at the polls.

Clark and Wilson lump status rewards with solidary incentives such as congeniality. This seems a basic error, since status is much more a material reward, though intangible. The machine politico who wanted (and needed) a public job shares certain rewards with the new-style activist who seeks public recognition but does not want a public job (and does not need one). To separate tangible material and intangible status rewards is to obscure some relevant facts. The modern affluent politician may not seek a public position because he can carn more privately. What he receives from public participation is exalted status, or even electoral office, that will undoubtedly augment his economic or social position indirectly. Tangible patronage is no longer desirable, but "intangible patronage" may be eagerly pursued.

The joy in participation for the machine precinct worker was the joy in finding a community or home where the heterogeneous city life could become homogeneously secure. Myths about the machine politician too easily obscure his motivational complexity.

If I emphasize material incentives as differentiating traits of the regular, I may be concentrating upon the less useful attributes. What in fact may produce a gap between the regular and the insurgent in motivations is the centrality and singularity of issue-oriented politics for the reformer. It is not, however, the absence of this source of motivation for the professional, but rather its combination with other rewards that may distinguish the two groups. These issue-directed motivations, described as purposive ones by Clark and Wilson,[29] require that the amateur become involved in order to influence policy, determined on its own merits and implemented for the good of all. The success with which he fights for the adoption of these policies provides all the satisfaction he desires.

Much of the literature stresses the purposive goals of the amateur, his vital concern with issues and/or some objective definition of the general interest. This view of the amateur is supported not only by Wilson, but also by Hirschfield, Swanson, and Blank in their study of Manhattan activists.[30] Carney found the same orientation in the California reform movement.[31] If there is very little doubt about the purposive incentives necessary to mobilize the reformer, it is not self-evident that the regular does not exhibit this preference for policy-directed goals. In a study of Michigan parties, Eldersveld found that seventy-four percent of the Republican regular precinct leaders began their careers with impersonal motivations.[32]

Michigan politics seems to have a strong issue orientation. Thus one might expect regulars there to display this type of entrance motivation. What I hope to discover is whether this is unique to Michigan, or whether regulars are also motivated by purposive goals. I expect them to be. There are indications that other local regulars display impersonal entrance motivations.

Marvick and Nixon's examination of campaign workers in Los Angeles concluded that public issues were considered very important by eighty-three percent of Democratic and seventy-one percent of Republican workers in explaining their own activity. Strong party loyalty was next in importance for sixty-one percent of the Democrats and seventy-eight percent of the Republicans. Third was a sense of community obligation. Fifty-six percent of the Democratic and sixty-one percent of the Republican respondents stressed this factor.[33]

With the multiple reasons offered to explain political exertions, one moves away from simplistic definitions of individual motivation. Yet I do suggest that the amateur has a more single-minded focus for his beginning concerns. He will claim solidary or material reasons less often than the regulars will. According to research, then, purposive motivations do not segregate the reformer from the professional as entering forces. Both groups may describe purposive motives to explain their entrance into politics.

The reformer who stresses purposive ends and the regular who also does so will fall into two distinct groups. I expect the N.D.C. member to mention more specific issues than the professional, who might emphasize a general interest in political participation. Furthermore, a strong dedication to party as a precipitation to activity will be absent from the amateur's frame of reference. The amateur is called an insurgent for good reasons. His motivations will be more purely issue-dominated than the professional.

Although I hypothesize that entrance motivation will indicate some differences between the two groups, the more meaningful distinction is projected in continuing motivation. A shift from purposive to either material or solidary incentives has been recorded for Eldersveld's regular: only twelve percent of the same Democrats and twenty-two percent of the Republicans, mentioned above, maintained their original impersonal motivations.[34] Thus, even in Michigan, issue-oriented reasons are hard to sustain as a source of incentive.

This movement from impersonal motivation to personal, and especially to solidary rewards, is important for the regular. The issue-directed activist can not receive philosophical rewards from organizations that are predicated upon nonideological foundations. This suggests that the activist so involved must either revise his incentives or stop his party work.

Although the participant does not find ideological satisfaction in party work, he finds the party meets other needs, such as sociability. And if he incorrectly believed that party work would fulfill his philosophical yearnings, he soon discovers his error. The ideological activist has two choices. He can either "fight or switch." The regular is likely to switch his motivations to conform to the incentive system of the party, which is a source of identification for him.

Simply recall the other motivations that overlapped with issue concerns in Marvick and Nixon's study. The loyalty to party was itself an incentive for action. This remains as a foundation upon which to build.

The reformer, on the other hand, loosely tied to party, does not have this underlying source of attraction, which would convince him to adjust to the party's structure of rewards. Thus the reformer will fight the definition of party as a group of happy playfellows and will continuously urge policy-oriented activities upon the organization. If this fails, then the activist is likely to drop out, agreeing with his own prophecy that the party system is corrupted by material incentives, and that it is too late to save anyway.

The pure-type amateur will continue to demand a purposive organization. He is also the individual most likely to be frustrated by politics. The amateur who consistently participates in politics is almost a contradiction in terms. For those motivated by issues, an issueless brand of politics must constantly lead to political disillusionment. Such activists seek rewards that the traditional party system does not produce. This, more than anything, may explain the erratic activity of the amateur politician.

The amateur who remains continuously active has been able to revise his incentive system to mesh with the party's, accepting solidary rewards to replace his purposive ones. In this way he differs from the ideal-type of disillusioned amateur.

I continue to claim that issue orientation as a motive for the reformer is paramount. That I anticipate finding a continuous purposive motivation of the reformer, however, is not accepted by Wilson, who states that the reformer either loses his issue orientation or becomes disillusioned and withdraws. Wilson joins others in locating strong social impulses to support political activity that began with issue involvement.[35]

This emphasis upon solidary satisfactions for the reformer and regular does not have to replace the essential nature of issues for the reformer. It may, rather, enhance his ability to continue working when defeat over the issues might frustrate him. It can also introduce flexibility into a rigid motivation structure.

In support of this contention that the amateur is sustained by impersonal inclinations, I cite the one study that continues to discover this form of incentive. In suburban Nassau County, New York, executive-committee members exhibit an initial and continuing rationale for participation that is purposive.[36] It is appropriate that this style appears in an area that I hypothesized would illustrate amateur politics. While Nassau regulars are not necessarily "amateurs," Ippolito's study does illustrate the possibility of maintaining purposive rewards under certain conditions.

On what other grounds do I intend to prove that the amateur continues to be stimulated by impersonal motives? To rely completely upon queries about motivation seems to leave out the relationship between motivation and actual behavior. Motivation, at best, appears to be an amorphous concept. Much confusion has been introduced by the attempts to operationalize motivation by means of questions about what one would miss if he stopped working in politics, or why one is working now.

The satisfactions one derives from a job are rather abstract, compared to the reality of the task itself. I shall, therefore, concentrate on motivations as they interact with behavior, through career patterns, role descriptions, and role performance.

A secondary benefit of this approach will be to separate rhetoric from action. It is likely that most people describe their reasons in selfless terms. Would one admit to materialistic desires as a basis for political activity? Probably not. But whether or not one has a background of political jobs is a concrete example of one's reward structure. The history of a reformer who is motivated by impersonal designs will be barren of government or patronage appointments, quite contrary to the professional, if there are purposive orientations for the former and material ones for the latter.

Besides government jobs, activists also have subjective views of their political roles and tasks. While income might be an essential part of their motivations, specific party activities require some other rationale. Will a participant emphasize electoral chores, educating the electorate, reforming the system, helping his constituents with governmental problems (brokerage)? One would assume that electoral and brokerage functions would be more important to the regular and education and reform would be more essential to the N.D.C. member.

Part of this distinction between reformers and regulars is visible in the brokerage function often assumed by the regular. The political broker provides a line of communication between government and individuals. He serves as a mediator between the bureaucracy and the troubled citizen. Of course, N.D.C. members are not necessarily party officials, so the fact that they have not helped constituents get jobs or shown people how to pursue their rights might be part of their differing formal positions. Yet the reformer precinct-leader will do noticeably less of this social service work than the regular precinct-leader, according to this hypothesis.

Thus I expect the professional to perceive his political activities more often in terms of helping others than the reformer will. The concern of the reformer with issues will color his definition of his tasks.

Past research, already discussed, makes one expect the regular to emphasize campaign-related activities, while the amateur would stress educational tasks. About this likelihood occurring, I am not sure. One of the reasons that past descriptions of "amateur" politics seems less applicable to the N.D.C., concerns this organization's awareness of elections to implement policies. What led to the dissolution of the N.D.C., in fact, was conflict over how the group might best pursue such goals through electoral politics. For this reason, in discussing the N.D.C., I have chosen to use the terms *reformer* or *insurgent,* rather than *amateur.* The campaign emphasis of the N.D.C. makes that organization seem as "professional" as the regular organization in certain respects.

I have emphasized the interrelationship of issues and motivations for the reform politician. Yet the content of those issues is another series of variables. The fact that the insurgent defines his role in issue-oriented terms indicates that he cares deeply about policies. The policy or programmatic variables illustrate another way in which these concerns of the reformer and regular may be interpreted through differing political styles. The myth of the professional politician, totally devoid of issue concerns, is not validated by the literature. The distinction, however, may lie in the intensity and direction of the amateur's obsession with policies. One also can not ignore the kinds of policies for which he raises the battle cry.

C. Issue Orientation

First, I shall look at the liberal-conservative continuum of amateurs and regulars to indicate the direction of the issue preoccupation. One has to remember that this is a discussion about grass roots leadership, not the general public. Democratic and Republican voters are not as clearly separated by their policy commitments as their party's leadership is. Democratic leaders are usually judged as liberal compared to Republican leaders.[37]

In addition to interparty differentials, there are also wide ranges of attitudes toward specific policies within each party. Some studies contend that the lower echelon leaders differ essentially from the upper levels. In California, the substructure is more liberal than the superstructure, while in Michigan the reverse is true within the Democratic Party.[38] On a local level in Los Angeles, Democrats indicate little relationship between issue orientation and power position within the party, but Republicans with power positions are substantially more conservative than those without.[39]

It should be clear, then, in studying the grassroots activists within the Democratic Party, one can not generalize about the upper echelons of the organization nor about all party leadership. Yet if the kinds of demographic variations expected within these groups' class structure do appear, such findings might be relevant to political opinions. The hard-hat syndrome of toughness on military issues, civil rights, and civil liberties is associated with lower-middle-class backgrounds. This possible relationship must be examined, as one considers specific policies.

Liberalism as a mere function of class differentials must be analyzed. In the context of this study, however, one would expect

such class-related attitudes to be unimportant. I do not think variation between the groups can be explained by demographic variables
alone. Lower-class activists will not be more alike in attitudes than
will middle- and lower-class participants within the same organization. Liberalism, distinct from background characteristics, will
separate the regular from the reformer.

My anticipation of distinct liberal-conservative dimensions between the two groups is not supported by the literature. In analyzing Democratic amateurs, Wilson stresses not liberalism as
much as issue orientation as a *motivation* for these insurgents.
Liberal and regular Democratic candidates are plentiful. What
characterizes these liberal regulars, however, is their purpose,
which focuses upon winning elections, not merely promoting
liberal issues.[40] For Wilson, the distinction between regular and
reform Democrats may not be liberalism, but rather the emphasis
and intensity with which these positions are espoused. Carrying
this possibility one step further, Soule and Clarke found that
liberalism or conservatism were unrelated to amateurism.[41]

Unlike Wilson or Soule and Clarke, I do not expect to find
strong and significant divisions between the two groups, even on
substantive issues. I hypothesize that reformers will be distinguished from regulars in most opinions, especially in regard to
Vietnam, since the war was a precipitating force for their support
of such candidates as Eugene McCarthy and Robert Kennedy.
I anticipate that the amateur position will be "isolationist" in
Vietnam and Cambodia. A definite unwillingness to commit further resources to Southeast Asia is also hypothesized as a difference between the two groups. Aroused by Vietnam, the N.D.C.
member turned to domestic issues, involving poverty and racism
only after his primary interest in the war.

The policy direction of the insurgent is liberal, but it is also
national in scope. The reformer is characterized by his concern
with the great national issues of the day, as opposed to the local
ones. Even his definition of issues will be in broader terms than
that of the regular. This will be evident in the pattern of political
activity as well as the frame of reference of his political interest.

Combined with a policy of foreign retrenchment, the reformer
associates himself with government intervention domestically.
He conceives of himself as a liberal, but as an economic liberal he
may be no different from the Democratic regulars who are also
willing to spend funds on housing, education, and unemployment.
These are the economic concerns of the New Deal coalition, which
are relevant to all Democrats.

I anticipate a distinction on civil rights issues. Both professionals and reformers will support government intervention to defend the legal rights of blacks. The variation will appear in the intensity of this support. Also, regulars, relatively committed to the system of government and defending the years of Democratic national control, will perceive a great deal of improvement in the status of the black in America. The more dissatisfied (even alienated) reformer will perceive little change in the black's position. This intensity of feeling for the black is in keeping with the reformer's perception of himself as a deeply liberal individual.

More important than foreign affairs, economic issues, and civil rights in segregating the regular from the insurgent will be civil liberties. The reformer's concern with civil liberties is tied to his political commitment to democratic procedures. Reform for the insurgent very often meant procedural intraparty reform in decision making, a point discussed in the last chapter. In the area of civil liberties, the reformer is expected to take a much more permissive stand than the regular.

This is in keeping with the contention of Prothro and Grigg, as well as McClosky, who believe support for such civil libertarian issues resides mainly within the elite.[42] Jackman now claims that education (once region, sex, and city are controlled) explains the attachment to democratic principles, rather than elite consensus.[43] In anticipating distinctions between regulars and reformers in such civil liberties questions, I do so even when education and income are held constant for both groups.

Procedural issues are the ones usually associated with amateurs who stress democratic mass participation to open up the party. The Stevenson reformers of the 1950s were deeply concerned with an issue-oriented party. These issues, however, were mainly those of democratic procedure — means of making decisions — not the end or substantive policy itself. Thus they were greatly involved with internal revision of party rules about personnel or policies.

The role of organization has been so central to the reform movement that one must remember the 1950s amateur too often considered organization and leadership to be diametrically opposed to democracy. Ever since Robert Michels, left-wing participants have been prone to confuse the absence of total democracy on every issue — substantive as well as procedural — with autocracy.[44] Much of the amateur bent had a basically antiorganization/antileadership bias. The major issues were: "patronage," "bossism," and "undemocratic parties." Any reform leader who won elections or accepted patronage became suspect. Who should distribute party patronage, a basic focus for reform, is one of the "procedural" issues that split the two groups. I suggest that a willingness to leave these decisions to party leadership groups distinguished the regular from the reformer.

One reason I contend that the insurgent will differ from the regular on substantive as well as procedural issues is that the literature on the post-World War II reformers mainly analyzes the Stevenson group of the fifties. The 1952 amateur was motivated by the inability of Stevenson supporters to activate the Democratic Party for their candidate. This problem was interpreted as a procedural one and led to proposals to "democratize" the party. For the 1968 reformer, a substantive policy — the war in Vietnam — was the instigating force. This emphasis upon the war for the more recent insurgents makes one expect issues to be central for them. Thus one hypothesis is that procedural as well as substantive positions distinguish liberal reformers from more conservative regulars.

Although I do expect the reformer to be divergent from the regular in issues supported, even if he were indistinguishable from the professional, it would not have disproved an essential hypothesis of this study: issues are central in importance to the attitudes and behavior of the reformer, while they are secondary for the regular.' The content of these issues is irrelevant to this point. After all, the Goldwater supporters of 1964 provide a clear view of amateurism on the right. A coherent dedication to principles indicates what I mean by my rather loose construction of the term *ideology*. Ideology will be discussed in greater detail in later chapters.

D. Ideological Orientations

It is also important to note that the literature on party supporters discovers little consistency in their attitudes between domestic and foreign-policy orientations. Liberals on one set of policies are not necessarily to the left on others.[45] Thus ideological constraint between varying abstract as well as specific ideas seems quite limited in the United States.[46] Since sensitivity to ideology increases as one ascends in degree of participation, it is likely that activists will be more coherent and consistent in orientations than the mass public. Yet the overriding importance of issues for the reformer leads one to expect some differences between the groups in terms of consistency and intensity.

These ideological characteristics of the amateur provide the last component in the analysis. Motivations, task perceptions, and policy content are intrinsically related to ideological variables, yet they are distinct. The first three sets of properties dealt with the individual, his background, his incentives, and his policy penchants. Now I seek to emphasize the extent to which an activist judges the proper role of the party in ideological or issue-oriented terms, as well as the interrelationships between various issue positions.

The purposive motives of the amateur will be tied to an ideological definition of the party's positions. This emphasis upon principles helps to explain the demand for motivational purity by the reformer, who often rejects the regular with positions quite in accord with his own liberalism. Positions must be taken on their own merits, never for personal gain or to win elections.

The regular is viewed as a pragmatist; therefore his dedication to specific policy alternatives is influenced by the electoral utility of the position, unlike the insurgent. Another hypothesis expects the professional to be more receptive to the party as a pluralist amalgam of different interests and as a vehicle for compromise.

William E. Wright has developed an Ideological-Pragmatism Scale, which does not tap liberalism or conservatism, but rather commitment to ideology.[47] These questions use conceptions of the role of the party and thus permit one to compare the regular and the amateur along this continuum. This study not only makes comparisons possible between reformers and regulars on this ideological continuum, but also permits one to identify the overlap between the two organizations, for example, N.D.C. members who were also Democratic committeemen. A hypothesis is that this group will illustrate an intermediate position between willingness to compromise and eagerness to remain intransigent.

After reviewing the amateur politician in his historical settings, as well as the grass roots activist displayed in the social science literature, it seems evident that the amateur has been replaced by the reformer. The insurgent's political wisdom seems to be growing far beyond his amateur origins. Demographic, motivational, liberal, and ideological analyses of these past and present regulars and reformers only contribute to this original contention that change is in the winds. Before passing to the technical discussion of methodology, let me conclude this section with a summary of the hypotheses derived from the previous analysis. After this presentation, I shall describe the means developed for testing the hypotheses and outline the plan for the remainder of this work.

E. Hypotheses and Methodology

Demographic Hypotheses

Hypothesis 1 — There will be a significant difference between reformers and regulars in their cosmopolitan orientations.

Hypothesis 2 — There will be a significant difference in the class status of reformers and regulars.

Hypothesis 3 — There will be a significant difference in the upward mobility patterns of reformers and regulars.

Hypothesis 4 — There will be a significant difference in the ethnic and religious backgrounds of reformers and regulars.

Hypothesis 5 — There will be a significant difference in the socialization experiences of reformers and regulars.

Hypothesis 6 — Reformers will be significantly younger than regulars.

Hypothesis 7 — Reformers will be significantly more suburban in life-style than regulars.

Motivational Hypotheses

Hypothesis 8 — Entrance Motivation: There will be no significant difference between reformers and regulars in purposive motivation.

Hypothesis 9 — Continuing Motivation: Amateurs will be significantly more purposive than regulars.

Hypothesis 10 — Role Perceptions: There will be a significant difference in the ways reformers and regulars perceive their roles.

Hypothesis 11 — Career Patterns: Reformers will be significantly less likely than regulars to hold high-party positions.

Hypothesis 12 — Political Tasks: Reformers will be significantly less likely to perform election-oriented tasks than regulars.

Issue-Oriented Liberal Hypotheses

Hypothesis 13 — There will be a significant difference between the liberalism of reformers and regulars.

> a. Regulars will be significantly more supportive of the status quo than reformers.
> b. There will be a proportionately greater difference between reformers and regulars on procedural rather than substantive issues.
> c. Reformers will be significantly more likely to perceive themselves as liberals than will regulars.

Ideological Hypotheses

Hypothesis 14 — Reformers will be significantly more constrained in their issue concerns than regulars.

Hypothesis 15 — Reformers will be significantly more ideological about party activity than regulars.

To operationalize these hypotheses, a mailed survey was developed, which made use of questions designed by Eldersveld, and Marvick and Nixon in previous surveys.[48] The questionnaire is displayed in Appendix A and the cover letters in Appendix B. In the chapters that present and evaluate the findings, the relevant questions will be cited.

This questionnaire was administered throughout New Jersey. New Jersey is not necessarily the typical state, but it provides a laboratory for my analysis on two divergent bases. In the first place, the state exhibits a wide range of demographic characteristics, thus permitting one to test hypotheses in different settings. New Jersey is the most urbanized state in the country, and yet it still includes several counties with rural-agricultural economies. While this extreme urbanism illustrates one of the unique traits of New Jersey, the balance of rural and suburban districts also indicates the usefulness of a study that includes an entire state.

A statewide study of precinct leaders and reformers, furthermore, permits one to hold constant size of place or interparty competition, thus enabling one to see if previous findings can be tied to the uniqueness and limited base of the areas selected. Perhaps from there I can generalize about areal attributes that influence party activity, combining survey and aggregate data for two types of political activists.

Exhibiting much variety, New Jersey also reflects trends evident in the country at large: growing urbanization and suburbanization, migration patterns of whites and nonwhites, increasing education, and changing composition of labor force. Furthermore, as one historian has noted: "In a remarkable way New Jersey's industrial profile is representative of that of the nation as a whole; 62 of the nation's 75 largest industrial corporations, for example, operate in the state.[49]

Heterogeneous and yet reflective of national trends in social and economic characteristics, the same can be said for certain political aspects of the state. Growing competitiveness evident nationally is visible in New Jersey. Selecting Democratic electors for President in recent times three out of seven times, dividing its Senatorial representatives between each party, and selecting Representatives who lean slightly toward Democratic dominance, New Jersey is competitive by any standard in national elections.

Competitive on a state basis, New Jersey illustrates a wide variety of two-party relationships on a county level. One can find traditionally Democratic counties — Hudson and Cumberland — traditionally Republican counties — Bergen and Atlantic — plus competitive ones such as Essex, Passaic, and Union, all in the same state. City-level data are also available to illustrate a wide range of competitive types.

The tradition of one-party dominance on a county level is evident in a further unique trait of New Jersey: the long and durable history of machine politics. Jersey City Mayor Frank Hague may be the most famous example of this syndrome but "the dominant voice in statewide elections still tends to be the caucus of county leaders."[50]

In stressing the national representativeness of New Jersey, it is also essential to emphasize that reformers are not the mere product of demographic forces. "Take one part upper status, three parts suburbanism . . ." is the extreme absurdity of such an approach. The N.D.C. did not arise in the vast majority of states. Thus, while New Jersey can provide a laboratory for understanding the insurgent politician, one can not then expect to discover reformers — ipso facto — in all suburban areas.

While New Jersey does reveal certain national trends, it is thus useful to keep in mind some of the unique qualities of the state. My next concern after describing the laboratory for the research is to review methods for operationalizing "reformer" and "regular."

Tracing the development of reform movements, I have focused upon New Jersey's New Democratic Coalition as the source of reformers. By joining the N.D.C., a political activist chose a reform organization. This self-selection eases my burden of sampling considerably. Since I was interested in the reformer as active politician, the more involved members, the 1,000 who went as delegates to the New Democratic Coalition Founding Convention, 22 March 1969, were chosen. Seeking a comparative group of low-echelon regulars for my study, I concluded that a sample of the 9,000 Democratic precinct committee members (also called county committee members), elected locally, would illustrate the closest level of involvement to the N.D.C. activist. The committee member sample was stratified by sex and county to match the proportions evident in the N.D.C.

Both groups were mailed four-page questionnaires in the spring and summer of 1970. There were several follow-ups of all N.D.C. delegates and of a stratified random sample of the committee members, through postcards, a second questionnaire, and telephone calls. The questionnaires were accompanied by a cover letter either signed by an organization leader, as they were in the case of the regulars and one county N.D.C., or signed by me with an academic letterhead and endorsed by various factional leaders, as they were in the case of the vast majority of N.D.C. mailings.

The response rate in the regular group was thirty-three percent for the stratified random sample. The N.D.C. group had a return rate of sixty-two percent. Before one leaps to any conclusions about the response rates, I must mention that regulars were not pursued as intently as the amateurs. Telephone calls were directed at all nonreturning amateurs but not regulars, since resources were limited. Response rates indicate little bias according to the percentages by sex and county who returned the questionnaires. Both groups illustrate a similar proportion of women or of county respondents, reflective of the original stratification. Furthermore, early and late respondents within each group were analyzed for variations in selected variables. No differences seemed to be important here.

Yet if there are certain biases in response rates, these might even be useful for the study. I sought the activist who feels most attached to his group — whether the Democratic Party of the N.D.C. Since the cover letters indicated the organization's support of the project, respondents are likely to be purer types of their organization's loyal adherents. One can argue that respondents were more highly motivated than nonrespondents to react to the questionnaire, either because they were truly the active members of formal organizations, or because they felt a responsibility to cooperate with a study endorsed by their leaders.

The laboratory, the subjects, as well as the hypotheses, are presented above. I have one short task before beginning the actual analysis of the data: this is to mention the measures, that is, the statistics used to interpret the findings. Basically I shall employ Goodman and Kruskal's Coefficient of Ordinal Association — the gamma — to find strength of association between N.D.C. affiliation and demographic, motivational, liberal, and ideological variables.

Since most of the data are not interval, the gamma and analysis of variance are more suitable. Yet tests of significance, deriving from an analysis of variance, are not terribly useful within the context of this study, since this statistic is so closely tied to the size of the sample. With a sample as large as this one to analyze, almost every finding becomes "significant" statistically. Furthermore, the results of significance tests do not indicate the strength of relationship between variables, but rather — and only — the likelihood that the finding resulted from sheer chance.

Of greater concern and more practical worth is a statistic that provides one with the power of the interrelationship between variables. For this purpose the gamma coefficient does permit one to compare rankings of ordinal data along two dimensions.[51] The degree to which these rankings match each other determines the strength of the statistic. The statistic "is a ratio of the amount of predominance of agreement or inversion between two sets of rankings to the maximum possible agreement or inversion."[52] Gamma in this study will be used comparatively to indicate strengths and weaknesses in various relationships with N.D.C. membership. Thus the number, which ranges from +1.00 to -1.00, should be viewed in comparison to the other gammas that appear in the analysis, rather than as absolute themselves.

Since the gamma is sometimes influenced by extremes in the distribution of responses between the possible answers, I also concentrate upon percentages that help to rectify any misleading gammas. In fact, in most cases, the percentages present a more important picture than the gamma for understanding the similarities and distinctions between reformers and regulars.

Where the data are not ordinal, but interval in scope, I make use of a more appropriate statistic, such as Pearson's r. Also in drawing together my findings in the concluding chapters, multiple regression will help determine the strength of various relationships explored. One of the main contentions of this study is that certain variables will be more potent than others.

I would like to suggest that the root of the amateur lies less in the demographic variables than in the motivational, ideological, and liberal ones. Multiple regression will help test this supposition. The insurgent is distinguished by his attitudes, not his class or ethnicity. Not all middle-class people are positively oriented to amateurism. They are not, I suggest, because of the variation in their liberalism and the intensity with which this commitment is held. These are the foundations of the amateur style. If I relate these reform actions to socioeconomic characteristics or mere issue-oriented motivations, I might be able to predict a predisposition toward amateurism, but this is a far cry from understanding the forces that impel one individual from a similar background to opt for insurgent politics and another to be totally indifferent or to choose the professional path.

Explanation is more my purpose than prediction, for while reform movements may seem to be waning, it is my strong conviction that these very structures represent the growing trend in party organization. The affluent, nonpatronage politics of the second half of the twentieth century is more likely to bring success to the party that makes use of amateur styles than the party that does not.

Support for this contention lies in the changing nature and growing numbers of Independent voters. Once the uninformed, uninterested nonparticipant, the Independent now is becoming more the reverse of his predecessor.[53] Converse relates this change to the increased flow of information that upsets the inertia involved in party loyalty.[54] While the trend is a slight one, it does indicate a direction that American party politics is taking. Once the natural attraction of party identification lessens, other lures must be found to draw voters and workers. The direction that amateurism points is then the road down which American politics might be moving.

In describing the historical setting and research findings about reformers and regulars, I have been able to draw together certain hypotheses and indicate how they will be tested in this study. In delineating the findings, I have remained rather close to the four sets of variables — demographic, motivational, liberal, and ideological — that were used to organize the past two chapters.

The pattern of the remainder of the work parallels this presentation with a minor addition. General socialization experiences have been separated from political socialization experiences in the following two chapters on demographic variables. The political socialization chapter also includes the data on career patterns, since growing political involvement is seen in the context of adult socialization. A separate chapter will emphasize the attitudes and perceptions of the activist according to his initial and continuing motivations, as well as their relationship to his political-role interpretations. Next any distinctions between the groups according to degree of liberal orientation to various issues will be presented. Following this analysis I will discuss the ideological versus the pragmatic bent of reformers and regulars.

After these four sets of variables have been studied, an attempt will be made to weigh the potency of each set of variables in explaining the most essential traits that might predict reform or regular organization membership.

Notes to Chapter 2

1. Kenneth S. Lynn and Everett C. Hughes, "Professions," in *The Professions in America,* ed. Kenneth S. Lynn and Everett C. Hughes (Boston: Houghton Mifflin Company, 1965), p. 2.

2. Bernard Barber, "Some Problems in Sociology of the Professions," in *Professions in America,* ed. Lynn and Hughes, p. 18.

3. Ibid.

4. Ibid.

5. Max Weber, "Politics as a Vocation," in *From Max Weber: Essays in Sociology,* trans., ed., and with an Introduction by H. H. Gerth and C. Wright Mills (New York: Oxford University Press, 1946), p. 84.

6. Wilson, *Amateur Democrat,* p. 3.

7. Riordon, *Plunkitt,* p. 22.

8. Anthony Downs, *An Economic Theory of Democracy* (New York: Harper & Row Publishers, Inc., 1957), p. 28.

9. William C. Mitchell, "The Ambivalent Social Status of the American Politican," *Western Political Quarterly,* 12 (September 1959): 683-98.

10. Forthal, *Cogwheels of Democracy*; William E. Mosher, "Party and Government Control at the Grass Roots," *National Municipal Review* 24 (January 1935): 15-18, 38; Gosnell, *Machine Politics*; Riordon, *Plunkitt.*

11. Dwaine Marvick and Charles Nixon, "Recruitment Contrasts in Rival Campaign Groups," in *Political Decision Makers,* ed. Dwaine Marvick (Glencoe, Illinois: Free Press of Glencoe, 1961), p. 200; Thomas A. Flinn and Frederick M. Wirt, "Local Party Leaders: Groups of Like-Minded Men," *Midwest Journal of Political Science* 9 (February

1965): 77-98; Leon D. Epstein, *Politics in Wisconsin* (Madison, Wisconsin: University of Wisconsin Press, 1958), pp. 88-89.

12. Samuel J. Eldersveld, *Political Parties: A Behavioral Analysis* (Chicago: Rand McNally & Co., 1964), pp. 52-53.

13. Phillip Althoff and Samuel C. Patterson, "Political Activism in a Rural County," *Midwest Journal of Political Science* 10 (February 1966): 39-43.

14. M. Margaret Conway and Frank B. Feigert, "Motivational Incentive Systems and the Party Organizations," *American Political Science Review* 62 (December 1968): 1,162-64.

15. Althoff and Patterson, "Political Activism," pp. 42-43; Eldersveld, *Political Parties*, pp. 28-29, 52.

16. Leon Weaver, "Some Soundings in the Party System: Rural Precinct Committeemen," *American Political Science Review* 34 (February 1940): 79-80.

17. Forthal, *Cogwheels of Democracy*, p. 33.

18. Wilson, *Amateur Democrat*, p. 13.

19. Hirschfield, Swanson, and Blank, pp. 489-506; Soule and Clarke, p. 891.

20. Soule and Clarke, pp. 891-92.

21. C. Richard Hofstetter, "The Amateur Politician: A Problem in Construct Validation," *Midwest Journal of Political Science* 15 (February 1971): 37-38.

22. Conway and Feigert, pp. 1,159-73; Dennis S. Ippolito, "Motivational Reorientation and Change Among Party Activists," *Journal of Politics* 31 (November 1969): 1,098-1,101; Dennis S. Ippolito and Lewis Bowman, "Goals and Activities of Party Officials in a Suburban Setting," *Western Political Quarterly* 22 (September 1969): 572-80; Dennis S. Ippolito, "Political Perspectives of Suburban Party Leaders," *Southwestern Social Science Quarterly* 49 (March 1968): 80-115.

23. Altoff and Patterson, "Political Activism," pp. 39-51; Hugh A. Bone, "Grass Roots Party Leadership," mimeographed; (Seattle, 1952) Lewis Bowman and G. R. Boynton, "Activities and Role Definitions of Grass Roots Party Officials," *Journals of Politics* 28 (February 1966): 121-43; Lewis Bowman and G. R. Boynton, "Recruitment Patterns Among Local Party Officials: A Model and Some Preliminary Findings in Selected Locales," *American Political Science Review* 60 (September 1966): 667-76; Conway and Feigert, "Motivation, Incentive Systems," 1,159-73; Phillips Cutright "Activities of Precinct Committeemen in Partisan and Nonpartisan Communities," *Western Political Quarterly* 17 (March 1964): 93-108; Phillips Cutright, "Measuring the Impact of Local Party Activity on the General Election Vote," *Public Opinion Quarterly* 27 (Fall 1963): 374-86; Phillips Cutright and Peter H. Rossi, "Grass Roots Politicians and the Vote," *American Sociological Review* 23 (April 1958): 171-79; Eldersveld, *Political Parties*; Richard T. Frost, "Stability and Change in Local Politics," *Public Opinion Quarterly* 25 (Summer 1961): 221-35; Hirschfield, Swanson, and Blank, "Profile of Political Activists," pp. 499-506; Ippolito, "Motivational Reorientation," pp. 1,098-1,101; Ippolito, "Political Perspectives," pp. 80-115; Ippolito, Bowman, "Goals and Activities of Party Officials," pp. 572-80; Henry J. Jacek, "The Urban Political World of Black and White Party Officials" (unpublished paper presented at 65th Annual Meeting of the American Political Science Association, New York, September 1969); Daniel Katz and Samuel J. Eldersveld, "The Impact of Local Party Activity Upon the Electorate," *Public Opinion Quarterly* 25 (Spring 1961): 1-25; Marvick and Nixon, "Recruitment Contrasts," in Marvick, pp. 193-217; Peter H. Rossi and Phillips Cutright, "The Impact of Party Organization in an Industrial Setting," in *Community Political Systems*, ed. Morris Janowitz (Glencoe, Illinois: Free Press of Glencoe, 1961), pp. 81-116; Phillips Cutright and Peter H. Rossi, "Party Organization in Primary Elections," *American Journal of Sociology* 64 (November 1958): 262-69; Robert H. Salisbury, "The Urban Party Organization Member," *Public*

Opinion Quarterly 29 (Winter 1965-66): 550-64; David C. Schwartz, "Toward a Theory of Political Recruitment," *Western Political Quarterly* 22 (September 1969): 552-71.

24. William J. Crotty, "The Party Organization and Its Activities," in *Approaches to the Study of Party Organization*, ed. William J. Crotty (Boston: Allyn and Bacon, 1968), pp. 247-306; Epstein, *Politics in Wisconsin;* Flinn and Wirt, "Local Party Leaders," pp. 77-98; Samuel C. Patterson, "Characteristics of Party Leaders," *Western Political Quarterly* 16 (June 1963): 337-41; Gerald M. Pomper, "New Jersey County Chairmen," *Western Political Quarterly* 18 (March 1965): 186-97; Robert Lee Sawyer, Jr., *The Democratic State Central Committee in Michigan, 1949-1959: The Rise of the New Politics and the New Political Leadership*, Michigan Governmental Studies, no. 40 (Ann Arbor, Michigan: Institute of Public Administration, University of Michigan, 1960); Lester G. Seligman, "Political Recruitment and Party Structure: A Case Study," *American Political Science Review* 55 (March 1961): 77-86; Frank J. Sorauf, *Party and Representation: Legislative Politics in Pennsylvania* (New York: Atherton Press, 1963).

25. Wilson, *Amateur Democrat*, p. 20.

26. Forthal, *Cogwheels of Democracy*, pp. 16, 35.

27. Kurtzman, "Methods of Controlling Votes in Philadelphia," p. 47; Mosher, "Party and Government Control," p. 18.

28. Frank R. Kent, *The Great Game of Politics* (Garden City, N. Y.: Doubleday, Page and Company, 1923); Edward J. Flynn, *You're the Boss* (New York: The Viking Press, 1947); Riordon, *Plunkitt.*

29. Clark and Wilson, "Incentive Systems," p. 135.

30. Hirschfield, Swanson, and Blank, "Profile of Political Activists," pp. 499-506.

31. Carney, *Rise of the Democratic Clubs*, p. 5.

32. Eldersveld, *Political Parties*, p. 287.

33. Marvick and Nixon, "Recruitment Contrasts," in Marvick, p. 208.

34. Eldersveld, *Political Parties*, p. 287.

35. Brown, "Fun Can be Politics," pp. 27-28; Mitchell, *Elm Street Politics*, p. 45.

36. Ippolito, "Motivational Reorientation." p. 1,099.

37. Herbert McClosky, Paul J. Hoffman, and Rosemary O'Hara, "Issue Conflict and Consensus Among Party Leaders and Followers," *American Political Science Review* 54 (June 1960): 406-427; Flinn and Wirt, "Local Party Leaders," pp. 94-95; Althoff and Patterson, "Political Activism," p. 51; Marvick and Nixon, "Recruitment Contrasts," in Marvick, p. 211; Gerald M. Pomper, "New Jersey Convention Delegates of 1964," *Southwestern Social Science Quarterly* 48 (June 1967): 31-33; Eldersveld, *Political Parties*, p. 187; M. Kent Jennings and Norman Thomas, "Men and Women in Party Elites: Social Roles and Political Resources," *Midwest Journal of Political Science* 12 (November 1968): 489.

38. Edmund Constantini, "Intraparty Attitude Conflict: Democratic Party Leadership in California," *Western Political Quarterly* 16 (December 1963): 956-72; Eldersveld, *Political Parties*, pp. 184-88.

39. Marvick and Nixon, "Recruitment Contrasts," in Marvick, p. 211.

40. Wilson, *Amateur Democrat*, pp. 150-53.

41. Soule and Clarke, "Amateurs and Professionals," p. 895.

42. Herbert McClosky, "Consensus and Ideology in American Politics," *American Political Science Review* 50 (June 1964): 361-82; James W. Prothro and Charles W. Grigg, "Fundamental Principles of Democracy: Bases of Agreement and Disagreement," *Journal of Politics* 22 (May 1960): 276-94.

43. Robert W. Jackman, "Political Elites, Mass Publics, and Support for Democratic Principles," *Journal of Politics* 34 (August 1972): 753-73.

44. Robert Michels, *Political Parties: A Sociological Study of the Oligarchical*

Tendencies of Modern Democracy, trans. Eden and Cedar Paul (Glencoe, Ill.: Free Press of Glencoe, 1915), esp. pp. 377-93.

45. Campbell, et al., *The American Voter: An Abridgement*, p. 113.

46. Ibid., pp. 111-13; Philip E. Converse, "The Nature of Belief Systems in Mass Publics," in *Ideology and Discontent*, ed. David E. Apter (New York: Free Press of Glencoe, 1964), pp. 206-261.

47. William E. Wright, "Ideological-Pragmatic Orientations of West Berlin Local Party Officials," *Midwest Journal of Political Science* 11 (August 1967): 381-402.

48. Marvick and Nixon, "Recruitment Contrasts," in Marvick, p. 208; Eldersveld, *Political Parties*, pp. 547-602.

49. Richard P. McCormick, "Perspective on New Jersey," in *New Jersey: Spotlight on Government*, League of Women Voters of New Jersey (North Plainfield, N. J.: Twin City Press, 1969), pp. 9-10.

50. V.O. Key, Jr., *American State Politics: An Introduction* (New York; Alfred A. Knopf, 1956), p. 92.

51. Leo A. Goodman and William H. Kruskal, "Measures of Association for Cross Classifications," *Journal of the American Statistical Association* 49 (December 1954): 732-64; Linton C. Freeman, *Elementary Applied Statistics: For Students in Behavioral Science* (New York: John Wiley & Sons, Inc., 1965), p. 79.

52. Freeman, *Elementary Applied Statistics*, p. 82.

53. Philip E. Converse, "Information Flow and the Stability of Partisan Attitudes," in *Elections and the Political Order*, ed. Angus Campbell, Philip E. Converse, Warren E. Miller, and Donald E. Stokes (New York: John Wiley & Sons, Inc., 1966), pp. 145-47; Walter Dean Burnham, "The End of American Party Politics," *Trans-action* (December 1969), pp. 12-22.

54. Converse, "Information Flow," in Campbell, et al., *Elections*, pp. 156-57.

3
The Socialization
of Reformers and Regulars

The "style" of the reformer, as opposed to his demographic traits, are viewed as the essence of the insurgent. "It is not his liberalism or his age, education, or class that sets the new politician apart and makes him worth studying. Rather, it is this outlook on politics, and the style of politics he practices."[1] Soule and Clarke found that 1968 delegates to the Democratic convention who were designated "amateurs" could be separated from professionals in demographic terms only according to their youth. Education was unimportant in analyzing convention delegates; income level was weak and insignificant.

Thus previous research would arouse few expectations that background characteristics could offer a salient dimension to this analysis of the insurgent. A few differentials were anticipated. The essentially upper-middle-class reformer could be compared with the lower-middle-class status of the regular.

More important than the reformer's own socioeconomic status, however, would be his social and physical mobility patterns. The reformer would derive from middle-class parents, while the regular would not. The reformer would exhibit much geographical mobility in his life-style, compared with the regular. From these findings on mobility, one expects political socialization patterns to vary somewhat, influenced by such other factors as ethnicity and religion.

From these general hypotheses, let me become more specific by describing the operational hypotheses employed to make these rather vague propositions detailed and, hence, testable.

These hypotheses were presented with the assumption that relatively minor distinctions between the groups would be evident in objective demographic traits. And yet the findings strongly upset this rather facile expectation. The thrust of previous research seems to be counteracted by this study. In fact, some of the major results of this analysis involve the demographic variables so lightly brushed aside. There may be interesting reasons for this contradiction.

Since Wilson would have scholars concentrate upon the amateur's "outlook on politics" instead of the demographic labels, he may minimize the role such economic, social, and parental characteristics play in shaping the "style of politics [the amateur] practices." Depicting the amateur as a "cosmopolitan," Wilson uses this concept to describe the reformer's focus upon the national or international scene. This contrasts with the local or parochial activist whose roots and interests are deep within the community where he resides.

These constructs, *local* and *cosmopolitan,* have a long sociological history from Toennies to Merton.[2] The terms have been employed to explain an individual's orientation toward all social relations, as well as his perceptions of relevant facts. Ethical interpretations are also involved.

Most of the literature stresses the implications of such attitudes, rather than the causes of its development. Thus Merton analyzes the social participation of cosmopolitans compared with locals and ties this behavior to a particular orientation. The cosmopolitan may join more voluntary associations than the local, but type of organizations joined is even more indicative of these attitudes than a mere quantitative listing. The professional group, in which one applies knowledge, is attractive to the cosmopolitan, while the fraternal or civic club, where one makes personal contacts, is appealing to the local.

Socialization Hypotheses

Hypothesis 1 — There will be a significant difference between reformers and regulars in their cosmopolitan orientations.

    a. Reformers will have higher proportions oriented to national media than regulars.

    b. Reformers will have higher proportions oriented toward cosmopolitan-voluntary organizations than regulars.

    c. Reformers will be significantly more physically mobile than regulars.

Hypothesis 2 — There will be a significant difference in the class status of reformers and regulars.

      a. Reformers will have a higher education level than regulars.

      b. Reformers will have higher proportions in professional occupations than regulars.

      c. Reformers will have higher proportions in technical occupations.

      d. Reformers will have higher proportions in the legal profession than will regulars.

      e. Regulars will have higher proportions self-employed than reformers.

      f. Regulars will have significantly more government jobs than reformers.

      g. Reformers will be significantly more wealthy than regulars.

Hypothesis 3 — There will be a significant difference in the upward mobility patterns of reformers and regulars.

      a. Reformers' parents will be significantly more often from middle-class backgrounds than regulars' parents.

      b. Higher proportions of reformers' parents will be native Americans than will regulars' parents.

Hypothesis 4 — There will be a significant difference in the ethnic and religious backgrounds of reformers and regulars.

      a. Reformers are more likely to be Jewish than regulars.

      b. Reformers are less likely to be black than regulars.

      c. Regulars are more likely to be white-ethnic than reformers.

      d. Regulars are more likely to be Catholic than reformers.

      e. Reformers will be significantly less observant in their religious affiliations than regulars.

Hypothesis 5 — Reformers will be significantly younger than regulars.

Information gathering is an individual's way to create "facts" about reality. Thus the cosmopolitan is found to read such newspapers of national scope as the *New York Times*. The parochial, on the other hand, depends upon local papers or tabloids that deal with "human interest." In short, the locals become influential because of "whom they know," while the cosmopolitans attain prestige because of "what they know."[3]

Perceptions and behavior are essential in understanding the local or cosmopolitan activist. Yet ethical questions are also imbedded in these distinct orientations. Hofstadter's study of the value conflict between lower-class immigrants and indigenous middle-class Yankees derived from ethical views of the best way to make political decisions. It is worth citing part of this view again.

> Yankee-Prostestant . . . traditions, . . . assumed and demanded the constant, disinterested activity of the citizen in public affairs, argued that political life ought to be run . . . in accordance with general principles and abstract laws apart from and superior to personal needs. . . . The other system, founded upon the European backgrounds of the immigrants, . . . took for granted that the political life of the individual would arise out of family needs, interpreted political and civic relations chiefly in terms of personal obligations, and placed strong personal local ties above abstract codes of law or morals.[4]

Banfield and Wilson characterized these different systems of political ethics as "public-regarding" and "private-regarding." They developed the constructs to explain either a selfless or a selfish brand of politics.[5] Later revising these categories, they accepted the formulation that individuals may simply define "the public interest" in different ways. These orientations toward public affairs became "unitary" or " individualistic."[6] Such attitudes lead one set of activists to concentrate upon interest as defined by the "best" solution for the whole, while the other might look for an outcome through compromise that contributes a little to each separate interest.

These descriptions recall the stress upon "specialization" and "technical skills" that the early reformers developed to combat governmental inefficiency. In tandem with these attitudes toward government went very specific ethnic identifications. The past reformers were segregated from regulars not only by motivations and attitudes, but also most clearly by demographic traits.

The focus upon cosmopolitan or local orientations provides other advantages. It helps to move the study of demographic variables into a more fruitful realm, for example, the salience to the individual actors of specific characteristics. For it is the value of that objective trait to the politico that is most likely to influence his attitudes and behavior. To describe an activist in terms of occupation, when he reacts politically because of his ethnic or religious ties, reveals the weakness and impossibility of separating objective from subjective analysis.

Kleppner's historical study of the Populists illustrates the ideal of replacing mere lists of attributes with a more thoughtful dissection of the values that truly salient traits arouse.[7] To note that the Populists were farmers is to overlook the point that they were pietistic farmers. Furthermore, and even more important, these religious values were most likely to have electoral implications, compared to the less essential occupational status. Thus orientation of the individual toward politics can be a most useful way to analyze his demographic characteristics.

The emphasis in this study on locals and cosmopolitans does provide just such an advantage. Furthermore, recent research does indicate continuing demographic variations between those that can be considered locals compared with cosmopolitans.[8] Merton also finds status contrasts between these groups, but claims that "educational and occupational differences may *contribute* to the differences between the two types of influentials but they are not the *source* of these differences."[9] Bearing in mind Merton's warning, and yet finding his analysis historically relevant to reformers, I will attempt to draw a demographic picture of the reformer as cosmopolitan and the regular as local.

Instead of using cosmopolitanism to distinguish the present political behavior of these activitists, it will be applied to their past socialization experiences. This method will illustrate — not the causality of the demographic variables, but rather — the important influences that might direct one more easily toward a cosmopolitan or local focus. Demographics provide the precipitants to present activities, but many intervening variables can turn a "demographic cosmopolitan" into an "attitudinal local" and vice versa.

Thus, by testing the local versus the cosmopolitan orientations of these activists, one can in later chapters determine the strength of such attributes in influencing motivations, liberalism, and ideology. If cosmopolitanism is merely a causal reflection of demographic characteristics, controlling for these variables would provide sharp diminution in attitudinal differences. But if cosmopolitanism is more than the summation of demographics, strong contrasts will continue to exist between professionals or mobiles who are either regular or reform Democrats. Approaching the demographic findings in this fashion, a portrait of the reformer as cosmopolitan and the regular as local can be sketched.

Demographic variables can also be interpreted separately as early socialization or later adult experiences. The attributes tied to parental background would appear to be early, unchangeable influences upon attitudes. One can hardly reverse the implications of being born into a Catholic or working-class family. These ascriptive variables influence the adult activist in his reflection of such achievement-based characteristics as occupation or economic and physical mobility. Yet the two forces — early socialization and adult experiences — seem separable for purposes of this analysis.

Integrating these categories of cosmopolitan-local with different socialization experiences produces demographic models of these activists. The early socialization picture of a cosmopolitan differs from that of a local. Cosmopolitans come from upper-status homes: Protestant or Jewish middle-class, native-born parents. Locals, on the other hand, are expected to derive from lower-status homes with lower-class Catholic or immigrant parents.

Adult socialization experiences that depict the cosmopolitan stereotype are social and geographic mobility, college education, professional occupation, upper-middle-class status, participation in many specialized voluntary organizations, and national media focus. For the local, little mobility, high-school education, business or craft occupation, lower-middle-class status, participation in fewer voluntary associations, and local-media orientation are expected. After tracing these models, the next step is to apply them to the findings discovered through this survey.

In examining the socialization patterns of reformers and regulars, the stereotype of cosmopolitans versus locals appears quite relevant. Parents of reformers were more likely to be native-born than were parents of regulars. Sixty-eight percent of N.D.C. fathers were born in the United States, as were seventy percent of these mothers. For the regulars, fifty-five percent of their fathers and fifty-eight percent of their mothers were born in this country. A gamma of .26 relating reformers to nativity of parents was discovered.[10]

This same slight differential is apparent in occupations of parents. Reformer homes were slightly more likely to have working mothers, since 30 percent of these women were employed compared to 19 percent of regular mothers. Jobs of the working mother gave a status advantage to the reformer, for 41.1 percent were professionals, while only 25.7 percent of regular working mothers were professionals. The same pattern is evident with fathers: fathers of reformers were more than twice as likely to be professionals (29.8 percent to 12.3 percent). While clerical and business occupations do not differ markedly, there are noticeable variations in the percentage of blue-collar skilled and nonskilled workers among fathers of reformers and regulars (21.8 percent to 38.9 percent). These occupational comparisons can also be summarized statistically.[11] A gamma of .28 relates occupations of mothers and .34 correlates fathers' occupations in the two groups.

Combining these distinct occupational categories into more general measures of middle-class status that include professionals as well as self-employed businessmen, managers, and officials provides continuing support for the upper-status nature of the reformer. Fathers of reformers are much more likely to be middle class than are fathers of regulars. Fifty-five percent of the former fell into this objective ranking, compared with thirty-three percent of the latter.

The class dichotomy between parents of regulars and reformers contributes positively to the models of locals and cosmopolitans presented above. Further evidence about religious and ethnic identification continues to support this distinction.

Probably the most noticeable trait of regulars is that they are overwhelmingly Catholic in religious identification. Fifty-eight percent of them came from such backgrounds, compared with sixteen percent of the reformers (Table 1). Examining the variable of religion, as Catholics and non-Catholics, produces a significant inverse relationship between reform identification and Catholicism with a gamma correlation of -.75.

Reformers indicate a more dispersed pattern of religious identification, since 27.7 percent are Jewish, 27.7 percent are agnostic, 16.3 percent are Catholic, 15.8 percent are Protestant, and 12.5 percent are other. Regulars who declare themselves Jewish account for only 12.9 percent of the total, Protestants for 20.1 percent, and agnostics 6.6 percent.

This religious upbringing of the regular has had a lasting effect. He attends services as an adult frequently compared with reformers. Fifty-two percent of the regulars attend services once a week or more, compared with 17.1 percent of the reformers (gamma = -.61). Before one jumps to hasty conclusions that Catholicism explains much of this variation between regulars and reformers, it is interesting to note that frequency of attendance at religious

TABLE 1

RELIGIOUS IDENTIFICATION OF
REFORMERS AND REGULARS

Religious Identification	Reformers (N = 614)	Regulars (N = 752)
	%	%
Catholic	16.3	58.1
Jewish	27.7	12.9
Protestant	15.8	20.1
Other	12.5	2.3
None	27.7	6.6
Total	100.0	100.0

services is not only related to the large proportion of Catholics in the regular group. Controlling for Catholicism does not affect church attendance very much. Catholics in the two organizations vary significantly from each other according to number of services attended: Catholic regulars attend services much more frequently than do Catholic reformers (gamma = -.46). Except for Protestants, who are similar, reformers, whatever their religious identification, attend services less frequently than do regulars.

The literature on the locals leads one to expect large proportions of Catholics in this group. This anticipation is consistent with these findings. And yet religion does not explain church attendance. This discovery harks back to questions about objective demographic criteria for discriminating locals and cosmopolitans. If one can not say that it is Catholicism that influences behavior and attitudes, then demographic descriptions of these activists may not contribute very much to an understanding of the cosmopolitan direction of the reformer, in contrast to the local one of the regular. The correlations in themselves may be unrelated to the distinct attitudes probable between the two sets of activists. With this hesitation in mind, one can examine the other socialization characteristic of these politicians with the same caveat relevant.

It is interesting that 43 percent of the regulars claim minority-group identification, while 53 percent of the reformers do. The ethnic pattern for the entire regular and reform group parallels these differences in religion. Approximately one-quarter of the regulars who claim minority status say they are Italian-Americans (compared to ten percent of the reformers) and slightly over one-quarter more identify themselves as Irish-Americans. Afro-Americans in both groups are approximately equal to their proportion in the state population: 11.6 percent regulars, 9.9 percent reformers.

These findings deny any racial bias of the amateur groups, yet reinforce expectations that early socialization experiences of regulars have differed essentially from those of reformers. While one might identify regulars as predominantly Catholic, one can only say of reformers that they are overrepresentative of Jews and agnostics.

Some light is thrown on the role of religion in explaining cosmopolitanism by these data. One might ask why Jews should display a cosmopolitan orientation. In his research, Dobriner finds Catholics the most localistic group and Jews quite cosmopolitan. He relates this tendency of the Jew to his marginal status within his town. Sensing himself apart from the community, it would be quite difficult for the Jew to develop a local identification.[12] This sense of marginality appears in the answers to the question on ethnic identification:

> If you are a member of any of the following minority groups, please check one: ( ) Italo-American   ( ) Afro-American   ( ) Irish-American   ( ) Puerto Rican   ( ) Eastern European   ( ) Other————————————————————————.

Jewish does not appear in the choices, since it was listed under the question on religion. Of all the responses, however, reformers wrote in Jewish as an ethnic identification 33.4 percent of the time. The comparable figure for regulars in only 8.2 percent. The Jewish reformer sees himself as a member of a minority group. The fact that he volunteers this information is important.

The ethnic Jew might merely have been the agnostic in the question on religion, in which case ethnicity would be his opportunity to emphasize his Jewish identification. But an ethnic analysis of religion does not support this hypothesis for the N.D.C.

member. In fact, 41 percent of the N.D.C. members who are Italian-Americans claim to be agnostics, while only 21 percent of the Jewish ethnics identify with no religion. For regulars, the figures are 3.7 percent and 15.4 percent.

This discovery only reinforces the questions raised by religion and church attendance, since ethnicity seems to have differing effects in the two groups. Italian-Americans are much more likely to be agnostics if they are N.D.C. members than if they are regulars. In terms of religious and ethnic behavior, reformers are much less parochial than are regulars. This finding upholds the cosmopolitan nature of the reformer, but not in terms of objective demographic variables.

Not formal religious identification but church attendance, not ethnicity as much as its interpretation in marginal status seem to separate the cosmopolitan reformer from the local regular. Merton is correct. It is useful to develop his model further: it is not the quantitative or objective analysis of these variables, but rather their qualitative or subjective aspects that count.

The ascriptive characteristics of these political activists do display some differences between the two groups. On the whole, reformers are born to higher-status homes than regulars, but the occupational differentials are not large. These status variations cohere to expectations about cosmopolitans and locals. Yet the relevance of such objective demographic criteria for understanding political behavior seems more and more questionable. Perhaps focusing upon both quantitative and qualitative distinctions for adult socialization experiences of reformers and regulars can clarify some of these confusions.

Turning to this analysis, one notes immediately that the status differences between parents of these activists increases when one looks at their offspring. The gamma correlating regular and reform occupational status is a rather strong .62. Table 2 illustrates this occupational breakdown by broad groupings. Reformers and regulars seem more varied in occupation than one would expect. Yet the reformer as upper-middle-class professional certainly reflects the picture of a cosmopolitan drawn previously.

More than twice as many reformers as regulars are professionals, 71.1 percent to 32.7 percent. The surprising finding, however, concerns the slight difference between the two organizations in the percentage who are employed in business or management. While more regulars follow such occupations (18.6 percent) than do reformers (15.9 percent), the difference is slight. Combining

TABLE 2

Occupational Distribution Of
Reformers And Regulars

Occupation	Reformers (N = 596)	Regulars (N = 485)
	%	%
Service workers	.2	5.4
Unskilled labor	1.4	6.0
Skilled labor	2.7	18.1
Sales	5.2	8.4
Clerical	3.5	10.7
Managers and business	15.9	18.6
Professional	71.1	32.7
Total	100.0	99.9*

Gamma = .62

*Total percentages may not add up to 100% due to rounding.

these categories of business and professional work to derive the measure of middle-class status used previously, 87 percent of the reformers but only 51.3 percent of the regulars can be so classified (gamma = .73).

The original hypothesis had claimed that most of the contrast between the two groups would be evident within the middle class, according to type of occupation, rather than between broad occupational classifications. In some ways, this is supported by the data. Examining professional versus nonprofessional occupations, one finds a very strong relationship (gamma = .66) — illustrated by the percentages — between this variable and reformed membership. Yet the data go quite far beyond this expectation, since variations are great even between the percentages of each group who hold blue-collar jobs. Over one-quarter of the regulars, 29.5 percent, are employed in blue-collar occupations. Compare this with only 4.3 percent of the reformers. As for clerical and sales people, 20 percent of the regulars' employment can be categorized this way, while only 8.7 percent of the reformers' can.

Discovering large proportions of professionals among the N.D.C. ranks, however, is not enough to develop the distinctions between cosmopolitans and locals. Closer examination of the kinds of professionals or the kinds of businessmen is necessary. Thus one expects the cosmopolitan's status to be predicated upon technical skills, while the local's rests upon personal relationships. This is what Merton meant by the qualitative behavior of the influentials he studied.

Detailed analysis of the professional's occupation does not prove too instructive. Similar percentages are lawyers (16.9 percent of the regulars and 15.7 percent of the reformers). For other "learned professionals," such as accountants, architects, and college professors, the percentages are alike: 31.6 percent of reformers and 29.2 percent of the regulars. Technically trained professionals — for example, engineers, chemists, and optometrists — are in greater proportion in the regular professional category, 26.3 percent, compared with 17.4 percent for the N.D.C. Reformers are slightly more likely to be from such middle-status groups as noncollege teachers or social workers (32.5 percent of these reformer professionals, while 25.2 percent of the regulars who are professionals can be so classified).

Merton does suggest that the distinction between locals and cosmopolitans may not even be in the distinctions between types of professionals, but rather in the role perceptions a worker brings to his tasks. While approaching this factor only indirectly, one may infer personal contact versus the skill from the business orientation or other employment patterns available in this study. The cosmopolitan manager is more likely to come from the top level of the bureaucracy, where technical and organizational needs are paramount, while the local, uninvolved in such skills, would probably own his own business.

The first suggestion is supported by the data: 28.4 percent of the regulars who are in business or management, while 49.3 percent of the reformers who are, come from top bureaucratic levels. Only 20.4 percent of the reformers and 25.7 percent of the regulars, however, own their own businesses. This latter finding does not contribute any certainty to the suggestion that skills versus contacts are differential sources of competence. Since this occupational category included not only private business, but also public managerial positions, one must find other ways to examine specific occupational distinctions.

Part of this problem is resolved by a separate question, which asked:

Are you employed by: ( )   government   ( )   institution
( ) private business ( ) self ( ) other＿＿＿＿＿＿＿＿＿.

Regardless of occupational classification, 54.6 percent of the regulars are involved in private business. The percentage of reformers in private business is only 39.7 percent. Conversely, 24 percent of the reformers are employed by institutions and only 6.9 percent of the regulars are. Once again, the business orientation of the regular stands out. The institutional affiliations of reformers also sustains the argument of technical and specialized skills.

It is no surprise that both regulars and reformers are so equally and infrequently likely to be self-employed (18 percent for both groups). The growth of corporations and diminution of small enterprises is a fact of American industrialism. Nor is it unexpected that government jobs are unavailable to regulars, only 19.5 percent of whom hold such positions. The total was not much lower, 15.2 percent, for reformers. Just as corporatism is a way of life, so, too, the civil servant in a large government bureaucracy is not likely to be a patronage appointee. Specialization and expertise, as Weber noted, become the necessary adjunct of a bureaucratic state.

Furthermore, not value-free expertise, but instead the values of science and technical skills permeate the relationships of these professionals. Apter emphasizes this point when he claims that science is an ideology that glorifies "planning, calculation, and rationalistic goals."[13] Such orientations in one's work carry over into one's political life, where, more and more, experts make policy decisions that the nonprofessional can not even begin to evaluate.

Such cosmopolitan perceptions have loosened the ties of the activist to his traditional moorings. Thus, while class can be important in discriminating locals from cosmopolitans, an even more essential question involves occupational and physical mobility. If the N.D.C. member conforms to this picture of cosmopolitanism, he will display these traits quite visibly.

Recalling findings cited earlier, one should note that parents of reformers and regulars are more alike in their occupations than are their activist offspring. The class differentials appear to be exaggerated between generations. On the whole, however, reformers' parents who are middle class produce children who "inherit" this status more often than do regulars' parents. Table 3 illustrates this point.

TABLE 3

PARENTAL AND RESPONDENT'S MIDDLE-CLASS OCCUPATIONAL STATUS

| | Father's middle-class occupation | | | |
| | Reformer | | Regular | |
Occupation of respondent	Professional (N = 107)	Management (N = 147)	Professional (N = 67)	Management (N = 121)
	%	%	%	%
Professional	78.5	76.9	58.2	33.1
Management	13.1	12.9	13.4	31.4
Clerical	4.7	2.0	9.0	9.9
Sales	.9	6.1	7.5	9.1
Skilled	.9	.7	4.5	7.4
Unskilled	1.9	1.4	3.0	1.7
Service	—	—	4.5	7.4
Total	100.0	100.0	100.1*	100.0

*Percentages may not add up to 100% due to rounding.

Fathers who were professionals have middle-class children 91.6 percent of the time if N.D.C. members, but only 71.6 percent of the time if regulars. A similar pattern exists for managerial fathers. Their children who become reformers are more likely to be middle class than are regulars (89.8 percent to 64.5 percent). Either there is some downward mobility for the regular in comparison to his father, or the occupational measure of status exaggerates the middle-class nature of certain jobs. "Self-employed businessmen" could represent the small grocerystore owner, whose middle-class position is more likely to be of lower status than the partner in a larger clothing business. For the shopkeeper father, in fact, his son's involvement in a skilled craft might illustrate upward mobility. These categories, however, can not deal with such fine distinctions.

Middle-class parents of reformers produce middle-class offspring. While one can not say this with the same strength for regulars, the pattern does not appear to be dissimilar. The specific issue of mobility from lower-occupational status of the father to upper status for the offspring has yet to be discussed. While the numbers of reform parents are small compared to the regulars, the greater mobility of the reformer is clearly shown in Table 4.

TABLE 4

INTERGENERATIONAL MOBILITY FROM LOWER TO MIDDLE CLASS FOR REFORMERS AND REGULARS

Father's lower-status occupation	Middle-class status of offspring	
	Regulars (N = 355)	Reformers (N = 194)
	%	%
Clerical	55.0	76.4
Sales	66.6	89.2
Skilled	44.3	79.7
Semi- or unskilled	39.6	76.2
Service worker	40.7	89.7

Even those activists whose parents exhibited a lower status illustrates differentials in mobility between regulars and reformers. Insurgents became middle class in larger proportions than did regulars, even if their parents were not. The middle-class nature of the reformer is evident. Only fifty-one percent of the regulars, compared with eighty-seven percent of the reformers, can be categorized as middle class according to occupational variables. Yet these middle-class reformers did not all inherit their status. Coming from lower-class homes, the reformers are more likely to achieve occupational advancement than are the regulars.

The cosmopolitan is mobile. While the reformer seems to be deeply embedded in a family middle-class tradition, there is some occupational mobility. Even more evident, and certainly related, is his geographic mobility.

No distinction exists between regulars and reformers as to birth in the United States (91.4 percent to 92.8 percent). Yet a majority of regulars were born in New Jersey, 55.9 percent, compared to 40.5 percent of the reformers. While this difference seems slight, the same pattern holds for adult physical mobility. Reformers are less likely than regulars to reside for a long period in their present countries. The average number of years reformers have lived in their country is 18.6, compared to 31.1 for regulars.

Since physical and social mobility have been found together,[14] it makes sense that the picture of the reformer as one of high status, both because of parental occupation and also because of his own achievement, is not contradicted by the data on physical mobility.

> The more movement there is within the society, the more likely people are to be exposed to different agents of social learning and to different political norms and attitudes. Much of the social and political meaning of mobility stems from the resulting exposures to new agents of political socialization.[15]

The reformer, both by birth and by upward mobility, is more likely to be touched by the values of an upper-middle-class orientation toward politics associated with cosmopolitanism. The findings here seem to suggest that a class-based politics of well-to-do against less well-to-do is reappearing in the guise of reformer versus regular. An analysis of other demographic variables continues to raise this possibility.

In terms of education, there is a moderately strong correlation between years of school and N.D.C. membership. A gamma of .57 clearly confims the hypothesis of reformers' higher educational status. The statistic alone does not illustrate the importance of this point. Over 68 percent of the N.D.C. had *at least* a four-year college degree, compared with 30.8 percent of the regulars. The obverse of this is the fact that only 13.4 percent N.D.C. delegates were educated less than or equal to a high-school degree, while 42.1 percent of the regulars fell into this category.[16]

It has been suggested that education, with its emphasis upon civic virtues and democratic participation, might be the cause of the "reform" style of politics. The highly educated reformers have certainly spent more time in institutions that purvey these values. Perhaps the reformers have adopted their attitudes toward politics through educational exposure. I shall return to this point in later chapters when such demographic factors can be related to specific political attitudes and behavior.

In this discussion of education and socialization, it might also be appropriate to note the age differences between regulars and reformers. Reformers are considerably younger than regulars (gamma = -.52). A majority of the N.D.C. members are under forty years of age (59.4 percent to be exact). Only 30 percent of the regulars are this young. The main point, however, is that 30 per-

TABLE 5

FAMILY INCOME DISTRIBUTION FOR REFORMERS AND REGULARS

Annual income	Reformers (N = 601)	Regulars (N = 721)
	%	%
Less than $4,999	1.8	4.3
$5,000 to $9,999	16.1	25.1
$10,000 to $14,999	19.8	33.3
$15,000 to $19,999	23.6	16.9
$20,000 to $24,999	15.5	10.4
$25,000 and over	23.1	10.0
Total	99.9*	100.0

*Percentages may not add up to 100% due to rounding.

cent of the N.D.C. members are under thirty years of age. The corresponding figure for regulars is 5 percent. This is very similar to Soule and Clarke's finding.[17] Perhaps this age discrepancy between the groups might reflect incomplete socialization into the norms of party activity. As the reformer ages and becomes experienced in party work, he may adopt the values of more traditional party activists. This possibility can be kept in mind until later discussion of political attitudes.

Income is moderately related to reform participation and seems similar in effect to education. Sixty-two percent of reformers earn over $15,000 a year. For regulars, only 37.3 percent have incomes at this level. Regulars, however, are not poor. Few activists in either group earn under $5,000 a year: only 4 percent of the regulars and 2 percent of the reformers do. As one can see in Table 5, 30.4 percent of the regulars have an income below $10,000 per year, while only 17.9 percent of the reformers have such low earning power. Reformers are much wealthier than regulars, but for both groups there is considerable spread in income distribution.

Income differences do not highlight the actual status variation between the groups as accurately as do education and occupation. Since occupations of reformers appear to be of high status, but not necessarily high income, the actual difference between the groups is minimized if one concentrates on income as a variable.

The interrelationship between the three main demographic variables (education, income, and occupational class) is reviewed in Table 6.

TABLE 6

INTERRELATIONSHIP OF OCCUPATION, INCOME, AND EDUCATION (GAMMA CORRELATIONS)

Demographic variable	Reformers		Regulars	
	Gamma	N	Gamma	N
Occupation and education	.69	(485)	.60	(593)
Occupation and income	.13	(471)	.48	(579)
Education and income	.23	(601)	.57	(717)

Any correlation with income for the N.D.C. lowers the strength of the relationship considerably. While occupational status related to education indicates a strong tie for reformers and regulars, no such pattern exists between income and either occupation or education for the insurgent.

If one interprets these data as status consistency for regulars, that possibility is far from true for the reformers. Their educational attainments and their middle-class occupations are limited by incomes that are below what one might expect according to these other demographics. Lipset has suggested that the intellectual considers himself deprived in terms of status. This deprivation, in turn, makes him responsive to leftist political ideologies.[18] Perhaps this same pattern is operating for the reformer whose income is not in line with his educational and occupational status.

In describing the objective demographic characteristics of reformers and regulars, a distinct status difference is evident. More than these quantitative descriptions are important, however, in locating the cosmopolitan tendencies of the N.D.C. member. Here perceptions and values are essential. The cosmopolitan is not only exemplified by his higher status and mobility, but also in his orientation toward applying his technical skills: such an activist is likely to belong to different kinds of voluntary associations than the individual who sees such organizations as a way to increase his social contacts.

Yet reformers and regulars are just as likely to belong to organizations. In fact, both groups average 2.2 associations for each member. Reformers, however, are more likely to belong to professional and political associations (not party) than are regulars. Forty percent of the reformers join professional organizations, while the figure for regulars is only twenty-two percent. This makes sense in terms of both occupational self-interest as well as application of one's skills.

The non-party political orientation of the reformer (fifty-three percent belong to such groups) is quite distinct from the regular (only thirty-one percent of whom do). Regulars, on the other hand, are more likely to participate in associations that are: social or fraternal (thirty percent to fourteen percent), religious (thirty-eight percent to twenty-three percent), veterans (fifteen percent to two percent), or labor union (fifteen percent to six percent). No differences appear in the activists who join charitable business or civic, and ethnic associations. The localism of these groups can only be inferred from their labels. Yet the regular does seem to lean toward the kinds of organizations promoting social contacts that have been associated with local versus cosmopolitan orientations.

The heart of the distinction between these perceptions lies in an interpretation and direction of one's interests. A veterans' group could have a local or a national focus, either providing social activities or economic and military pressures. From these data, one can not do more than suggest such attitudes. An indirect way to focus upon this dimension of cosmopolitanism would be to explore an activist's media patterns. The cosmopolitan is expected to have a national orientation, which would be evident in his reading, viewing, and hearing.

When asked to describe their political reading and listening habits, 59.2 percent of the regulars say theirs is an equal mixture of national, state, and local coverage. Fewer reformers claim this balance (47.1 percent), as is shown in Table 7. Reformers are considerably more involved in national media than are professionals (38.4 percent to 11.7 percent).. In keeping with local expectations about the regular, one notes that he is clearly more community bound in his media coverage.

TABLE 7

POLITICAL MEDIA ORIENTATION OF
REFORMERS AND REGULARS

Media focus	Reformers		Regulars	
	Percent	N*	Percent	N*
Local	7.0	(44)	20.0	(154)
State	4.6	(29)	6.5	(50)
National	38.4	(243)	11.7	(90)
Equal mixture	47.1	(298)	59.2	(456)

*Since respondents could check more than one answer, the number of respondents is provided for each distinct category.

The information on newspaper reading also supports the cosmopolitan nature of the reformer. Regulars read an average of 1.69

newspapers each, compared with 1.76 for the reformer. The real distinctions, however, lie in the types of papers. While 37.8 percent of the regulars read the *New York Times*, 80.6 percent of the reformers depend upon it regularly. Newark newspapers, such as the *Newark Evening News* (now defunct) and the *Newark Star Ledger*, were more popular among regulars that reformers (33.6 percent to 21.3 percent), while other New Jersey dailies illustrated a similar pattern.

The national involvement of the reformer is complemented by his magazine reading habits. Reformers were also more likely to read magazines regularly. N.D.C. members follow an average of 1.45 periodicals compared to .88 average for regulars. More important, however, is the continuing picture of the reformer as one to whom political opinions and a broadly cultural focus are essential. While both groups are likely to read such general news magazines as *Look, Life, Newsweek,* and *U.S. News and World Report* (47 percent of the regulars and 44.4 percent of the reformers do), reformers are much more likely to follow the political opinion magazines of the left, such as *New Republic* and *Nation* (32.2 percent to 4.1 percent). Cultural magazines such as *Saturday Review, Harpers,* and *Atlantic Monthly* are noticeably more attractive to the N.D.C. group (25.8 percent to 4.5 percent).

Merton places great emphasis upon the media habits of influentials. The information these activists obtain is used to implement their prestige and status as interpreters of events.[19] Thus the sources of this influence are very indicative of their viewpoints.

The reformer who depends upon the *New York Times* perceives his world in national and international terms. There was little mention of New Jersey-state, let alone local, politics in that newspaper when this survey was completed. State or local newspapers provide a quite different source of "facts" and information. Whether this cosmopolitan status is reflected in political perceptions and behavior is something to be discussed in the next chapter. But if one could conclude anything about the demographic variables that have characterized the reformer so far, it would appear that he can be described quite comfortably as a cosmopolitan. The regular, on the other hand, is more typically the model of a locally oriented individual.

Thus it seems that the socialization hypotheses that were thought to be so unimportant seem to be rather strongly confirmed. A class differential was discovered, as well as some variation within the professional class. While the overall hypothesis of professional occupations for reformers seems confirmed, others related to occupational characteristics were not. Thus more regulars were employed in private businesses, but few in both groups were self-employed.

Ethnic, religious, age, and income distinctions were also supported by the data, while racial differences were not. Most important, however, does seem to be the cosmopolitan orientation of the reformer. This was discovered in the insurgent's media focus, mobility patterns, and membership in voluntary associations. But even the class, ethnic, and religious variables suggest that their salience resulted from implications they held for the orientation of a particular activist.

In turning to the next task, it is necessary to place the socialization of the reformer into a political context: Is this cosmopolitanism relevant? How can one best depict the early political experiences as well as the adult interest and eventual participation of the reformer? The following chapter will present the political socialization of reformers and regulars in the continuing context of cosmopolitanism.

Notes to Chapter 3

1. Wilson, *Amateur Democrat*, p. 2.

2. Merton, "Patterns of Influence," in Merton, p. 393.

3. Ibid., pp. 400-409.

4. Hofstadter, *Age of Reform*, pp. 8-9.

5. Banfield and Wilson, *City Politics*, chaps. 3, 16.

6. James Q. Wilson and Edward C. Banfield, "Political Ethos Revisited," *American Political Science Review* 65 (December 1971); 1,049.

7. Kleppner, *Cross of Culture*.

8. Thomas R. Dye, "The Local-Cosmopolitan Dimension and the Study of Urban Politics," *Social Forces* 41 (March 1963): 239-46; William M. Dobriner, "Local and Cosmopolitan as Contemporary Suburban Character Types," in *The Suburban Community*, ed. William M. Dobriner (New York: G. P. Putnam's Sons, 1958), pp. 132-46; Wilson and Banfield, "Political Ethos Revisited," pp. 1,048-62.

9. Merton, "Patterns of Influence," in Merton, p. 402.

10. In the analysis of the data, N.D.C. membership is treated as a dichotomized variable: 1 equals N.D.C. membership, 0 equals absence of reform membership. Thus a positive finding means a variable is directly related to reformism, while a negative correlation indicates an inverse relationship with N.D.C. membership.

11. This coding of occupation depended upon seven distinct categories: professional, managerial or business, sales, clerical, craft workers, unskilled workers, and service

workers. In developing a variable middle class, the first two categories — professional and managerial or business — were combined to create middle-class status, while the other categories were collected to indicate lower-class background. To discuss professional versus nonprofessional occupations, category 1 — professional — was dichotomized from all other occupations.

12. Dobriner, "Local and Cosmopolitan," in Dobriner, pp. 140-46.

13. David E. Apter, "Introduction: Ideology and Discontent," in Apter, p. 40.

14. Richard E. Dawson and Kenneth Prewitt, *Political Socialization* (Boston: Little, Brown & Co., 1969), pp. 58, 93.

15. Ibid., p. 93.

16. These N.D.C. percentages are even lower if one omits the twenty-eight N.D.C. members who were under the age of twenty-one.

17. Soule and Clarke, "Amateurs and Professionals," p. 891.

18. Seymour Martin Lipset, *Political Man: The Social Bases of Politics* (Garden City, N. Y.: Anchor Books, Doubleday & Company, Inc., 1960), pp. 332-63.

19. Merton, "Patterns of Influence," in Merton, p. 391.

4
Political Socialization
and Career Patterns

Past studies, as well as the hypotheses of this research project, firmly expected the demographic characteristics of the reformer to be far less important than his issue orientation and motivation. In depicting the insurgent as an upper-status cosmopolitan, the focus has been upon the effects of certain background traits on an individual's perceptions and attitudes. Less important than the class of the reformer and regular will be their interpretation of political reality through the lens of localism or cosmopolitanism. How these orientations influence participation of the activists in quite different organizations is the main thrust of this study, not merely the enumeration of certain demographic attributes.

Class may be relevant to any study of politicians, but an even more immediate interest directs one to the kinds of motivations that intervene between such variables as demographics and liberalism to precipitate and support political involvement. For this reason the following two chapters will concentrate upon the more specifically relevant question of motivations.

In this chapter motivation will be approached indirectly by relating political socialization to career patterns. In the next section the personal motivations and role interpretations of these activists will be discussed.

The contrasting motivations between reformers and regulars has been previously tied to class differentials. The machine loyalist was a recent immigrant whose desperate material needs were met by the party. In turn, the recipient gave emotional fealty to the boss and did him little electioneering favors by simply getting his friends and neighbors to vote the ticket.

The reformer — from the Progressive Era on — had few economic demands the machine could meet. Middle class or upper, these solvent groups found politics and politicians a rather disreputable bunch. Class and ethnic identification, above all, clarified the distinction between the groups of activists, as I have shown in the historical analysis.

Strict immigration laws, the New Deal, growing prosperity, and upward mobility, plus civil service reform, dried up not only the patronage available, but also the nurturing motivations that led an individual to respond to patronage as an incentive. This machine-style participation had involved an immediately satisfying exchange relationship for political or economic gain.

Not all new immigrants, however, had sought politics as an avenue for mobility. And not all the middle class joined the ranks of the urban reformers. Different motivations and incentives must, therefore, have been enticing to different people. The political vocation is not a deterministic choice.

Obviously, since activists are said to be of different classes, a certain class background alone did not turn one into a certain type of activist. Ethnic background alone did not produce one kind of politician. Demographics might shape the underlying factors that set the path of one's early socialization. These paths, in some sense, structure reality as well as choices available to an individual. Yet the choices still remain multiple. To explain the modern-day reformer and the regular in terms of general demographic variables does not seem to be much of an improvement in understanding the motivations and incentives that can operate in different types of voluntary organizations.

Furthermore, the demographic findings of this study do not reveal an immigrant or lower-class background for the regular. While he is distinct from the reformer in ethnicity and status, these differences are not the same as those one would anticipate from the "machine-age" professional. For this reason, political variables and influences must be examined. It is useful to continue the cosmopolitan-local differentiation, and to apply it to such questions that political socialization might raise.

There are two rather distinct components of the cosmopolitan spectrum. One involves the foundations of social interaction. For the cosmopolitan these relationships and attitudes are based upon "objective" criteria of skill, efficiency, and welfare of the whole community. One discovers for the local, however, an orientation predicated upon personal contacts, loyalty, and concern for separate interests.

A second aspect of cosmopolitanism regards national and international events as primary sources of political facts and information. For the parochial, information is developed locally since interest and involvement are so focused. The use of information for the reformer requires a different kind of fact gathering to meet his national concerns. Thus, after describing the political goals of these activists in terms of personal loyalty versus objective criteria, one can explore national or cosmopolitan orientations as they relate to initial political involvement. Then the continuing career patterns of these activists will be an important part of the discussion, as will analysis of tasks that reformers and regulars perform.

The application of cosmopolitanism to political phenomena develops the train of argument begun in the last chapter. Certain general demographic traits of reformers and regulars could be fruitfully organized around the concept of cosmopolitanism. Now its usefulness can be expanded to understanding the political socialization and career patterns of N.D.C. and regular Democrats.

Before proceeding in this discussion, it will be helpful if the same method pursued in the last chapter can be applied here. I shall first make the general propositions of the study more concrete by presenting the detailed hypotheses with which they were operationalized. These hypotheses are numbered in accord with their derivatives from the conclusion of chapter 2 for reference purposes.

Political Socialization Hypotheses

Early Socialization Experiences

Hypothesis 5 — There will be a significant difference in the socialization experiences of reformers and regulars.

    a. Regulars will come from homes that are significantly more Democratic than reformers.
    b. Regulars will be significantly more interested in politics at a younger age than reformers.
    c. Reformers will be significantly more likely than regulars to come from apolitical homes.

Adult Political Cosmopolitanism

Hypothesis 1 — There will be a significant difference between reformers and regulars in their cosmopolitan orientations.

a. Reformers will have higher proportions interested in national politics than regulars.

Hypothesis 7 — Reformers will be significantly more suburban in life-style than regualrs.

a. Reformers live in areas that are proportionally more Republican in voting habits than do regulars.

Political Tasks and Career Patterns

Hypothesis 12 — Political Tasks: Reformers will be significantly less likely to perform election-oriented tasks than regulars.

Hypothesis 11 — Career Patterns: Reformers will be significantly less likely than regulars to hold high-party positions.

a. Reformers will be significantly less likely to hold patronage appointments than regulars.

The overarching concern still remains cosmopolitanism. The political socialization of a local is characterized by firm ties to the primary group, while the cosmopolitan displays an orientation toward such secondary influences as schooling or specific issues. These variations, if relevant for insurgents and regulars, may be apparent in parental influences. One would expect that the strongly Democratic household might exert the kind of influence upon a child that could produce a political attachment equivalent to the local's orientation toward the primary group. One does, in fact, discover rather obvious differences between party loyalty of parents in the two organizations.

Approximately seventy percent of the regular parents belonged to the same political party as their offspring, while only fifty-five percent of the reform parents did. The findings are not conclusive in relation to past research. Campbell, et al., in *The American Voter*, discovered that among parents who identified with the Democratic Party, this same party loyalty was transmitted to offspring in seventy-six percent of the cases.[1] Since Campbell's study made use of data from 1952 and 1956 at the latest, one can not rely on it comparatively, because shifts in party identification are becoming visible in the electorate.

The growing number of Independents, evident in 1968, is paralleled by a decrease in the percentage of strong party identifiers.[2] This seventy-six percent transmission rate for the general population is slightly above that evident for the regulars, who follow their parents' party in seventy percent of the cases.

A more recent study discovered that 59 percent of a parent-student national probability sample agreed in their party identification.[3] Thus reformers may not differ essentially from recent population trends in party identification, while regulars indicate an older pattern of high cohesion between parent-offspring party affiliation.

Since the regular's identification is not in greater accord with his parents' than one might expect from Campbell's study of the general electorate, can the real distinction be in the level of parents' party commitment? Such a possibility is not supported by my findings. Regular parents played a minimal role in party, much less public office. Thus parental loyalties to a party, combined with lower occupational status, do not necessarily produce party activism. Mothers in *both* groups held party offices in approximately four percent of the cases; fathers in *both* groups did so in eight percent of the cases. These percentages are only worth mentioning for the surprisingly low party involvement of the regulars' parents. Parents of regulars exhibited rather a passive loyalty to the Democratic Party, although loyalty of some degree is evident in comparison with reformers.

This loyalty and its transmission to children would be more in keeping with the local's orientation toward primary-group ties. Besides this commitment to Democratic Party politics, the hypotheses also anticipated an early interest in politics for the regular. This youthful fascination was related to the socialization process, in which party loyalty would predispose the youth toward the Democratic Party. The impact of parents, as opposed to secondary-group influences, was much in keeping with the supposition that the regular becomes attuned to the political orientations of the local. Motivated by such early attachments, his political beliefs would rest upon the importance of loyalty to family and the personalization of politics.

Instead of this finding, however, I discovered the lack of interest in politics for the young regular. The vast majority of them (69.6 percent) claim to have become interested in politics as adults. Only 46.5 percent of the reformers waited this long to whet their appetites (Table 8). Thus there appears to be a negative but significant relationship between age of first political interest and reformism (gamma = -.37). This is contradictory to Soule and Clarke's analysis of amateurs at the 1968 convention.[4]

TABLE 8

AGE OF FIRST POLITICAL INTEREST
FOR REFORMERS AND REGULARS

Age of first interest	Reformers (N = 628)	Regulars (N = 757)
	%	%
Childhood	18.6	12.7
Adolescence	34.9	17.7
Adult	46.5	69.6
Total	100.0	100.0

Gamma = -.37

Socialization literature does support the contention that one of the few political attitudes to be "inherited" by children is party identification.[5] Yet this adoption of parental values does not implicity lead to active participation in politics. The value system might, however, provide a foundation upon which interest, once aroused, would take on a predictable and positive affinity for the Democratic Party. Thus to note that twenty-eight percent of regulars and twenty-four percent of reformers attribute their first interest in politics to family indicates that similar proportions have been influenced by these forces. This does not reveal, however, the content of the influence and does not permit one to guess about the underlying conditions that attract an activist to reform-oriented politics. One conclusion possible, however, is that parents of regulars do not illustrate unusually strong and active ties to the Democratic Party.

In the first two chapters, the survey of historical developments rejected the traditional view of the regular as a machine politician, motivated only by a desire for material rewards. These demographic findings support this decision, since the parents of regulars so rarely held party or public office that one could hardly equate the socialization of the regular with an increasing orientation toward machine politics.

TABLE 9

SOURCE OF FIRST POLITICAL INTEREST
FOR REFORMERS AND REGULARS

Source of interest	Reformers		Regulars	
	Percent	N*	Percent	N*
Family and friends	36.0	(225)	63.8	(484)
Issues	36.6	(229)	15.9	(121)
School, reading	24.8	(155)	8.8	(67)
Job	2.2	(14)	4.6	(35)
Candidate	15.5	(97)	14.6	(111)

*More than one response was possible.

Party allegiance for the regular may have been inbibed early, yet it remained remarkably latent, until adult interests aroused political involvement and channeled it in the direction of party work. Perhaps a clearer understanding of this precipitating interest can be reached if other information is presented.

In describing not only the time of their first interest in politics but also the reasons for this interest, it becomes evident that reformers and regulars differ considerably, as is shown in Table 9. The importance of primary group attachments for the regular is in keeping with the view of him as a local to whom personal contacts are important. Family and friends provide the foundation for political interest for 63.8 percent of the regulars, while only 36 percent of the reformers stressed such reasons.

Impersonal, intellectual experiences are stressed by reformers as reasons for political arousal. Issue concerns (36.6 percent) and school (24.8 percent) are mentioned more often by reformers than by regulars (the percentages for regulars are 15.9 percent and 8.8 percent, respectively). This might very well be the cosmopolitan orientation. For the cosmopolitan, not primary-group attachments, but eagerness to serve the general good through policy commitments evoked one's interests. The effect of school and reading also induce one toward "civic responsiveness" and "issue orientation." Occupation influences very few, while the attraction of a candidate is equally, but not very important for N.D.C. and regulars.

One can pinpoint the effects of primary-group influences on regulars even more by relating age of first political interest to source of first interest (Table 10). Friends and family ties are important as precursors of political interest for the regular at any age compared to reformers. Even more important, as reformers age, they become subject to new influences. Regulars are much more likely to remain within this network of primary-group loyalties.

TABLE 10

SOURCE OF FIRST POLITICAL INTEREST RELATED TO AGE OF FIRST INTEREST (GAMMA CORRELATIONS)*

Source of interest	Reformers Gamma (N = 623)	Regulars Gamma (N = 751)
Family, friends	-.53	-.20
Issues	.60	.29
School, reading	-.42	-.48
Job	.66	.65
Candidate	.45	.36

*A positive sign means direct relationship between cause of interest and older age of first interest.

The older a reformer was when he became interested in politics, the less likely he was to be influenced by primary-group loyalties (gamma =-.53). Age of first interest only slightly relates to the influence of family or friends for the regular (gamma = -.20). Issues become paramount for the reformer as he ages, but seem relatively unrelated to chronological age for regulars.

The first component of cosmopolitanism emphasized relationships based upon impersonal criteria. For such activists it makes sense that school or issues should arouse their interest. Also quite in keeping with the picture of the regular as a local are the primary-group networks that precipitate political interest. In the following chapter this interest will be traced into motivations for activity, where one can see whether this cosmopolitan pattern holds. For the present, however, I shall turn to the second component of the political interpretation of cosmopolitanism, one's national or local perspective.

In the past chapter the leanings of the reformer toward national newspapers, such as the *New York Times*, were noted. Another suggestion was that this information served a purpose for the individual who sought out such material. If this media focus is related to "political cosmopolitansim," there will be a complementary interest in national over state and local political affairs. National campaigns will be more a focus of interest and involvement than local ones. Such hypotheses are clearly supported by the data.

The discussion of political interest shifts from attitudes toward overt political action. The first campaign in which a reformer participates is three times more likely to be a national one than is this involvement for the regular. This distinction, which is illustrated in Table 11, produces a rather strong gamma of .75. The responses that elicit a more local orientation come overwhelmingly from the regulars, as is shown in Table 12.

TABLE 11

COSMOPOLITAN ORIENTATION OF REFORMERS
AND REGULARS IN FIRST CAMPAIGN

Campaign	Reformers (N = 610)	Regulars (N = 738)
	%	%
National	66.7	22.6
Nonnational	33.3	77.4
Total	100.0	100.0

Gamma = .75

TABLE 12

LOCAL ORIENTATION OF REFORMERS AND REGULARS IN FIRST CAMPAIGN*

Campaign	Reformers (N = 610)	Regulars (N = 738)
	%	%
Local	20.2	47.2
Nonlocal	79.8	52.8
Total	100.0	100.0

Gamma = -.56

*Tables 11 and 12 are separated, since respondents could check both national and local as well as state elections.

A rather interesting finding is the invisibility of state politics as a precipitator to action. As few regulars as reformers become involved through a state election (the figures show that .3 percent of the regulars first took part in a state campaign, while .2 percent of the reformers did). This finding closely follows the invisibility of state media for both groups.

The N.D.C. as an organization is so new that one may forget the long history of political involvement its members had before its inception. Thus not only did the kinds of campaigns differ for regulars and reformers, but also the actual year of first participation varies.

Twenty-eight percent of this group became involved for the first time in 1968, mobilized by the circumstances of one particular recent election. No such concentration in one year can be found for the regulars. The pattern for these professionals, instead, can be described as one of dribs and drabs.[6] The largest proportion of regulars to enter politics in any year occurred during the 1960 presidential campaign with 11 percent of the total. This is even larger than 1964 (6.9 percent), an electoral windfall year for the Democrats, or 1968 (9.0 percent).

It is easy to equate party activism with political participation. Yet involvement in the N.D.C. was not the reformer's first attempt at politics. While longevity and continuity are on the side of the regulars, the reformers did not appear full-blown from nowhere in 1968. When this survey was completed in 1970, two-fifths of the reformers had been active in politics — not necessarily Democratic politics — for four years or less, compared with one-fifth of the regulars. Slightly over half the regulars had been involved for ten years or less, compared with two-thirds of the N.D.C. While these figures support the ephemeral nature of the reformer, they do not, by contrast, describe the regular as the Rock of Gibraltar. A rather weak relationship exists between N.D.C. membership and recentness of political activism (gamma = .23).

When Plunkitt, in speaking of early reformers, referred to them as "mornin' glories" whose persistence in politics was doomed, he could also be estimating the behavior of present-day reformers and perhaps even regulars. Lacking the material rewards that Plunkitt found so desirable, the insurgent had nothing but good will to encourage his participation. Obviously this was not enough. Rather interesting, however, is the noticeable turnover among regulars, as well as reformers. Later I shall examine this issue of material rewards directly.

The lack of continuity in political participation can be related to other factors besides the motivations suggested by Plunkitt. These explanations stress the problem for cosmopolitans that continuous participation might entail. Youth and physical mobility may account for much of this recent development of political activism for the reformer.

One can recall from an earlier discussion that almost sixty percent of the N.D.C. members were under forty years of age. The percentage of regulars in the category was half that figure. Also influencing political continuity would be physical mobility. Reformers do seem to move about much more than regulars. Thirty percent of the N.D.C. members had lived in their present county less than five years. Only eight percent of the regulars were so mobile.

Even taking into account these factors, reformers do not claim to be active in politics year in and year out. Ninety-one percent of the regulars are active every election. While significant numbers of reformers are also continuous participants (67.8 percent), the contrast between the groups is evident (gamma = -.65).

Such a finding clearly relates to the national orientation of the more cosmopolitan reformer. National elections, such as presidential campaigns or congressional races, take place every two years at the most. One would, in fact, expect the percentage of N.D.C. members who are continuously active to be even lower than it is. This rather high proportion of N.D.C. members may point to a growing political persistence of the new reformer, which makes him rather distinct from the amateur of the past. I have suggested this possibility in the historical analysis. The discovery of substantial numbers of N.D.C. members active every year may support this contention of the changing nature of reformers.

The interest and participation of these politicos should also be viewed in terms of their specific career patterns and activities. One would surely expect the local politician to display greater interest in grass roots party positions than the cosmopolitan. This behavior, reflected in formal positions, does show substantial variation on the grass roots level of politics. Simply from the construction of the sample, one would expect regulars to be much more involved in party offices than reformers. Yet forty-five percent of the reformers have entered party primaries at one time or another, a surprisingly large figure. Furthermore, fifty percent of the regulars have won more than four primary victories, compared with twenty-five percent of the reformers who entered contests. The regular's longer and more successful involvement in politics is evident, compared with the reformer. Yet the N.D.C. member also makes some impact on the party.

Another way to interpret these electoral victories emphasizes not the comparative nature of N.D.C. versus regular involvement, but rather the limited participation of the regular. For fifty-nine percent of them to win fewer than five primaries actually illustrates relatively brief commitments, much in keeping with the earlier discovery of rather short periods of political involvement. There must, in fact, be an immense turnover in committeemen and committeewomen if the numbers of primaries entered are so low.

Perhaps, however, limited longevity as committee people is indicative of mobility within the party ranks. Yet here the findings continue to support the limited participation of the regular. Aside from the office of committeeperson, very few distinctions exist between the two groups, as illustrated in Table 13.

Committeepersons have few avenues for party mobility leading either to elected or appointed office. The fine old days of the Plunkitt-type machine, dispensing patronage to the faithful, is

TABLE 13

POLITICAL OFFICES AND JOBS HELD
BY REFORMERS AND REGULARS

Office	Percent who ever held jobs	
	Reformers	Regulars
Party office		
Committeeman	26.2	100.0
Ward chairman	4.1	10.4
Municipal chairman	6.8	9.5
Miscellaneous party office	26.2	7.1
Elected office		
Municipal	3.6	7.4
County	.8	1.3
State	.9	.4
Appointed jobs		
Municipal	12.9	19.1
County	4.3	7.0
State	6.8	4.3
Federal	8.0	4.2

gone, just as it was suggested in previous chapters. This finding about patronage jobs contrasts markedly with earlier studies, that discovered large proportions of party activists on the public payroll in Chicago, Philadelphia, and Albany.[7] Such a change, however, reflects some of the trends in American politics discussed previously.

While regulars are still more likely to hold the positions of ward and municipal chairmen than are reformers, the reverse is evident for such miscellaneous party offices as delegates to conventions or appointments to party committees. This figure may not be reliable, because many N.D.C. members might have meant attendance at their own N.D.C. convention. Discounting this correlation, one discovers no important differences between the two groups according to elected or appointed office. In fact, reformers might even have the advantage over regulars in certain paid jobs.

Twenty percent of the regulars claim to be presently employed by government, compared with 15 percent of the reformers. Of those who have ever had a government job, 26.6 percent of the reformers could be categorized as professionals, such as teachers. Professionals only composed 6.7 percent of the jobs held by regulars. Much more often the regulars cite such positions as tax assessor, Board of Health office worker, county clerk's office worker. Over an individual's entire career in politics, 31.4 percent of the regulars and 26.7 percent of the reformers held some job that could be categorized as governmental. Yet the distinction one might make between teachers and the more overt patronage appointments to the clerk's office appears obvious.

Schools and other institutional affiliations require expertise that placement in a clerical job does not. Furthermore, while teachers are state employees, their hiring is by local school districts, entities legally separate from the political parties. Jobs in the county clerk's office and on the election board, however, involve payment for party activity. Even this pattern of government positions points to the models of cosmopolitans and locals. The former political jobs would be earned because of expertise and skill, while the latter derived from rewards for personal commitments to the party.

The picture sketched of the regular and reformer in terms of their political careers is not that dissimilar. If the reformer can be characterized as a "mornin' glory," then the regular has become, over the years, a rather inconsistent annual, who must be replanted each spring and nurtured carefully. The fertilizer of patronage has weakened with time.

In examining the career patterns of both sets of activists, one finds a rather low level of patronage appointments. While this may differ from the previous literature, it supports my suggestion that material rewards, such as patronage, can no longer be expected to motivate the party worker. The rewards of jobs are few and far between according to the data. Although the reality depicts no political careers, it is interesting how many regulars would be willing to accept a county or state job, if it were offered. More reformers than regulars, in fact, would take a state appointment, sixty-four percent to sixty percent (gamma = .08). More regulars would prefer local patronage (gamma = -.16). It is rather surprising that sixty-five percent of the N.D.C. would accept a local appointment. This is almost the same as the seventy-two percent of the regulars who would. The differences between the groups are so slight, however, it seems fair to conclude that patronage is somewhat desirable to both groups, if not very likely for either. Where is the reform force against patronage jobs? While patronage is disappearing, the new breed of reformers has become willing to accept political positions.

Receiving few material benefits in return for political energy, reformers and regulars may not be that disparate in their incentives. This query about motivations will be answered more fully in the next chapter. But it does seem relevant to ask about an activist's participation, "Why bother?" If one receives so little out of politics, does not that explain the rapid turnover of both the morning glory and the annual? Yes, but it does not explain the staying power of those more hardy individuals of each species. Uncovering few overt supports to continued party and political activity, one still finds that certain tasks do get done.

Just as the patterns of interest and involvement help to fill in certain political areas of the cosmopolitan-local continuum, so too may the chores politicians do for their party depend upon personal relationships or technical skills. Thus one would expect the reformer to be rather uninvolved in the election-oriented tasks that require personal contacts, but to be more involved in the skills aspects of campaigns, such as giving speeches. Above all, however, I anticipated that the regular would display greater involvement in campaigns. Also, any tasks that required helping people are expected to be more evident in the regular group.

In turning to descriptions of activity, such as career patterns and work accomplished, I am laying the foundation for later discussions of motivation, that is, what rationale regulars and reformers impute to their actual behavior. For this reason, it is important to illustrate that behavior first.

As an aside one might note that political activism requires certain attitudes toward the possibility of successful involvement. In some ways, it is important for both regulars and reformers to share an optimism about political success. It is noteworthy, then, that one of the few variables that shows absolutely no difference between the two groups deals with this very trait. For both there is equally strong disagreement that the respondent is politically ineffectual. While 77.4 percent of the regulars disagree with this statement, compared with 78.4 percent of the reformers, what is even more interesting is the similar percentage distribution between gradations of strong and weak responses. A gamma of .01 clearly indicates this point.

Both regulars and reformers come to political activity with underlying beliefs that they will be able to accomplish certain goals. What varies then, according to my hypotheses, is the content of these goals and the particular activities performed by cosmopolitan or local activists. Yet the kinds of jobs that regulars claim to carry out for their organizations are not quite in accord with these expectations.[8] One discovery of this survey is that election-oriented tasks are carried out by *both* groups in rather high numbers, as shown in Table 14. While committeemen and N.D.C. members are unlikely to take over the leadership of campaigns or internal organization management, they are both fairly committed to contacting voters and distributing literature.

Equal numbers of reformers and regulars will participate in all tasks, yet the conclusion one draws from this material is that reformers seem to be even *more* campaign oriented than are regulars. This fits my previous finding in relation to the rather weak sanctions that support and urge on the regular to great electioneering. The discovery also meshes with Wilson's contention that non-material motives such as solidary or purposive rewards are not effective for activating campaign workers.[9] What can the party do to the committeeperson who does not fulfill his job energetically? It has practically no sanctions to force him to mend his ways. This might also explain the ease with which reformers can replace regulars on a local level, given a strong commitment of time and energy.

The reformer has changed his stripes and shows a political awareness concerning the nitty-gritty of election tasks. Both groups share this interest. The one stereotype of the regular that still distinguishes him from the reformer in the data, however, is in the brokerage function, that is, helping people get jobs. One might try to account for this in the low number of N.D.C. members who are actually committeemen. Not having access to patronage would certainly limit any social-service functions. But if one compares regular committeemen with N.D.C. members who are also committeemen, the difference persists (thirty percent help constituents get jobs, compared with 9.4 percent for the reformers).

TABLE 14

POLITICAL TASKS PERFORMED BY REFORMERS AND REGULARS (GAMMA CORRELATIONS)

Political tasks	Reformers (N = 633)	Regulars (N = 770)	Gamma
	%	%	
Election oriented			
Contacted voters	85.5	86.6	-.05
Distributed literature	81.4	76.5	.15
Gave speeches	35.2	30.9	.10
Managed campaigns	30.5	22.2	.21
Gave money	66.8	52.2	.30
Organizational			
Made policy	29.4	25.1	.11
Chose candidates	30.5	40.8	-.11
Brokerage			
Help get jobs	8.1	29.5	-.65
Show people how to get rights	29.2	34.2	-.11
Did all tasks	69.2	64.2	.11

Yet showing people how to pursue their rights indicates little variation between the groups. Costikyan, a Tammany reformer, emphasizes that the requests he received for help did not involve patronage or fixing tickets, but rather information on how a constituent can wend his way through the massive bureaucracy in search of his rights.[10] Thus the reformer offers a brokerage function in this area similar to the regular.

The reform committeeman is probably the most energetic worker in both groups. Looking at three categories, those who are only committeemen and committeewomen, those who are only N.D.C. members, and those who are both, shown in Table 15, it is evident that this latter group is more likely to give campaign contributions, manage campaigns, make policy, and select candidates. These tasks require leadership roles as well as a more intense involvement.

TABLE 15

POLITICAL TASKS PERFORMED BY REFORMER AND REGULAR
COMMITTEEMEN AND REFORMER NONCOMMITTEEMEN

Political Tasks	Committeemen		Noncom-mitteemen reformers (N = 537)
	Reformers (N = 96)	Regulars (N = 770)	
	%	%	%
Election oriented			
Contacted voters	88.5	86.6	84.9
Distributed literature	79.2	76.5	81.8
Gave speeches	37.5	30.9	34.8
Managed campaigns	42.1	22.2	28.5
Gave money	71.9	52.2	65.9
Organizational			
Made policy	37.9	25.1	27.9
Chose candidates	44.2	40.8	28.1
Brokerage			
Help get jobs	9.4	29.5	7.8
Show people how to get jobs	30.1	34.2	29.1
Did all tasks	67.7	64.2	69.5

On the whole, the efforts of reformers and regulars are directed along similar paths. Neither their career patterns nor the tasks they perform seem remarkably varied. As the sources of patronage politics dissipate, party activists may become more alike in their behavior. Finding new types of rewards available, perhaps a new type of activist is attracted to politics, replacing the old patronage seeker. Thus not only is the reformer a different breed of amateur, wiser in electoral machinations, but also his foe, the regular, appears very unlike the machine politician, receiving material rewards and working assiduously for his political party.

Before concluding this chapter and turning in detail to the kinds of motivations that an activist attributes to his behavior, it is useful to explode two other myths about reformers and their political attributes. These two myths concern the geographic characteristic of reform areas. The assumption that Republican dominance and suburbanization foster reform-style politics relates to an underlying contention that the amateur's upper-middle-class status will influence the brand of politics he selects. Furthermore, Republican and suburban areas are described, in this view, as homogeneous and, hence, predictive of one particular style of participation.

The confusion with this approach can be seen when one relates aggregate data to surveys of individuals. Suburbanism, an aggregate characteristic, predicts, causes, or determines reform politics, a quality analyzed through individual attributes — according to this view.

Another difficulty with this supposed relationship is the way it simplifies and homogenizes suburban or Republican communities. Thus the strength of the reformer is supposed to be in the weakness of the regular Democratic Party. These relatively upper-income areas are Republican strongholds, according to Wilson's study.[11] In my statewide survey, however, this idea is not supported in the least. Looking at a correlation between percent Democratic in two elections — one for freeholder and one for congressman — I find no relationship between the strength of the Democratic Party and weakness of the reform movement. A Pearson's correlation of -.02 for congressman and -.05 for freeholder is only worth mentioning for the lack of support it indicates for one of my hypotheses.[12] The status of reformers might be remarkably different from regulars, yet the political aspects of municipalities in which they reside do not appear to be noticeably different from each other.

Distinct from the details of party dominance is the question of suburbanism and the nature of amateur politics. Studies of regular-party organizations in suburban counties locate an "amateur" style of purposive politics, at least in terms of entering motivations.[13] But these analyses are rather bound by the case-study approach and the uniqueness of the areas chosen. Recent information, in fact, emphasizes the vast heterogeneity of the supposed areal type, "suburb."[14]

According to my study, 25.6 percent of the regulars reside in suburban New Jersey, compared with 30.5 percent of the reformers (gamma = .12). Since the category of suburban was derived from an in-depth study of New Jersey municipalities,[15] the classification was much more precise than that of the Census Bureau's Standard Metropolitan Statistical Area. S.M.S.A.'s include both the core city and all nonagricultural counties surrounding it.

Since New Jersey counties are rather heterogeneous in composition, classifying all noncore cities and towns together would, in effect, mix a city like East Orange with a town like Millburn. This approach, instead, permits one to recognize the great internal heterogeneity of various counties. This county heterogeneity also explains why one can stratify the samples of this study by county and yet not affect suburbanization as a finding. Matching counties does not eliminate the variation within each area, where complexity is quite evident.

In terms of other demographic variables, suburban life-styles make a greater difference for regulars than reformers. Forty-six percent of the nonsuburban regulars are middle-class, compared with sixty-four percent of the suburban regulars. The pattern is similar but less extreme for the reformer, of whom 85 percent of the nonsuburbanites are middle class, while 91 percent of the suburbanites can be so classified. Basically, suburbanism relates to income and status rankings within both groups of activists. Suburbanites are also younger and more professional in occupations, yet the important distinction lies in wealth. For those who earn over $15,000 a year, only 28 percent of the regulars and 54 percent of the reformers live in nonsuburban areas. Compared with those in the same income category, 62 percent of the regulars and 82 percent of the reformers live in suburban municipalities.

The percentages are similar for regulars and reformers who dwell in central cities, as well as for those who live in the already developed cities near the core city areas. Approximately fourteen percent in both organizations live in major cities. Slightly more reformers than regulars live in these settled, older municipalities:

twenty-seven percent to twenty-three percent. The remainder in both groups live in smaller cities on the more distant rim, outside the central city and immediate areas.

Whether or not suburbanism also reflects relevant political motivations and attitudes will have to be shown later. But at this point the cosmopolitan orientation of the reformer can be supported by his higher status, his national orientation to media and politics, and his purposive initial political interests. Suburbanism and Republicanism, however, do not seem very relevant in describing the political cosmopolitanism of the insurgent. In fact, cosmopolitan orientations do not seem to make any differences in political positions held or tasks performed. In this respect reformers and regulars appear rather similar, in spite of the variations evident earlier between cosmopolitan reformers and local regulars.

One major conclusion of this chapter, then, supports a previous argument that objective demographic characteristics, such as religion or status, do not necessarily have political implications for reformers and regulars. Thus, while the major hypotheses of the chapter on socialization were rather strongly confirmed, those in this chapter, where political socialization is interpreted through political careers, illustrate a much more varied outcome.

The early political socialization of reformers and regulars did differ somewhat, but not in the expected directions. Regulars came from families that were more strongly Democratic in party affiliation than N.D.C. members, yet for both groups, family was rarely active in politics. This party attachment, moreover, did not influence an early fascination with politics for the professional politician. In fact, reformers were interested at a younger age. The source of interest did confirm the cosmopolitan orientation of the insurgent: intellectual criteria, such as school or issues, were especially important for reformers, while the personal contacts of friends and family influenced the regular.

The national focus of the reformer's involvement became quite clear once political activity commenced. Yet this perception was not reflected in the more suburban or Republican areas in which N.D.C. members were expected to reside. Only slightly more suburban in life-style than regulars, no difference appeared to confirm the hypotheses that reformers live in strongly Republic areas.

Even more essential, except for committeemen and -women positions, reformers and regulars do not differ markedly in upper-echelon party appointive or elective public office. The career patterns do not confirm expectations of major distinctions between the groups. Patronage seems of limited viability to cement the regular to his party work. This weakness might help to explain another finding, that regulars are not more likely to perform election-oriented tasks than are N.D.C. activists. One must conclude that orientation toward politics can support the cosmopolitanism of the reformer, yet this focus does not then require different activities and career patterns.

The ultimate importance of these findings must wait until the concluding chapter, where multiple regression will permit a determination of the relative strength of such background data in predicting reform or regular-party attachments. The next series of chapters will explore the attitudes and opinions of these politicians. Only as demographic variables help to explain these motivations and positions are such background data important. In themselves they merely help lay the foundation for this later analysis.

Notes to Chapter 4

1. Campbell, et al., *The American Voter*, pp. 147-49.

2. William H. Flanigan, *Political Behavior of the American Electorate*, 2nd ed. (Boston: Allyn and Bacon, Inc., 1972), pp. 42-43.

3. M. Kent Jennings and Richard G. Niemi, "The Transmission of Political Values from Parent to Child," *American Political Science Review* 62 (March, 1968): 173.

4. Soule and Clarke, "Amateurs and Professionals," p. 892.

5. Campbell, et al., *The American Voter*, pp. 147-49; Jennings and Niemi, "Transmission of Political Values," pp. 179-84.

6. Of course, these percentages are not necessarily the actual number of activists who first became involved in any one year, but rather are the proportion who continue to be participants, no matter when they first entered the political arena.

7. Forthal, *Cogwheels of Democracy*, pp. 16, 35; Kurztzman, "*Controlling Votes in Philadelphia*," p. 47; Mosher, "Party and Government Control," p. 18.

8. The specific questions asked can be found in the questionnaire, Appendix A. Refer to question 19.

9. Wilson, *Amateur Democrat*, pp. 356-58.

10. Edward N. Costikyan, *Behind Closed Doors: Politics in the Public Interest* (New York: Harcourt, Brace and World, Inc., 1966), p. 92.

11. Wilson, *Amateur Democrat*, pp. 259-62.

12. Pearson's correlation was used here because the data are interval in nature.

13. Conway and Feigert, "Motivation, Incentive Systems," pp. 1,161-62; Ippolito, "Motivational Reorientation and Change," p. 1,098.

14. Frederick M. Wirt, et al., *On the City's Rim: Politics and Policy in Suburbia* (Lexington, Mass.: D. C. Heath and Company, 1972), esp. chaps 3 and 4.

15. George Sternleib, et al., *Housing Development and Municipal Cost* (New Brunswick, N. J.: Center for Urban Policy Research, forthcoming).

5

The Motivational Framework Applied To Initial Incentives

Cosmopolitanism has provided a useful focus for the analysis of reform characteristics. Yet in applying the concept to socialization, career patterns, and performance of specific tasks, much of the distinction between amateur and regular politics seems to have become blurred. Varied socialization experiences of the two groups do not predict large differences in overt behavior. Contrary to past research, reformers seem to be as election-oriented and job-oriented as regulars. Yet one must also conclude that for neither does a willingness to accept political patronage seem to be a viable source of potential reward, since so few hold patronage positions.

While these objective characteristics may not have provided the political effects that previous studies anticipated, the main thrust of this survey has been upon the perceptual and more subjective interpretations and orientations of a particular activist. For this reason, cosmopolitanism has permitted one to interpret these findings in a rather positive light. Not tasks performed, but rather their interpretation through the eyes of the actor becomes important. Thus in turning toward the underlying motivations that promote and sustain political activism, this analysis is proceeding along the same path that was charted in the selection of cosmopolitanism as an essential organizing construct.

Perceptions of a politician can be quite usefully displayed through his motivations and incentives. This focus is ideal, since it is possible that participation leading to the same behavior — a pattern detected in the last chapter — can be supported by quite varied motivations.

For this reason the research has explored self-descriptions of entrance and continuing motivations in the context of actual political behavior, encompassing the activist's political career, his performance of political tasks, and his conception of his role. I shall first examine motivation in relation to initial involvement in this chapter. Then, in chapter 6, continuing motivation will be examined in the context of political behavior. Finally, entrance and continuing motivations will be related to each other.

The reformer has been described as a cosmopolitan through demographic variables. The more general demographic explanations paint a distinct portrait of the N.D.C. member in contrast to the localism of the regular.

The original purpose in applying such descriptions implied that these traits would have consequences for political behavior. Yet one does not find either the pattern of political careers nor the activities of regulars and reformers to be in line with such expectations. Studying that behavior in greater detail does not appear to be a very fruitful approach. Instead, it is necessary to turn to the motivations that these politicians attribute to their behavior. In so doing, I am temporarily moving away from the framework of cosmopolitanism to the motivational constructs of Clark and Wilson. Their development of the categories — solidary, purposive, and material rewards — has been a most useful foundation for this analysis.[1] My contribution to their analysis expands and develops their theory in a rather major way. In using this different frame of reference to discuss motivations, categories have been found that seem indirectly related to cosmopolitanism. After all, the local, dependent upon personal contacts and friendships for advancement, is more likely to describe his motives and rewards as social or solidary than is the reformer. For this latter participant, expertise and use of principles as mechanisms for occupational success might direct him toward political rewards that emphasize the "general good" and are purposive. Not questions of personal loyalty, but rather how fine a job an individual might do would determine political support from a reformer.

While material motives are more likely for regulars than reformers, their appearance in either group is expected to be minimal. This is rather different from previous research cited earlier. The reason has to do with the diminishing base of patronage as

well as the unappealing nature of those clerical or unskilled positions available. Certainly the small proportions of patronage jobs
held by either group supports this contention that material rewards
are shrinking in importance. Yet this is the very basis of traditional
politics: the material or divisible reward that supposedly makes
voluntary participation attractive and permits a tightly knit
organization.

Mancur Olson, Jr., in *The Logic of Collective Action,* makes this
very argument about divisible goods: the power of various economic-
interest groups derives not from the shared interests of its members,
forcing them to participate, but rather from the fact (fortunate for
the groups in question) that they provide important services for
their members other than common economic interests.[2] The
"other benefits" are essential to explain any organized and continuous participation in associations. This is especially true if one
realizes that the universal and indivisible benefits that derive from
these associations' successes will accrue to all those with the same
interests, whether they participate in the organizations or not.

Underlying Olson's thesis is an implicit assumption that divisible
benefits are essential to the formation of ongoing voluntary groups
to represent these interests.

Olson gives very little space to political parties, except to note
their inherent weakness as formal organizations. He relates the
amorphousness of national party organizations to his theory.

One explanation is that political parties usually seek collective
benefits: they strive for governmental policies which, as they
say, will help all of the people (or at least a large number of
them). Though most people feel they would be better off if
their party were in power, they recognize that if their party is
going to win, it will as likely win without them, and they will
get the benefits in any case. The average American has about
the same attitude towards his political party that Dr. Johnson
said the English people had toward the exiled Stuarts in the
eighteenth century. Johnson said that "if England were fairly
polled, the present king would be sent away tonight, and his
adherents hanged tomorrow." They would not, however, "risk
anything to restore the exiled family. They would not give
twenty shillings to bring it about. But if a mere vote could do it,
there would be twenty to one." The point is that the average
person will not be willing to make a significant sacrifice for the
party he favors, since a victory for his party provides a collective
good. He will not contribute to the party coffers or attend
precinct meetings. There are on the other hand many people

with personal political ambitions, and for them the party will provide noncollective benefits in the form of public office. . . . There are also many bussinessmen who contribute to the political parties in order to get individual access to officials when matters of importance to their own firms arise.

Political "machines," on the other hand, have massive organizational structures. But the political machines do *not* work for *collective* goods. A machine is at best interested in patronage, and at worse in outright graft. . . . Political machines are able to develop well-articulated organization structures, then, because they strive mainly for benefits that accrue to particular individuals, rather than for the common interests of any large group.[3]

In many ways, the diminished patronage and power of bosses and parties attest to Olson's point. The divisible benefits might appear to be smaller and smaller crumbs of an inadequate pie. Yet parties do attract workers and even reform-style counterorganizations do bud every now and then. How can this occurrence fit the insights developed by Olson? Olson directs one to questions concerning attraction and motivation of workers in organizations that have lost their traditional sources of material or divisible rewards.

The question about motivation becomes not simply a description of different activists, but rather a query as to why anyone would invest so much energy in what appears to be so little return. Because Olson assumes the central focus of any activist would be a divisible benefit, he describes only the old-time machine. While noting the dissipation of patronage, he relates this to the concurrent weakness of party organization. My concern was also with shrinking patronage, but it is clear that parties do continue to function and workers do maintain a certain involvement. In fact, according to the Michigan Survey Research Center, there are increasing numbers of citizens active in politics.[4]

The need for traditional material incentives may be changing as a catalyst for political activism. I have attempted to answer Olson's question by elaborating upon Clark and Wilson's categories. Before presenting these possible revisions and potential models, there is an important point to clarify.

This assumption of the inadequacy of purposive rewards derives from the implicit belief that "no one does something for nothing." "Nothing" is then defined as anything that does not involve divisible benefits. In the literature, this distinction between the regular and the reformer is quite clear. Basically, it reduces to the description of the amateur as purposive in orientation, compared with the material orientation of the regular.

Believing that these constructs tend to provide a stereotype of both the motivations of regular and reform politicians, I propose that whatever motivates an activist, his final rewards are ego-centered. The purposive reformer and the material regular both derive some personal satisfaction from what they do.

Personal satisfaction — no matter how it is interpreted by the activist — is a kind of reward, which, like material rewards, is based upon ego-centered motivations. One might, in fact, conclude that, at some level, personal satisfaction is evident in even purposive or solidary motives, similar to material rewards. Therefore, it might be useless to distinguish between motives that are other-directed and those that are self-directed. All activities voluntarily selected by an individual fulfill some basic need. The reduction of all motives to ego-centered benefits — whether they have socially beneficial results or not — makes me search for more useful ways to understand the different motivational patterns of reformers and regulars.

The amendment of these material, solidary, and purposive models is required by both theoretical underpinnings, as well as methodological problems. It seemed that the solidary category, which combined such diverse motives as hunger for status or fun of participation, were really quite different incentives that should not be grouped together. The former represents a superior-subordinate relationship between people, while the latter implies peer-group interactions. In fact, one might argue that recognition is closely related to material and divisible rewards. Solidary rewards such as fun and excitement, however, are indivisible and available to all participants.

In fact, the relationship between recognition and material incentives provides one of the strongest positive relationships, when all continuing motivations are correlated with each other (gamma = .79 for reformers and .66 for regulars). Material incentives can be reexamined as a category related to such status rewards as recognition if one views the models in slightly different terms. Both material and status rewards emphasize the distribution of scarce goods. This is true whether the scarce goods are intangible status or specific jobs and public office. With the decrease in tangible material incentives related to the shrinking patronage available or sought, the growth of such nonmaterial but scarce rewards as status should rise in importance.

The fun of the political game and the purposive goals of issue formulation both represent *nondivisible benefits,* to use Olson's term. The party group, either reform or regular, does not exclude participants from equally enjoying and sharing such rewards. Besides lumping these divisible and nondivisible solidary rewards together, Wilson had also equated divisible with tangible benefits in his description of the regular politician.[5] Yet since status rewards are divisible but intangible, this grouping clouds the distinctions that may exist.

It is the divisibility of material and status rewards that separate these two motives from the goals of friendship or issues. For the purpose of this study, I shall differentiate within solidary motives between status orientations or pure sociability.

Another important distinction relates to purposive rewards. Wilson and others who have studied the amateur emphasize that he is motivated by a need to be a good citizen, to participate in his community because of duty.[6] Yet purposive motivations also contain another component that is substantive. To understand this aspect, one would ask: participation for what goal? If that purpose is described in policy terms or through issues, this orientation is "issue oriented," not merely "participation oriented." I make this distinction where possible in the analysis of the data and use the term *purposive* only to describe substantive issue incentives.

The rationale for the distinguishing features of these two motivations rests upon the belief that the two kinds of goals, participation and issue implementation, are qualitatively distinct. In fact, participation-oriented motives may be another category for the solidary grouping. If an activist becomes involved because of some amorphous need to participate, he is unlikely to be sustained over any long period of time only by that reward. This individual is expected to revise his "purposive" motivations and turn to such rewards as sociability or status, both suggested in his initial incentives.

Fulfilling one's duty implies recognition that others know how "good" a citizen one truly is. The activist, however, who became involved because of a commitment to substantive issues might very well maintain his original purposive orientation through his strong dedication to policy formulation. Thus, the distinction is drawn because of an assumption that entrance motivations, predicted upon one type of supposedly purposive incentive, may very well lead to nonpurposive continuing motivations.

The works of Olson, and Clark and Wilson provide a possible structure to discuss these diverse motivations. Abstracting from the previous analysis, I have dealt with two rather distinct aspects of motivation: the tangibility of the reward and the divisibility of the benefits sought. Adopting Olson's category of divisible and nondivisible benefits, it can be extended to another relevant dimension: the tangibility or intangibility of the reward.

This added distinction between kinds of motivations emphasizes the possibility that tangible divisibility of benefits does not explain all about an individual's political motivations. Intangibility or nondivisibility rewards may also play an important role.

Table 16 illustrates the matrix that is hypothesized between tangibility or divisibility of the incentive system, with some examples of the motives already analyzed in the discussion above.

TABLE 16

TANGIBILITY AND DIVISIBILITY OF POLITCAL MOTIVATIONS

	Tangible	Intangible
Divisible	Material (Business contacts)	Status (Recognition)
Nondivisible	Substantive Purposive (Policies)	Solidary (Primary group loyalties) (Sociability and fun)
		Participatory (Citizen duty)

In order to see how this matrix contributes to understanding the motivations of the activists concerned, details of the findings about initial and continuing motivations, their relationship to each other, and the effects, if any, of such motivations upon role interpretations will be presented. After finishing that analysis, it will be possible to return to this discussion of divisibility and tangibility to describe the reformer and the regular in more theoretical ways. The main hypotheses concerning motivations presented earlier stressed the single-minded purposive motivation of the reformer in contrast to the more complex entrance motivations of the regular. The entrance motives of the N.D.C. were expected to be more purposive in orientation, but it was their single-minded purposiveness that mattered. The regular was also expected to illustrate purposive entrance motivations. What characterized this activist, however, was the likelihood that with these purposive concerns, he would also stress party loyalty, sociability, as well as material goals. It is in the continuing motivations that switches were expected. I hypothesized that the reformer would be significantly more purposive in his continuing motivation than would the regular. The continuing multiplicity of motives was stressed for the regular committeeman, as well as the increasing importance of solidary rewards.

The questions to operationalize entrance and continuing motivation are adapted from Eldersveld's study of Detroit and from Marvick and Nixon's survey in Los Angeles.[7] Let me at this point continue the procedure of the previous chapters by delineating the specific hypotheses that helped to operationalize the more general ones of chapter 2.

Motivational Hypotheses

Hypothesis 8 — Entrance Motivation: There will be no significant difference between reformers and regulars in purposive motivation.

> a. Regulars will admit to proportionately more material incentives than reformers
> b. Significantly more regulars than reformers will stress party loyalty.
> c. Regulars will indicate significantly more complex entrance motivations than reformers.
> d. Reformers will emphasize significantly more single-minded purposive motivations.

Hypothesis 9 — Continuing Motivation: Amateurs will be significantly more purposive than regulars.

> a. Regulars will be significantly more multifaceted in their continuing motivations than reformers.
> b. Regulars will be significantly more solidary or material in these motives than reformers.
> c. Reformers who maintain purposive motivations will be significantly more disillusioned than those who switch to solidary incentives.

Hypothesis 10 — Role Perceptions: There will be a significant difference in the ways reformers and regulars perceive their roles.

a. Reformers are significantly more likely to perceive their roles in educational or reform terms than are regulars.

b. Regulars are significantly more likely to perceive their roles in campaign-centered or brokerage terms.

The literature on professional versus amateur motivational patterns continually identifies the amateur style of politics as one where concern for serving the community is associated with a citizen's obligation. Such motives are called either purposive, group- and society-related, or impersonal and coded with slightly different categories.[8] These studies do find large numbers who do describe their initial reasons in such ways. Yet it does seem that verbiage for public consumption on the desire of politicians to serve the community is hardly reliable data for understanding the actual motivations that distinguish regulars from reformers. In fact, it comes as no surprise that 78.5 percent of the regulars claimed a desire to serve their community was very important in their decision to participate in politics. This percentage is the highest of the many possible explanations offered by regulars for entrance motivation. What is more surprising is that reformers are not as likely to explain their behavior in such terms. Sixty-two percent of the reformers claimed serving the community was very important in reporting their first reasons for political activity. Eldersveld considered such responses impersonal ones and discovered them rather widely in Detroit.[9]

While regulars seem slightly more prone to use the rhetoric of public service than do reformers, such a dependence upon flattering explanations would be misleading to explain the attitudes and experiences of the two different groups. Some of the other responses to the questions of entering motivation may be even more illuminating. Table 17 presents the data on entrance motivation, grouped according to the categories of divisible and tangible rewards developed in Table 16.

In the entire table, the only responses that strongly relate N.D.C. membership to recruitment motives emphasize policy concerns (gamma = .46). The amateur, while desiring to serve the community (along with the regular), stands out as much more concerned with policy matters than the professional. But even here, it is useful to note the percentages. Seventy-three percent of the regulars were very interested in issues, according to the figures. Another major conclusion from the survey is the total lack of party attachment as an important motivating force for the reformer (14.1 percent) in sharp contrast to the regular (48.6 percent).

Over forty percent of the regulars mentioned these diverse

TABLE 17

ENTRANCE MOTIVATIONS FOR REFORMERS AND REGULARS (GAMMA CORRELATIONS)

| Motivation | Percent who say very important | | Gamma |
	Reformers (N = 633)	Regulars (N = 770)	
1. Material			
a. Possibility of business or political contacts	2.8	10.6	-.36
b. My jobs experience	11.1	14.1	-.14
2. Solidary: Primary group loyalties			
a. Friends urged me	10.0	25.5	-.45
b. Family was always active	6.3	13.4	-.28
3. Solidary: Sociability			
a. Excitement of campaigns	16.8	31.1	-.23
b. Enjoyment of working with others in important jobs	22.7	53.2	-.47
4. Status			
a. Community recognition	7.0	21.3	-.40
5. Substantive purposive			
a. Concern with policy matters	88.1	72.6	.46
6. Participatory			

continued

a. Desire to serve community	62.4	78.5	-.38
b. Duties of citizenship	44.8	65.0	-.39
7. Miscellaneous (Unclassificable)			
a. Particularly interesting candidate	54.3	53.0	.05
b. Attachment to a political party	14.1	48.6	-.60

reasons: interesting candidate, enjoyment, issue concerns, desire to serve community, duties of citizenship, and attachment to a political party. One could categorize these motives as both solidary, purposive, and participatory. For the reformer, however, fewer and more similar motives are mentioned as very important by over forty percent of the respondents: interesting candidate, issue concerns, desire to serve community, and duties of citizenship. All these motivations can be described by the terms *purposive* and *participatory*. The patterns vary between the two groups quite obviously.

A specific reason, support for a given candidate, can result from different motivations. Compare the rather impersonal source of activity on behalf of Eugene McCarthy with the solidary purpose derived from interest in the campaign of a friend. Reformers and regulars are equally likely to emphasize the precipitating effect of an attractive candidate, but the meaning behind the overt act can be very different.

One non-ambiguous finding, however, tends to support the underlying hypothesis that the main distinction between reformers and regulars does not reside in their varied entrance motivations, but rather in the more single-minded purposive motivations of the reformer. The importance of solidary ties was essential to the regular even in his recruitment. For thirty percent of the professionals, excitement of campaigns was a very important reason for initial activity. The regular begins political action enjoying his tasks, while the reformer commits himself to his study as a good, issue-oriented citizen. Personal pleasure is rather unimportant for him.

Few activists emphasize business or political contacts as reasons for involvement. Nor do they stress the role of recognition. Both explanations are rather unflattering descriptions of one's activities.

If, instead, one looks at the percentage who claim these reasons were *unimportant*, for regulars business and political contacts were unessential to 67.7 percent, compared with 81.6 percent of the reformers. With recognition, however, slightly under half the regulars find it totally unimportant, while two-thirds of the N.D.C. would fall into the same category. One might argue from these findings that the reformer is totally unattracted by such material or status rewards as recognition, but is aroused only by intangible philosophical goals.

This situation of multiple motivations for regulars becomes further highlighted if one explores the series of motives evident for both groups. In order to accomplish this for each entrance motivation, those who said this motive was very important were separated from all other respondents. Then each response was placed in the subcategories of tangible and divisible groupings presented in Table 16. Participatory motives contained responses that emphasized citizen duty and desire to serve the community, while substantive purposive motives dealt only with issue orientation. Material incentives combined both those who found their job experience or business and political contacts very important for their first participation.

The solidary category of Clark and Wilson was divided in several ways. Status, that intangible but divisible reward, was separated from sociability or fun. A distinct solidary category was also created for primary-group influences such as family or friends.

Candidate and party attachment were left uncategorized since one could interpret such reasons as either solidary or purposive. Any interpretation would depend upon an individual's perception of what party or candidate attachment meant. The correlations of these different entrance groupings are presented in Table 18.

The data highlighted is rather repetitious of Table 17. Yet there is a growing clarity in the lack of divisible rewards. The purposive N.D.C. member whose policy orientations remain paramount is similar to the multimotivated regular in one way. Neither group claims that divisible benefits — either tangible or intangible — were a force for incipient participation. While more regulars (approximately twenty percent) found these rewards very important, still the proportion is rather small. For both sets, their source of activity lies within the nondivisible benefits that are reputed to lead toward apathy, according to Olson. Since even Eldersveld found purposive motives among his Detroit regulars — at least as a reason for their original participation — such a discovery does not in itself

TABLE 18

ENTRANCE MOTIVATIONS FOR REFORMERS AND REGULARS
BY TANGIBILITY AND DIVISIBILITY
(GAMMA CORRELATIONS)

| Motivation | Percent who say very important | | Gamma |
	Reformers (N = 633)	Regulars (N = 770)	
Divisible-tangible			
Material	13.4	20.6	-.25
Divisible-intangible			
Status	7.0	21.3	-.40
Nondivisible-intangible			
Participatory	72.7	85.5	-.38
Primary-group loyalties	15.6	34.4	-.48
Sociability	31.7	59.3	-.52
Nondivisible-tangible			
Substantive purposive	88.1	72.6	.46
Uncategorized			
Party	14.1	48.6	-.60
Candidate	54.3	53.0	.05

become significant. The more important issue is whether or not these motives remain as pure when the reformer has been involved for some time.

According to Wilson and to Olson, one might almost conclude that any reformer who can not transform his entering motivational structure into something more supportable by the present-day party system is bound for disillusionment and probably retirement from the political arena.

Somehow, this stress upon material and solidary rewards implies that multiple motivations produce stronger support for continuing activity. The regular tied by party loyalty as well as a desire for patronage may stay involved in politics even though jobs disappear. Regulars are clearly more motivated by multiple reasons. Seventy-one percent of them mentioned three or more initial reasons as very important, compared with fifty-four percent of the N.D.C. Yet since these incentives for the reformer tend to be the non-divisible ones, there might be even weaker qualitative supports than quantitative ones.

Another way to approach this topic of multiple-entrance motivations is to examine the relationship between initial motivations that are stressed most often — that is, participatory and purposive — and all other motives.

Much stronger correlations appear between these entering non-divisible rewards and other divisible rewards for regulars than for N.D.C. members, as can be seen in Table 19. The picture of the regular exhibits a web of interrelationships. Purposive goals are related to participatory ones, such as citizen duty, much more strongly than they are for the reformer (gamma = .63, compared to .19). But these motives are also related to such divisible incentives as material or status rewards (gamma = .31, .33). The reformer with his purposive goals is, in fact, repelled by such divisible benefits that underlie his issue orientation.

Besides the relationship between entering divisible and issue-directed motives for the regular, social supports are also positively related to these purposive ends. For the reformer, a negative correlation joins initial issue orientation and the fun of the game.

The policy commitment of the regular, far from the isolation of the N.D.C. member, is related to entering solidary and divisible motives and also to candidate support and party loyalty. Solidary reasons are fused with purposive ones from the very beginnings of political involvement for the professional.

In fact, the enjoyment of the regular in participation correlates fairly well with almost every other motive proposed. The entering regular begins with a commitment to politics as fun and parties as essential. No wonder, with these multiple sources of incentives, the regular is pictured as a more lasting variety of politico. Compare this with the sparse motivational patterns evident for the reformer and one begins to understand some of the potential difficulties that the literature assumes will await the reformer.

Wilson and Olson do not stress the numbers of supports an activist claims, but rather the divisibility of the rewards. On both

TABLE 19

INTERRELATIONSHIP OF PARTICIPATORY AND PURPOSIVE
WITH OTHER ENTRANCE MOTIVATIONS FOR REFORMERS
AND REGULARS (GAMMA CORRELATIONS)

Motives	Percent who said both rewards very important		Gamma correlation between two motives	
	Reformers (N = 633)	Regulars (N = 770)	Reformers	Regulars
Purposive and material	11.4	22.2	-.12	.31
Purposive and status	5.6	16.6	-.23	.33
Purposive and participatory	64.4	65.9	.19	.63
Purposive and sociability	26.9	45.3	-.16	.35
Purposive and primary-group loyalty	13.9	23.2	.26	.00
Purposive and party	12.9	35.8	.23	.14
Purposive and candidate	49.4	41.8	.42	.45
Participatory and material	9.9	18.2	.16	.30
Participatory and status	6.0	20.1	.49	.63
Participatory and sociability	25.6	54.5	.31	.62
Participatory and primary-group loyalty	11.5	29.2	.14	.13

Participatory and party	11.1	43.1	.19	.37
Participatory and candidate	36.4	45.6	.26	.17

counts, however — quantity and quality of motivational foundations — the N.D.C. member would appear a less likely candidate for continuous involvement. Yet while illustrating potential weaknesses of reformers, questions have also been raised as to the nature of the party regular.

Some stronger correlations between divisible motives and professional identification may be shown, but a reexamination of Tables 19 and 18 through the percentages illustrates the rather limited nature of these material or status rewards.

The discovery that divisible rewards are rather weak as initial motivations does not support my prior contention of long-term shifts in party incentives. On the other hand, I have also doubted the universal necessity of these divisible benefits as support for continuous participation. The strongly purposive reformer who maintains this issue orientation may illustrate a pattern quite distinct from the purposive regular who soon bends toward solidary, nondivisible rewards.

This expected path from one source of motivation to another might also permit one to prove that divisible benefits are not a necessary foundation for sustained involvement. Continuing participation might come from such divisible rewards as status or patronage. But it also seems possible that an intense commitment to the goals of an organization can support ongoing participation. This intensity will be explored through ideology and intense liberalism in later chapters. Thus, the easily disenchanted, issue-oriented reformer may be as much a stereotype as the supposedly patronage-based reward system of the regular. While the traditional views of reformers and regulars might be questioned by this research, most of my hypotheses are validated for entrance motivations.

The single-minded purposive motivation of the reformer is confirmed by the data, as well as the more complex incentive system of the regular. While few activists in both organizations emphasize divisible goals, the hypothesis that claimed this would be more evident for regulars is supported by the evidence. The heterogeneity of the professional's motivations also provided proof for the salience of party loyalty for him. Thus the hypotheses for entrance motivations seem to be well confirmed by these findings.

In testing these hypotheses one also could make use of the models for incentives, which did prove quite helpful in characterizing the various rewards sought by regulars and reformers as they entered politics.

The importance of initial incentives was emphasized at length, since it clarifies the motivations of an activist before he becomes influenced by the organization of his choice. Once participating in a particular party structure, his original incentives may be revised and limited. Thus, my next concern in the following chapter is continuing motivation. This focus raises the question of what activists learn to accept in order to remain active. Can a reformer seeking issue-oriented politics find happiness in an organization that can usually offer only fun and games? Or — as I expect — can a reformer enmeshed in an issue-oriented structure like the N.D.C. maintain his purposive orientation in his continuing goals?

Notes to Chapter 5

1. Clark and Wilson, "Incentive Systems," pp. 129-66.

2. Olson, *Logic of Collective Action*, chap. 6.

3. Ibid., pp. 163-65.

4. Survey Research Center, University of Michigan, cited by Flanigan in *Political Behavior of the American Electorate*, p. 106.

5. Wilson, *Amateur Democrat*, p. 170.

6. Ibid., pp. 4-5; Mitchell, *Elm Street Politics*, p. 40.

7. Eldersveld, *Political Parties*, pp. 589; Marvick and Nixon, "Recruitment Contrasts," in Marvick, p. 208. The exact questions can be found in Appendix A. For entrance motivation *see* question 8; for continuing motivation *see* question 21.

8. Clark and Wilson, 'Incentive Systems," p. 135; Eldersveld, *Political Parties*, pp. 277-83; Conway and Feigert, "Motivation, Incentive Systems," p. 1,165.

9. Eldersveld, *Political Parties*, pp. 277-83.

6
Continuing Incentives: Their Development and Interpretation

The reformer or regular who selects a particular organization in which to enact his political role brings certain values and motivations with him. These have been described in chapter 5 as his initial motivations. The particular framework, divisibility or tangibility of the reward sought, remains untouched in this chapter, yet a new dimension is added: the effects of an organization upon the perceptions and behavior of an activist.

Perhaps the reason the reformer can derive his satisfactions so directly from purposive goals is due to the continuity with which his present issue-oriented goals are linked to his original entrance motivations. These entering incentives are transformed into continuing rewards through the active participation of an individual in the reform-or regular-party organization to which he belongs. Therefore, under certain conditions the entering motivations of an activist might be preserved and accenuated by the environment in which he works. In other situations, these entering motives may be transmuted by the kinds of rewards and the specific tasks necessary for the survivial of that organizaton.

The impact of groups upon the motivations and behavior of its members can be seen as a form of socialization. Participation is a learning experience, and learning can also be related to organizational socialization. There are two very distinct approaches to this process in the organizational literature. One is studying the large bureaucracy or business enterprise, emphasizing the "adaptive techniques" employees learn to turn themselves into good company men.[1] Formal rules and reward structures are analyzed. The other approach derives from small-group analysis and stresses the way "group norms" regulate behavior more informally.[2]

One area of similarity in these diverse analyses appears to be in the assumption that group structure has an impact on individual reactions. The shaping of the group member's perceptions does not necessarily come about because of any overriding interest in that individual's happiness or success. Instead the exchange between the individual and the group or organization takes place because of the needs of the larger whole. A corporation's main concern is production and profit. The incentives of the individual involved in that business might be materially oriented, too. Yet individuals have many other needs, as Maslow pointed out.[3] Enjoyment of the work experience is not unimportant. Thus, to the extent that corporate managers believe production will increase if their employees are contented or stimulated, these bureaucrats may attempt to satisfy these needs. Where no such belief exists — and no strong labor union makes nonmaterial incentives salient — other motivations and goals of the employee may never be met.

This comparison of corporations to the political party is not too farfetched. In fact, one might suggest that it is extremely relevant. It causes one to perceive the interrelationships between an organization — which is far more than the sum of its individual members — and its adherents. The goal of a professional party is to win elections. In order to do this it must attract workers and reward them for their efforts. The exchange between the organization and its members is quite similar to the exchange between a corporation and its employees.

This reciprocity between the group and the individuals can be quite complementary in nature. Their goals mesh nicely in this instance. In another case the ends come into conflict. The priorities of each, if followed, would limit the rewards of the other. Both of these scenarios fit the findings of this study. The former for the N.D.C., while the latter might better describe the regular organization. Before further interpretation, however, it will be useful to display the findings for continuing motivations and then relate them to the patterns for initial ones. After this, motivations will be analyzed in regard to their impact upon role perceptions. Only then will a discussion of organizational socialization be most fruitful.[4]

From the data assembled on continuing motivations (Table

20), one might feel rather comfortable in predicting the continuity of the purposive N.D.C. member. As hypothesized, the N.D.C. members seek substantive-purposive rewards in overwhelming numbers. Ninety percent declare they would miss most "supporting important issues and ideals." While the percentage of purposive reformers is huge, there is also evidence that sixty percent of the regulars claim a purposive continuing motivation — not an insignificant number by any means. As it is in entering motivations, these policy-oriented continuing motives present almost the only positive correlation between N.D.C. membership and any incentive. (The other exception is the response that an acti-

TABLE 20

CONTINUING MOTIVATIONS OF REFORMERS AND
REGULARS (GAMMA CORRELATIONS)

Motivation	Percent who say would miss most		Gamma
	Reformers (N = 616)	Regulars (N = 742)	
Divisible-tangible			
Business and political contacts	3.7	9.3	-.45
Divisible-intangible			
Community recognition	5.8	12.5	-.41
Nondivisible-intangible			
Working with friends	21.3	50.4	-.58
Nondivisible-tangible			
Supporting issues	90.1	62.1	.69
Uncategorized			
Knowing what's happening in the community	45.0	60.9	-.31
Nothing	8.1	5.9	.16

vist would miss nothing if he stopped political work tomorrow.)

Another pattern that repeats itself is obvious in the small proportion of activists who would miss divisible benefits of any sort. The percentages have dwindled noticeably even from their small number as entering motives. This discovery makes even more remarkable Olson's contention about the necessity of divisible benefits for volunteer activists. If this reward were a necessary cause for continuous participation, then both reformers and regulars would be nonexistent and grass roots parties would be dead. Rather than highlighting the weakness of the reform organization, I have found a similar fault within the regular party structure. Nondivisible yet tangible purposive orientations are selected by both groups in varying degrees, but divisible motivations are conspicuously absent for insurgents and professionals.

Besides this policy orientation, the regular is sustained by sociable rewards to a much greater degree than is the reformer. Over half the regulars would miss most this social component, compared with twenty percent of the reformers. This finding confirms an earlier hypothesis about the increasingly solidary goals of the professional.

A new motivation appears as a continuing reward: missing the inside knowledge of what is happening in one's community. Substantial percentages of regulars, 60.9 percent, and reformers, 45 percent, would miss this "inside dopester" reward, although the divergence between the groups is significant. How can one categorize this variable in terms of divisible and tangible benefits? Obviously, information is tangible. One can also claim that it is divisible.

The individual who would miss inside knowledge of what is happening in his community might be receiving some divisible status reward when he claims access to that scarce resource, information. Knowing what is occurring in one's town also implies that an individual rubs shoulders with the elite and hence receives status by contagion. This possibility is supported by Merton's discussion of media usage for cosmopolitan and local influentials.

It also seemed clear that the functions of the newsmagazine differ greatly for the rank-and-file and the influential reader. For the one, it largely serves a private, personal function; for the other, a public function. For the rank-and-file reader, the information found in the newsmagazine is a *commodity for personal consumption,* extending his *own* conception of the world of public events, whereas for the influential, it is a *commodity for exchange,* to be traded for further increments of prestige, by enabling him to act as an interpreter of national and international affairs. It aids him in being an opinion-leader.[5]

If I am correct in defining "inside dopester" rewards as non-tangible but divisible benefits, such as recognition, then the party worker has found a new kind of motivation, once he becomes involved in the organization. The strength of such an incentive to support frequent activity is something that develops only within the party.

However one looks at it, Olson would probably find the status conferred by inside information a rather weak incentive for continuous action. It would probably rank slightly below purposive on a list of the most feeble incentives. Yet knowledge and purposive rewards sustain each other and overlap in both organizations, according to Table 21.

TABLE 21

INTERRELATIONSHIP OF CONTINUING MOTIVATIONS FOR REFORMERS AND REGULARS (GAMMA CORRELATIONS)

Motives*	Percent who would miss both rewards		Gamma correlation between two motives**	
	Reformers (N = 616)	Regulars (N = 742)	Reformers	Regulars
Purposive and status	5.0	7.3	-.20	-.13
Purposive and material	2.6	5.1	-.63	-.16
Purposive and sociability	18.8	27.8	-.10	-.30
Purposive and knowing	41.6	37.7	.24	-.01
Purposive and nothing	3.6	.7	-.91	-.87

continued

Sociability and status	1.5	7.5	.11	.20
Sociability and material	1.8	6.9	.57	.51
Sociability and knowing	5.2	28.8	-.52	-.16
Sociability and nothing	.2	.5	-.87	-.84
Knowing and status	1.1	5.3	-.57	-.43
Knowing and material	.5	4.0	-.70	-.37
Knowing and nothing	.2	.9	-.96	-.81

*The motives were dichotomized so that a respondent either would miss it most or would not miss it most.

**A negative sign means an inverse relationship between the two motives. A positive sign can be interpreted as a direct relationship.

If the need for divisible benefits to support continuous activity is true, then such motivations as knowing, status, or material rewards will be directly related to other nondivisible rewards that are either purposive or solidary. Purposive issue-oriented rewards and social supports will not be directly related, however, since both are nondivisible and provide their benefits equally. Table 21 gives some support to Olson's belief in the importance of divisible benefits (if one allows "knowing" to be divisible), although not strong enough to leave his theory inviolate.

For reformers, the only direct relationship between issue orientation and other incentives exists with the divisible status reward of being an "inside dopester." Forty-one percent of the reformers would miss both issues and knowing what is happening in the community (gamma = .24). Reformers who are issue oriented are slightly less likely to require recognition or friendship (gamma = .20 for the correlation of status and issues; gamma = -.10 for the correlations of sociability and issues). With such rather weak correlations, it would appear that purposive motives operate independently of both a desire for sociability and for the status of community information. Yet one can also find a substantial "inside dopester" component supporting purposive goals. This divisible intangible motive was expected to support nondivisible tangible motives, although the relationship is rather weak.

It is also interesting that almost four times as many non-purposive reformers would miss business or political contacts compared to the percentage of purposive reformers who miss such material rewards (gamma = -.63). On the whole, these interrelationships for the reformer reflect similar patterns found in initial motivations. The negative correlations between sociability, status, material rewards, and purposive orientations remain. The reformer appears to have shifted in his motivations only slightly.

On the other hand, the initial purposive professional — for whom divisible and solidary incentives were so important — has become an activist whose purposive motivations seem unrelated to any others.

For the regular, issues as a motivating force stand in isolation. One interesting finding is the moderate inverse relationship between issue orientation and sociability for the regular. This correlation statistic is much stronger than that of the same relationship for reformers (gamma = -.10).

The relative importance of issues for reformers and regulars seems moderately related to quite different incentives. While issues and sociability are moderately and inversely related for the regular, and issues and knowing appear to be moderately and positively related for the reformer, the statistics and percentages do not indicate any strong correlations to accept.

The one exception exists between material and purposive motives for the reformer. The reformer who strongly rejects the divisible rewards of business or political contacts and — to a lesser extent — recognition is supported in his continuing efforts by concern for issues and his role as "inside dopester." This would be much in keeping with the view of the reformer as an upper-middle-class cosmopolitan whose fascination with ideas would lead him to cherish "knowing" above the local and more pragmatic regular. In effect, the importance of divisible benefits may exist for the reformer, although such rewards may have become less tangible in the shift toward "knowing."

One final comment on the negative relationship between issues and sociability for the regular. One can guess that there is within the regular organization a strain of purposive and reform-oriented activists. These people, motivated by issues, are more strongly repelled by sociability than are the same group in the reform organization. The socializing of a purposive reformer within the N.D.C. is the association of like-minded people with each other, while the same activity for the professional in a non-issue-oriented party organization might be a rather frustrating experience. Thus, while regulars are more often motivated by the nondivisible reward of socializing, purposive regulars are even less likely than non-purposive regulars to miss such motivations.

This influence of organization on motivation is an essential feature in any examination of an activist's continuing rewards. I can only approach the structure indirectly. Yet it does seem that rather than the picture of a frustrated reformer battling against pragmatic organizations, one finds in the N.D.C. a rather supportive environment for the sustenance of purposive motives, quite independent of the rewards of socializing.

The importance of sociability to fifty percent of the professionals and twenty-one percent of the reformers can not be ignored. Furthermore, for both groups, this motivation is clearly tied to the divisible material motives of business and political contacts (gamma = .57 for the reformers and .51 for regulars).

The support of friendship for both regulars and reformers is the only motive of the three most important ones (issues, knowing, and sociability) that can be related positively to the divisible rewards of either status or material benefits. While the data are only suggestive, they do pose the possibility that sociability is not enough to sustain an individual, nor does it direct him toward purposive rewards. Instead, divisible benefits may become important.

To conclude this section, it might be useful to emphasize that for regulars, the interrelationships of purposive, sociability, and "inside dopester" rewards are relatively independent of each other. The correlations are not strong. In fact, the only ones that could be considered moderately yet inversely related are purposive and socializing motivations. A similar moderately strong inverse relationship exists for reformers between socializing and "inside dopester" motives. These negative relationships also show the distinctive character of the incentives.

If categorizing knowing, status, and material rewards together as divisible benefits makes sense, then some interesting possibilities arise in discussing continuous motivations. Since material rewards appear to be in short supply, their possible replacement by intangible, yet divisible rewards, such as knowing and status, may produce the foundations for ongoing participation so vital to the parties.

It seems clear that the purposive reformer is also more likely to need the status of knowing than is the nonpurposive reformer. No such relationship appears for the regular. Thus, it may be that the purposive N.D.C. member is even more strongly sustained by complementary "inside dopester" status than is the purposive regular. If so, this reformer may be an even more continuously involved activist than the purposive regular, who has fewer divisible rewards to support him.

Besides this combination of continuing purposive motives with status rewards, one can not ignore the impact of entering motives upon these continuing incentives. This focus reintroduces the effect of an organization upon the rewards available to its volunteers. The relationship between an organization and the motivations of its adherents can be analyzed through this study indirectly in two rather distinct ways.

In the first place, it is possible to trace the congruence between the entering and the continuing motives of each activist. If substantive-purposive rewards can be discovered as both entrance and continuing motivations in the reform organization, but less often in the regular, one can suggest that the organization influences the incentives available. Thus, issue-oriented entering activists either remain purposive or change their reward system. Originally sustained by the same motives, what is the cause of their shifting goals? One possibility is that these purposive rewards are not as readily distributed in one party structure as in another. Another likelihood is that the incentive was not very strongly held.

A second way to explore the indirect effect or organization upon motives is to relate continuing motivation to an individual's own description of his role. Do certain kinds of purposive incentives structure one's role orientation? Is the way an individual interprets his political tasks also related to the kinds of demands made upon him by his party? And is it, furthermore, tied to the perception he has of what his organization expects of him?

To answer these questions about organizations and their rewards to activists, first the relationship between initial and continuing motivation will be explored. Then one can turn to this question of role perceptions.

With such high proportions of reformers (approximately ninety percent) claiming a purposive orientation toward initial and continuous involvement, it is more unlikely to think there would be any metamorphosis in policy concerns. The equally high percentage of activists who express a purposive orientation for their con-

TABLE 22

RELATIONSHIP OF ENTRANCE AND CONTINUING MOTIVATIONS FOR REFORMERS AND REGULARS (GAMMA CORRELATIONS)

Entrance motivations	Purposive	Material	Continuing motivations		Knowing	N
			Sociability	Status		
			Reformers			
Nondivisible						
Tangible						
Purposive	.68	-.29	.05	-.44	-.09	(527)
Intangible						
Participatory	.24	-.38	.05	.62	.17	(435)
Sociability	-.19	.34	.45	.39	.17	(183)
Primary group influences	.07	.16	.23	.18	.06	(88)
Divisible						
Tangible						
Material	-.39	.55	.44	.07	.06	(75)
Intangible						
Status	-.34	.40	.00	.81	.01	(39)
Unclassified						
Party attachment	-.05	.51	.48	-.15	-.10	(83)
Candidates	.18	.05	.09	-.06	-.02	(312)

TABLE 22

Relationship Of Entrance And Continuing Motivations For Reformers And Regulars (Gamma Correlations)

Entrance motivations		Continuing motivations				N
	Purposive	Material	Sociability	Status	Knowing	
			Regulars			
Nondivisible						
Tangible						
Purposive	.38	-.07	-.08	-.03	.20	(485)
Intangible						
Participatory	.31	.20	.03	.38	-.08	(612)
Sociability	-.20	.50	.49	-.59	.04	(397)
Primary group influences	-.35	.49	.37	.26	-.09	(222)
Divisible						
Tangible						
Material	-.39	.72	.12	.60	-.03	(127)
Intangible						
Status	-.42	.58	.33	.70	.07	(136)
Unclassified						
Party attachment	-.26	.42	.42	.38	-.06	(320)
Candidates	-.07	.28	.29	.26	.06	(353)

tinuing as well as entering political activism certainly does not fit with much previous literature.[6] Past research, however, did describe purposive entering motivations in a regular organization. Conway and Feigert, and Eldersveld, for example, found such incentives among regular-party activists.[7]

The more interesting issue is "Under what conditions do these purposive incentives remain operative?" The suggestion has already been presented that the party organization influences the kinds of incentives available — as well as the types of activists attracted to such rewards. In a pragmatic structure, purposive rewards would be difficult to distribute, but in a more ideological or purposive organization, such motives may be richly supported and even enhanced. Thus, in a pragmatic party, one would expect to discover a rather major shift from issue-oriented rewards to those that deal with solidary aspects of fun and status or even — to a lesser extent — material rewards. I have ruled out much expectation of these divisible tangible rewards from an understanding of the changes evident in party organization. Yet if they did appear, it would be more likely in the regular organization.

In keeping with the distinction drawn between substantive-purposive orientation and the mere desire to participate, one would expect a continuing purposive orientation for those who sought substantive issues, but a diminution of purposive incentives in relation to those whose motives were only participatory. There do seem to be some slight differences for regulars in this direction, but not for reformers.

Entering purposive motives are much more likely than are participatory ones to predict future substantive-issue motivations for reformers than for regulars. Correlating substantive motives that are both entering and continuing, one discovers a gamma = .68 for reformers and gamma = .38 for regulars (Table 22). Ninety-three percent of the reform group who entered because of their substantive issue orientation maintained this incentive, compared with 70.1 percent of the regulars. Yet participatory entering motives, related to continuing issue concerns, only produce a gamma = .24 for reformers and .31 for regulars. The percentages confuse the picture here. Ninety-two percent of the N.D.C. members who entered because of participatory motives continued because of purposive ones, compared with 65 percent in a similar group of regulars. What the percentages do not illustrate is that almost everyone in the N.D.C. claims to be purposively motivated as a continuing incentive, whether one was participatory or not in one's entering motivations. For this reason, the gamma correlation is the more useful statistic. The main point of these findings is that they indicate the usefulness of separating substantive purposive from participatory motives, since they do relate quite differently to continuing motivations.

Table 20 attests to the overwhelming continuity of purposive motives for the reformer, enmeshed in an amateur organization. No matter what other incentives seem important, purposive sustaining motivations remain predominant. Since the correlations offer another view of the data, it is useful to recall that ninety percent of the reformers still claim purposive motives. While the correlations illustrate the relative strength of one motivation in predicting another, the percentage of purposive reformers indicates that, on the whole, entering motivations seem unrelated to continuing motivation for the reformer. Whether an N.D.C. member joined because of the lure of status or material goods (note how small these numbers are, however), he is likely to be maintained by substantive rewards within his issue-oriented organization.

Another expectation that participatory motives are more related to the desire for recognition and other divisible benefits than to nondivisible-substantive rewards also is supported by these data. Entering because of citizen duty, both reformers and regulars are more likely to continue working because of material or status incentives than are activists who enter politics for more purely substantive reasons. For reformers, such a relationship with divisible benefits is reversed, if one compares substantive entering motives instead of participatory ones. In fact, the substantive entering reformer is repelled by such divisible benefits as status (gamma = -.44) or material rewards (gamma = -.29). No relationship exists for regulars between substantive entering motives and these divisible continuing ones.

Attempts to categorize such entering motivations as candidate or party attachment were avoided in an earlier chapter. One could argue that each implies issue orientation or sociability. By correlating these incentives with continuing ones, the patterns regulars and reformers develop from such initial motivations can be discovered.

For the reformer, candidate involvement is unrelated to any continuing motivation, except quite mildly to substantive purposes (gamma = .18). Thus, the reformer is more like the picture drawn of him: activated by Eugene McCarthy, but not by a personal friend. There is, then, a slight issue component in the candidate involvement of the reformer. Yet the regular illustrates a rather different picture of the activist who participated because of a candidate. Material rewards, sociability, and status are all correlated with such an entering motivation. (The gammas are .28, .29, and .26 respectively.) Issues, in fact, are noticeable by their absence. It would seem clear that candidate orientation means different things to different activists. The same could be said for the true "meaning" of party affiliation.

It appears possible that those who participate because of their attachment to a political party are implicitly making issue decisions. Yet party affiliation is inversely related to purposive continuing motivations for regulars (gamma = -.26) and unrelated to them for reformers (gamma = -.05). Instead, party attachment, like candidate motivations for regulars, coheres to material rewards, sociability, and status (gammas = .42, .42, and .38, respectively). While a similar pattern exists for material rewards and sociability for the reformer, it is not evident for status. (The relevant gammas are .51, .48, and -.15.) Party attachment shows no positive relationship with issue concerns, according to the data.

Sociability, relatively important for regulars as an entering motivation, but unimportant for reformers, is inversely related to purposive continuing motives for both groups (gamma = -.20 for regulars and gamma = -.19 for reformers). Entering sociability is positively related to such divisible benefits as status and material rewards and also to sociability, but more strongly for regulars than for reformers (gamma = .59, .50, and .49, respectively, for regulars and gammas = .39, .34, and .45 for reformers). While divisible benefits of status and material rewards are less strongly supported by the reform-style organization, sociability continues to indicate a similar moderate relationship in both party structures.

The relationship between entering social motivations and continuing divisible ones of status and material rewards also reflects the earlier discovery that among all continuing motivations, only solidary rewards are related to these divisible benefits. In fact, sociability is inversely tied to purposive motivations whether one looks at multiple motivations at one period of involvement or at entering and continuing incentives over time.

Sociability may lead to the desire for the kinds of divisible benefits, patronage, and status that are in very short supply. The other divisible benefit available, "knowing," is more clearly tied to the reformer's incentive system, although it is rather un-systematically but widely evident in the regular's.

Missing one's status as an "inside dopester" appears to be un-related to all entrance motivations for regulars and only slightly to participatory purposive and social motives for reformers. Since such a reward develops in conjunction with one's participation in an organization and may not itself stimulate activity, these corre-lations make sense.

So far, the concentration has been on individual activists. Yet indirectly, there are some implications for political organizations. The large proportion of regulars and reformers, who enter politics because of a commitment to purposive goals, find that motivation influenced by the party structure in which they work. Specific demands and activities shape the experiences of a politician. These functions can lead to revision of one's incentives, but they need not.

The reformer, enmeshed in the philosophy of issue-oriented politics, joins a reform movement, not to dissipate this purposive ethos, but rather to reinforce it. The results of his participation may socialize the N.D.C. member even further into the nondivisible rewards of policy-directed politics. The regular, however, partici-pating in a less issue-oriented group, may simply learn to adapt to new rewards. The shifting motivations of the regular, but not of the reformer, tend to confirm the N.D.C. member's rather single-minded purposive orientation.

Motivations are important variables in understanding how an individual interprets his role. The purposive reformer is expected to describe his job in educational, reform-producing, and, of course, issue-promulgating terms. The central question is how do such purposive motivations relate to the definition of one's role. Previously, the evidence showed that reformers and regulars tend to do fairly similar party organizational tasks. How they perceive these chores is another point. An individual interprets his own motives and role. This may be quite distinct from his objective tasks. Election-oriented chores may involve sociability, but they also can describe issue-orientation. Just as candidate attraction can mean different things to different activists, so can role defi-nitions. Therefore, in describing the perceptions each group holds of its role, my main concern will be in relating these views to the continuing motivations already analyzed. Table 23 presents the role interpretations offered by each group of activists in an open-ended question.[8]

TABLE 23

POLITICAL-ROLE PERCEPTIONS OF REFORMERS AND REGULARS (GAMMA CORRELATIONS)

| Role description | Percent who mention role | | Gamma* |
	Reformers (N = 487)	Regulars (N = 577)	
Reform	7.2	4.2	.28
Candidate support	3.1	3.1	-.01
Issue orientation	12.5	5.5	.42
Elections	32.4	41.8	-.20
Education	27.3	17.9	.27
Welfare	5.5	12.1	-.40
Formal job	11.7	17.3	-.23

*A positive sign means the role was directly related to N.D.C. membership, while a negative sign indicates an inverse relationship between N.D.C. membership and the specific role. More than one response was possible.

While numerous regulars and reformers declare they would miss most fighting for important issues and ideals, they do not, in an open-ended question, describe their most important tasks in such terms. Only 12.5 percent of the reformers and 5.5 percent of the regulars saw their most important job in issue-oriented ways. Although a gamma of .42 would indicate moderate differences between the two groups, the actual percentages are rather small, if one recalls the immense emphasis upon issues and general ideals that underlie the incentives for both groups.

Probably related to this concern about issues is the more often cited role of educating the electorate. Twenty-seven percent of the reformers see their activities in such a light, compared with 18 percent of the regulars (gamma = .27). For both groups, however, the role definition that appeals to most concerns electoral efforts (41.8 percent for regulars and 32.4 percent for reformers). While

professionals are more likely to emphasize this orientation, reformers are also concerned with such definitions of their most
important tasks (gamma = -.20). Reform-oriented jobs are more
important to the N.D.C., 7.2 percent of whom describe their
tasks this way, compared with 4.2 percent of the regulars. Yet
such low percentages lead one to question the traditional view of
the reformer as an "amateur" in politics, motivated by issues and
ignoring the salience of elections, just as was originally suggested
in the introductory chapters of this study.

This finding fits the previous discovery that reformers and
regulars do not differ in kinds of tasks performed. Specific chores,
however, do not necessarily reflect role interpretations. Both tasks
performed, as well as role perceptions, reinforce each other and
do clearly contradict other studies. My findings certainly do not
fit previous research that characterizes the reformer as rather inept
politically.[9] Yet here is confirmation in an open-ended question
that the reformer does, in fact, perceive his role in electoral terms.
Not only his actual chores, but also his perception of these chores
reflects this orientation.

Such a determination contributes support to the suggestion that
the N.D.C. member is distinct from the Stevenson reformer of the
1950s. Instead of the procedural niceties of past amateur organizations, the N.D.C. is committed to electoral politics. Issue-oriented
motivations may now be intrinsically tied to electoral combat for
the reformer as well as the regular. Insurgents who maintain political activism because of their concern with issues and ideals may
direct this purposive motivation toward electoral outcomes.

The picture of the reformer is of one committed to issue-
oriented politics through elections. Missing most working for issues and ideals, this new breed of reformer still describes his main
tasks in campaign-oriented terms, both through closed questions
regarding tasks he performs as well as more open-ended queries
of role definition. One may not see here the modification of the
reformer's purposive incentive, but rather its implementation in
ways that support his commitment. In order to prove this relationship between purposive motives and electoral roles, it is necessary
to examine these roles in relation to continuing motivation. There
is good reason for such an analysis.

If divisible benefits remain potent, yet those available, such as
material or status rewards, decrease in availability, then the continuing motivations of the regular may be weakened. It seems that
both sets of activists, in fact, display a rather shaky foundation

for continuous support. The sociability motive of the regular is strongly related to the less evident divisible benefits. This could mean that the regular desires what is no longer available. With the possibility of decreasing divisible benefits for the regular, intense efforts on his part are not as probable as when conditions permitted material or status rewards.

On the other hand, the reformer's purposive incentives are supported by the divisible reward of "knowing." This "inside dopester" reward appears quite potent in supporting the nondivisible benefits for the reformer in his orientation toward policy politics. It is possible that the reformer — rather than the regular — displays more easily satisfied motivations, given the evolution of party politics.

With the party needing electoral victory and the worker desiring personal rewards, the most fruitful individual motivations for the organization would be those that reinforced electoral activities. The major role interpretation for both sets of activists is this electoral role. Yet there appears to be an opposite relationship between this role and purposive incentives in the regular compared with the reform group. Fewer regulars who are motivated by issues describe themselves in electoral terms (gamma = -.24) than do nonpurposive regulars. Yet more issue-oriented reformers perceive their roles in this way (gamma = .16) than do nonpurposive N.D.C. members.

Certainly, these correlations are not outstanding for their strength, although they are rather interesting for the reversed relationship revealed. The percentages illustrate this difference and certainly support the possibility of a purposive yet electoral-oriented reformer. Thirty-three percent of issue-oriented reformers describe their tasks in electoral terms, compared with nonpurposive reformers, of whom only twenty-six percent claim such role interpretations. Yet in the regular group, this relationship is quite different. Approximately thirty-eight percent of the purposive regulars, compared with fifty percent of the nonissue motivated segment, emphasize electoral jobs.

So such difference between this role definition and continuing motives exists with "inside dopester" rewards. As it is with the social motivations for regulars and reformers, the informational rewards are directly related to electoral job interpretations. Regulars and reformers who would miss sociability are also more likely to interpret their tasks in electoral terms. Of those regulars who describe their jobs as electoral, 53.6 percent would miss friendships compared to those nonelectoral regulars of whom 44.6 percent would miss friends. The similar percentages for reformers are 25.6 percent and 21.5 percent, respectively.

The surprising relationship between continuing solidary and purposive motives for regulars (gamma = -.30), compared with the less strong negative relationship for reformers (gamma = -.10) was noted above. I hypothesized that this might be tied to the organizational supports available to purposive activists in reform organizations, but absent in the pragmatic party structure. Here are some further findings to support such a contention.

Approximately 50 percent of all regulars would miss sociability. Yet only 28.1 percent of those regulars who perceive their roles in issue terms would miss socializing, a rather impressive variation in motivations. For reformers, the percentage change is slight, but even more significantly moves the purposive reformer toward an increasing attachment to solidary ties. Thus, while 21.3 percent of all reformers would miss friendships, 29.5 percent of those who describe their role in issue terms would do so. The purposive activist is more supported by peers within the reform organization than within the regular structure, as was suggested previously.

For the regular, the nondivisible, nontangible rewards of sociability lead to electoral-role interpretations, while the nondivisible tangible incentives of issues guide the regular in the reverse direction. Sociability as well as purposive incentives for the reformer increase the likelihood (although slightly) that such an activist will define his job in electoral terms. One cannot help but surmise that the regular's decrease in receptivity to purposive incentives is related to his party experiences, while a very different involvement heightens and reinforces that prior leaning for the N.D.C. member.

The main emphasis at this point is upon the issue-oriented reformer. Far from the "amateur politician" of the past, he can quite successfully develop his purposive motives within the electoral arena, a finding that supports the relevance of such a study as this. No more the "mornin' glory" of Plunkitt, the reformer has been socialized into the pragmatic uses of the ballot to implement his policy goals. Furthermore, this N.D.C. member finds fairly great satisfaction in electioneering roles. While 8.1 percent of all reformers would miss nothing if they stopped political work, only 5.8 percent of those electoral reformers would. Electoral regulars, however, are no more nor less likely to miss nothing.

It would be absurd to overemphasize the political joy of the reformer. In fact, a core of underlying discontent with party work was evident in the reform group. This dissatisfaction with politics as a vocation is quite visible. When queried about these political efforts, 85.1 percent of the reformers could mention something they disliked, while only 47.5 percent of the regulars did so (gamma = .73). Thus, purposive motivations with few solidary supports produce rather widespread dissatisfaction with some aspects of political life. Yet solidary incentives for the regulars have appeared to be relatively ineffective without other divisible rewards.

Also indicative of dissatisfaction are the tasks and the continuity in their performance. Yet if one recalls the number of political chores that reformers and regulars shared in common, it does seem surprising that so many of these jobs should arouse so little intrinsic satisfaction and yet evoke such intense efforts. The hard-working but slightly discontented reformer is evident. He may perform the same campaign-oriented jobs as the regular, but he surely does not do so as often. Ninety-one percent of the regulars remained active every year, since their first campaign. For the reformers, only two-thirds have been so active (gamma = -.65).

Perhaps what these data indicate is that, while there is widespread dissatisfaction with some aspects of politics, this can not be interpreted as disillusionment with involvement. The reformer's purposive goals sensitize him to certain nonissue-oriented tasks, but on the whole, he has shown a remarkable flexibility in redefining these chores to fit into his incentive system. The main responsibility for this changing picture of the reformer can well be the development of the reform-style organization that satisfies his purposive incentives and role interpretations.

Now that the motivations and role structure of the reformer and the regular have been examined, these findings can be related to the theoretical propositions presented earlier in the chapter. Certainly very few reformers or regulars were supported by the divisible material benefits Olson claimed were so important in explaining political activism. Instead, one finds purposive entering and continuing motivations for reformers, who may receive some divisible status benefits from "inside dopester" rewards. These discoveries support the hypotheses presented above. But this finding certainly is not what Olson meant by noncollective goods.

For the regular, one discovers the importance of purposive incentives, also supported by "inside dopester" motivations as well as sociability. The great overlap between purposive and knowledge incentives and the lesser relationship between purposive and socializing motivations or socializing and knowledge rewards still can not be interpreted as Olson's divisible patronage.

While professionals do present more continuing solidary and material motives than reformers, the degree to which material rewards abound hardly confirms this aspect of the hypotheses.

Furthermore, the disillusioned and purposive reformer was not supported in the least. If anything, the ongoing purposive orientation of the insurgent leads him to greater political activism than the similar subtype in the regular group. This lack of disillusioned reformers is also supported by the role interpretations of these activists. While there is confirmation of the hypothesis that reformers perceive their roles more often than regulars do in educational and reform terms, and regulars are more brokerage centered, the main finding is of disconfirmation. The reformer and regular are almost as likely to see their roles in a campaign-oriented fashion.

One rather surprising discovery from these data relates to the similarity of the role perceptions, yet the discontinuity of underlying motivations that support these roles, if one compares regulars with reformers. As likely to describe their most important tasks as those that involve elections, these activists vary considerably in the extent to which purposive motivations encourage this orientation.

This discrepancy in the effects of similar motivations directs one back to the original discussion of organizational influences. It also, however, instructs one to reexamine cosmopolitanism. There seem to be two possible explanations for the differential effects of purposive incentives. One involves the kinds of people recruited to the organization, that is, cosmopolitans or locals. Different people differ in the way they interpret their motivations. Another possibility considers the effects that a structure has upon the reward system and behavior of an individual.

The reformer with his cosmopolitanism may enact his role as purposive activist in order to apply his technical talents to the confused and disorganized political arena. With a dedication, the reformer applies his skill to a tough political problem. Gouldner describes this very behavior of a cosmopolitan who has been recruited by a corporation. His lack of loyalty to the company results from his role as expert. In manipulating his "mysterious skills," his rewards are perceived in terms of his professional reference group, not the upper echelon bureaucrats of his company.[10]

The cosmopolitan who is free to exercise his technical skills finds intrinsic satisfaction in the application of this knowledge. An organization where these talents are respected and given loose rein is a group that will reward him amply.

Yet the analysis of issues, the development of politics — all-important priorities in the N.D.C. — would not be enough for his cosmopolitan soul. Like any good technician, not ivory-tower programs, but enactment and implementation of these ideals becomes necessary. Thus the campaign orientation of the reformer.

It is worth reiterating that the cosmopolitan reformer exists within an environment that encourages his purposive goals. In turning to the professional, no such assuption can be made.

It is also possible that the recruitment of the regular organization attracts a very different brand of purposive activist. One could theorize about the purposive with a local orientation. This may seem a contradiction in terms, yet it is likely that purposive motivations are held with varying degrees of strength by different politicians. These particular questions of the study did not permit the respondent to declare the intensity of his purposive commitments, only whether they existed or did not.

Furthermore, politicians are all supposed to describe their motivations in issue-oriented terms. This could encourage the expression of purposive goals that were weakly held. Also, much in keeping with the finding that regulars display multiple and complex motivational structures, it is possible that party loyalty might outweigh purposive goals when they conflict. Since incentives are multiple, it might be earier for the purposive regular to switch his incentives toward other rewards, when opposition to his goals becomes evident within the organization.

This whole question of intensity of purposive motives will be explored in the next chapter. It is raised here merely to pose a possible explanation for the discrepancies evident between motivations and role interpretations.

Another plausible description of the purposive regular involves returning to the question of organizational socialization. Perhaps the reformer and regular are similar in their initial purposive motivations. What differs is the way these incentives are rewarded in one structure, but not in the other.

In examining this new wave of reformers, one does find their continued purposive motivations reinforced by political involvement in such organizations as the N.D.C. I have attempted to explain this finding in relation to some of the theories of motivation discussed earlier. These discoveries suggest that the propositions of Olson might need to be revised as affluent living and leisure time propel more citizens into the political arena, which no longer provides divisible-tangible rewards. More subtle ego satisfactions may have replaced the overt patronage of the past.

In a society where technological improvements have created affluence, tangible-divisible benefits for voluntary activity may be replaced by new sources of divisible and intangible benefits of "knowing" the inside workings of government or being part of political decision making. For both groups, this motivation is an essential source of continued involvement. Mixed with knowing is the support of tangible, though nondivisible motivations that provide avenues for issue implementation.

For the affluent, middle-class activist with leisure time to spare, the ego satisfaction of seeing his policy concerns enacted may provide a concrete reward that replaces patronage as a motivating force. The overtly egocentric benefits of jobs and favors might have been replaced by the more subtly egocentric incentives of "power" and "influence" over policy formulation. Perhaps the tangibility of the outcome is important, whether the benefit produced is divisible or nondivisible.

In this chapter on role interpretations and continuing motivations, the original hypotheses have been tested. Yet in so doing, one raises more questions than are answered. Surely the intense rivalry between the two groups of activists can not be explained by the rather unimpressive distinctions drawn in this chapter on motivations. I can suggest a reason for the relatively mild importance of motivational attributes to discriminate the two groups that was touched upon in the preceding paragraphs.

In the first place, categorizing motives as nondivisible and tangible does not actually encompass the content of these goals. It is likely that most political activists will be concerned with issues. After all, they are clearly devoting their time to a political party, not some community-service organization.

It may well be these issue-oriented goals, so overwhelming to reformers and also important to regulars, must be further dissected. In examining the details of purposive motivations for both groups, I am answering questions about the content of these substantive orientations. The next discussion on liberalism and ideology will attempt to discover any deeper distinctions between the purposive motivations of these two groups. No findings available so far have led to a strong assertion that reformers are vastly different from regulars in their motivations or role perceptions or even tasks performed. Yet when this study explored role perceptions, certain interpretations seemed possible. Electoral roles are tied to divisible-tangible incentives more strongly for reformers than regulars. Perhaps these purposive incentives, espoused by both groups in large proportions, have different meanings for N.D.C. members and regulars. The following two chapters will help to answer this question by examining the qualitative aspects of this issue-orientation.

Notes to Chapter 6

1. Chris Argyris, *Interpersonal Competence and Organizational Effectiveness,* The Irwin Dorsey Series in Behavioral Science in Business (Homewood, Ill.: The Dorsey Press, Inc., and Richard D. Irwin, Inc., 1962), p. 33. The literature on this score is massive. I cite only a few sources: Alvin W. Gouldner, *Patterns of Industrial Bureaucracy* (Glencoe, Ill.: Free Press, 1954); Chester Barnard, "Functions and Pathology of Status Systems in Formal Organizations," in *Industry and Society,* ed. William Foote Whyte (New York: McGraw-Hill Book Company, 1946), pp. 46-83; Peter M. Blau, *Bureaucracy in Modern Society* (New York: Random House, 1956), esp. pp. 70-79; Cyril Sofer, *Organizations in Theory and Practice* (New York: Basic Books, Inc., 1972); Robert K. Merton, "Bureaucratic Structure and Personality," in Merton, pp. 195-206.

2. Muzafer Sherif, "Intergroup Relations and Leadership: Introductory Statement," in *Intergroup Relations and Leadership: Approaches and Research in Industrial, Ethnic, Cultural, and Political Areas,* ed. Muzafer Sherif (New York: John Wiley & Sons, Inc., 1962), pp. 3-23. The sources on the dynamism of small groups is legion. A few of the more relevant for the purpose of this study are: Robert T. Golembiewski, *Behavior and Organization: O. & M. and Small Group* (Chicago: Rand McNally & Co., 1962); Warren Breed, "Social Control in the Newsroom: A Functional Analysis," *Social Forces,* 33 (May 1955): 326-35; F. H. Roethlisberger and William J. Dickson, *Management and the Worker* (Cambridge, Mass.: Harvard University Press, 1947).

3. A. H. Maslow, *Motivation and Personality* (New York: Harper & Bros., 1954).

4. The more specific hypotheses are presented in the previous chapter. For details of the question, *see* Appendix A, question 21. Since multiple responses were possible, each response in analyzed as a separate variable.

5. Merton, "Patterns of Influence," in Merton, p. 391.

6. Conway and Feigert, "Motivation, Incentive Systems," pp. 1,169, 172; Wilson, *Amateur Democrat,* p. 171; Eldersveld, *Political Parties,* pp. 277-92.

7. Conway and Feigert, "Motivation, Incentive Systems," pp. 1,159-73; Eldersveld, *Political Parties.*

8. The exact wording is available in Appendix A, question 20. The open-ended responses were coded dichotomously as to whether the roles were or were not interpreted as: reform, candidate support, issue oriented, electoral, educational, welfare, or formal job as committeeman.

9. Wilson in the *Amateur Democrat* epitomizes this disdain for the reformer, but it can also be discovered in other works such as Costikyan, *Behind Closed Doors*.

10. Alvin W. Gouldner, "How People View Their Role in the Organization: Cosmpolitans and Locals," *Administrative Science Quarterly* 2 (December 1957): 282-92.

7
Direction and Intensity of Liberalism

The motivational thicket that was presented in the previous chapter was fraught with problems. No questions seem more bound to the rhetoric of public service and selfless reasoning than those that deal with personal motivation. It would appear quite likely that one would overestimate his own purposive orientations and minimize the more personally aggrandizing ones. In order to deal with this possibility, I have sought to detail the qualitative aspects of the purposive motives of reformers and regulars. Yet in turning to a description of liberalism and ideology, I may be leading from the thickets into the jungle — no great bargain for political explorers.

Most of this quagmire exists over the various meanings researchers have employed in their use of the term *ideology*, into which they lump not only *liberalism*, but also a multitude of other factors. Before discussing the issue-oriented philosophy of these politicians, it is necessary to develop clearer categories for such variables as liberalism and ideology. This diversion is especially useful, since I claim this section contains the most important distinctions between reform and regular Democrats. The qualitative aspect of the purposive motivations will help to clarify the actual meaning that an activitist imputes to his own nondivisible-tangible incentives.

There are several ways to approach these finer distinctions. In the first place, to be issue oriented as a motivation and also relatively intense in one's position would seem to be complementary evidence as to the strength of a purposive motivation. Such motivations combined with relatively moderate opinions, on the other hand, imply a rather different view of one's substantive orientations. In effect, the concept *ideology* contains several distinct elements. Reviewing how past researchers of grassroots activists have used the term will help delineate this concept a bit further and illustrate the many other approaches employed in this analysis.

After differentiating this terminology, a classification will be presented of two distinct components, liberalism and ideology. During this exposition my hypotheses will be reviewed and detailed. The remainder of this and the following chapter will then present the specific research findings.

The term *ideology* is used rather differently and broadly in past studies. Bowman and Boynton discuss ideological role orientations, when precinct committeemen describe their work as increasing the political information of the electorate or formulating policy.[1] Marvick and Nixon apply it to liberalism or conservatism.[2] Eldersveld's approach to ideology is similar to Marvick and Nixon's.

In discussing the party leader's "political perspective," Eldersveld defines his ideology as "the structure of his attitudinal positions on the critical public-policy questions of the day, and the extent to which his position coincides with the group's position, insofar as this is clearly definable and explicit."[3] A bit later he seems to consider ideology not only the direction of these attitudes, but also the intensity of these positions. By intensity, however, Eldersveld means the coherence of liberal responses on three specific areas: civil rights, government health insurance, and foreign aid.[4] Intensity meant that an activist took a liberal stand on two of these three issues consistently. Domestic issues were separated from the foreign-aid question. Thus, ideological liberalism for Eldersveld meant liberal responses to those two issue areas of health insurance and civil rights.

"Intensity" for Eldersveld is actually what Converse means by "constraint." Converse proposes that ideological orientations involve "a configuration of ideas and attitudes in which the elements are bound together by some form of constraint or functional interdependence."[5] Finding only ten to fifteen percent of the adult population fulfilling his requirements as ideologues, Converse concludes that belief systems are not in great evidence in the American political system, except among college educated and the political elite.[6] Thus, if belief systems are likely anywhere, political activists seem to be an ideal group to analyze.

Ideology, as constrained issues, tied together in either a coherent liberal or conservative fashion, place this concept apart from either direction or intensity of one's attitudes. My study employs Converse's concept to mean ideology. Yet another use of the term *ideology* that contains a liberal-conservative dimension connotes self-perception of an individual on such a scale. Hofstetter employs such self-placement in his analysis of reform and regular activists in Columbus, Ohio.[7] In discussing direction and intensity, this study of reformers and regulars treats such an analysis under the operational meaning of liberalism.

One final view of ideology is presented by Conway and Feigert and relates to motivations. Their ideological perspective would be the equivalent of my substantive issue-oriented motivation, described in previous chapters.[8]

Ideology has meant in turn: role definitions, political philosophy, intensity of these attitudes, interrelationship or constraint of such opinions, and, finally, the motivational source for purposive incentives. All definitions seem relevant to any study of reformers and regulars. But it is important to make their meanings distinct and to clarify the specific terminology of this study. While describing all of the above terms through the behavior of reformers and regulars, I do not group these totally distinct variables under the single rubric of *ideology*.

Ideology, in this study, connotes two rather separate orientations to political reality. It primarily depicts the interrelatedness of the various issue areas. Reformers will exhibit considerably more constraint between a wide variety of issue areas than will regulars. Besides these ties between issues, ideology also contains the notion of a world view. Apter speaks of "fundamental belief" and "outrage."[9] This emotional attachment to political objects displays more than internal consistency of issues. It also involves an interpretation of reality through a consistent application of principles or standards. Thus the ideologue finds issues salient.

This, however, does not explain all, for an individual may feel intensely about only one issue. He would not be considered an ideologue. The reformer is expected to illustrate intense responses to a whole series of issues, in conformity with his ideological approach to politics.

Thus a second aspect of this ideological orientation deals with the normative view reformers are expected to share about the proper role of the political party. The passion of an ideologue is expected to manifest itself in overt attitudes and behavior and is likely to be enacted through his political relations. Issue constraint plus intensity of concern are then linked to interpretations of ideal party activity. The politician not only catalogues his own attitudes, but also projects them as a value upon external organizations. The distinctions in party orientation would then be the range between ideological or pragmatic descriptions for political parties.

For those who perceive the party as an electoral coalition of diverse groups, compromise and winning are expected to evoke pragmatic party-role descriptions. I anticipate that the ideologue, however, will reject compromising and winning at all costs. By classifying the diverse meanings of ideology into the subcategories of normative party orientation and issue constraint, I have also begun to distinguish ideology from liberalism. Yet only half my task is completed. Just as the term *ideology* presented a forest of ambiguous meanings, so does the concept *liberalism*.

A. Philosophical Roots of Liberalism

Since all forces in American history seem joined to the liberal tradition, as Louis Hartz has well attested,[10] it may appear useless to describe the N.D.C. activist as liberal. Yet the distinction between the regular and the reformer is very much tied to the various concepts of liberalism and is, in fact, based upon the original context in which that philosophy developed. If one examines seventeenth- and eighteenth-century liberalism, the outstanding trait of such a representative theorist as John Locke was his eagerness to liberate the individual from the shackles of the past: either from authoritarian government, religion, or social conventions, through the application of reason.[11]

Thus liberalism developed in the past as a protest movement against external limitations on the potential of each and every man. The emphasis upon the individual who endorses the legitimacy of government only where it can safeguard what he himself can not protect, especially property rights, may have characterized the incipient liberal tradition. Yet its fundamental qualities were not in any specific policy, removed from cultural and historical perspective, but rather in an orientation toward change, toward progress, and toward tolerance that can be related to the liberalism of the N.D.C. This quality of mind provokes an "exploratory and experimental spirit in all fields."[12]

Thus, when liberalism became a doctrine wedded to the status quo through Manchester economics of laissez-faire capitalism, one might argue that it had lost touch with its "liberal" roots. After the "liberation" of the early liberalism, that philosophy grew to be the dominant ideology of middle- and upper-class industrialists. One might conclude that it was then a far distant cousin of the liberalism of Locke. When liberalism evoked natural order and natural selection to prevent the positive development of more and more individuals in their drive for self-expression, it then abandoned its origins.

Such philosophical support for the middle class was available in the sociology of William Graham Sumner, who argued that social classes owe each other nothing.[13]

The prostitution of that valued philosophy was bemoaned by such twentieth-century theorists as John Dewey, whose argument could be found even earlier in the works of the English philosopher, T. H. Green.[14] Rather than a negative view of man's social relationships, both these "new" liberals stressed the positive aspects of man's societal obligations. Not tied to Locke's natural rights preceding the state, Green described the state's powers as "necessary to the fulfillment of man's vocation as a moral being, to an effectual self-devotion to the work of developing the perfect character in himself and others."[15]   Dewey went even further toward espousing the social nature of men when he proposed structural reform to develop man's potential — a potential that could only be released through the positive role of government:

> Liberalism knows that social conditions may restrict, distort, and almost prevent the development of individuality. It therefore takes an active interest in the working of social institutions that have a bearing, positive or negative, upon the growth of individuals who shall be rugged in fact and not merely in abstract theory. It is as much interested in the positive construction of favorable institutions, legal, political, and economic, as it is in the work of removing abuses and overt oppressions.[16]

Thus government became an opportunity for self-expression rather than a hindrance endured for mere convenience. Out of this tradition and the experience of the New Deal arose the liberalism described as *pragmatic.*"[17] Positive government to moderate the inequities of an advanced technological society would hark back to the original tenets and certain implications .of eighteenth-century liberalism.

For it seems that two qualities are exhibited in any redefinition of the liberal tradition, capturing its earliest essentials. One is an attempt to unfetter each man further in his own personal development, while another claims the end of expanding this possibility to more and more individuals in a society. Whether one moves from majority rule to utilitarian theory or its revision, the goal of the true liberal is the expansion and expression of the worth of each and every individual in a community.

Dewey's and T. H. Green's attempt to come to terms with the laissez-faire tradition, which had solidified into a philosophy to prevent change, moved liberalism into its more recent social context. An individual does not merely bear the strains and inconveniences of social relationships and government to protect his material needs, but rather is himself qualitatively changed — for the better — by such social ties and commitments. Dewey's criticism of the New Deal was its short-range programs that permitted no long-term plan for the intellectual development of increasing numbers. While Dewey himself was classified as a nonideological pragmatist, he did yearn for the planning of social reconstruction that he believed would reduce suffering and expand possibilities for the masses.

Thus flexibility, rather than one particular program — laissez-faire — characterized the essence of liberalism. Identification with the underdog, rather than the elite, illustrates much of liberalism's dynamic. If one explored the history of American politics with these possibilities in mind, it does seem that the N.D.C. member, in his concern with individuals and his trust in their ability to judge what was best for themselves, reflects this underlying commitment to the "liberal" tradition as it first arose. The N.D.C. activist does, in fact, have more faith in his fellow man. Thirty percent of the regulars agree strongly that few people know what is in their own best interests. Only 12.7 percent of the reformers would subscribe to such beliefs. Faith in the individual, that touchstone of liberalism, seems quite evident in even this question that should have aroused the democratic rhetoric of both regular and reformer.

It is this very faith in mankind that led the New Deal to a positive view of government intervention in the economic sphere and in so doing remained true to the liberal heritage of equal development of individuals. This goal had not altered, but conditions had. Permitting the free rein of natural forces assumed that every person was equal in opportunity. Yet equality of opportunity, once the frontier closed and industrialization spread, was reduced to one of those general myths that is strongly contradicted by the plight of millions of poor and deprived Americans.

Thus, as American society changed, the definition of liberalism developed with it. From procedural liberties emphasized by Locke, it also incorporated substantive programs that entailed a positive government role. Procedural protections define government obligations in a rather negative way: abstaining from and preventing others from abrogating civil liberties. Substantive protections, on the other hand, commit government to an active, welfare role in reallocating wealth to diminish material inequities. Another way to characterize this distinction is the liberalism of means (democracy) versus that of ends (economic and social equality).

While this presentation provides only a brief introduction to the liberal heritage, it does permit me to describe the various methods this study employs to dissect the varieties of liberalism found in reform and regular Democratic groups.

My first subcategory of liberalism characterizes the reformer as a substantive liberal. He is expected to be much more liberal than the regular in the actual policies he espouses. But the reformer is also likely to demonstrate a liberal position on the procedures employed to reach these issue-oriented goals. Thus, a second category considers procedural liberalism. In fact, Wilson, in making this very distinction, claims that concern for the processes of decision making is characterized by an overwhelming interest in "democracy" at all stages of a decision.[18]   This procedural liberalism would be characterized by concern for civil liberties and mass involvement in decisions.

Besides the separation of substantive from procedural liberalism, there is a third and more generalized feeling about what liberalism means. This entails a willingness to support change and innovation, and follows directly from the historical development of liberalism. A conservative, according to this definition of the term, would defend the status quo. I expect the reformer to be favorable in his attitude toward change, in contrast to the regular. Furthermore, the extent of liberal orientation evident in an activist's opinions will combine objective as well as subjective definitions. An activist places himself on a liberal-conservative continuum (subjective liberalism). He also offers his opinions in specific issue areas (objective liberalism).[19] Besides the direction of these responses, their intensity will be very important in discriminating between reformers and regulars.

With this brief introduction to the different aspects of ideology and liberalism, I can review and expand the hypotheses — for liberalism as well as ideology — presented earlier. While the analysis of ideology will be reserved for the subsequent chapter, it is such an intrinsic part of the previous discussion, that the hypo-theses for both are offered together.

I anticipated that reformers would be more liberal than regu-lars on all issues. I did expect, however, an even greater distinc-tion between regulars and reformers on procedural issues com-pared with substantive ones — with the possible exception of Vietnam. Since the war provided the impetus to political action for many of these reformers during the 1968 campaign, I expect-ed Vietnam to be quite salient.

In analyzing the substantive issues, certain policies were expect-ed to be more divisive than others. I looked for little distinction on the issues concerning government involvement in the economy.

Liberal Hypotheses

Hypothesis 13 — There will be a significant difference between the liberalism of reformers and regulars.
> a. Regulars will be significantly more supportive of the status quo than reformers.
> b. There will be a proportionately greater difference be-tween reformers and regulars on procedural rather than substantive issues.
>> (1) Substantive Issues: Vietnam war will provide the greatest differences between reformers and regulars in substantive issues.
>>> (a) There will be little significant differ-ence between reformers and regulars on economic involvement of the government.
>>> (b) Reformers will be significantly differ-ent from regulars on civil-rights ques-tions.
>>> (c) Great Society issues will significantly differentiate reformers and regulars.
>> (2) Procedural Issues: There will be a significant difference between reformers and regulars on civil liberty issues.
>> (3) Intensity: Reformers will be significantly more intense in their opinions than regulars.
> c. Reformers will be significantly more likely to perceive themselves as liberals than regulars.

Ideological Hypotheses

Hypothesis 14 — Reformers will be significantly more constrained in their issue concerns than regulars.
        a. Reformers will be significantly more constrained
           in issue areas than will regulars.
        b. Reformers will be significantly more constrained
           across issue areas than will regulars.
Hypothesis 15 — Reformers will be significantly more ideological about party activity than regulars.
        a. Ideologues will be more liberal than pragmatics will
           be.
        b. Reformers will be more likely to vote against their
           party than regulars.

Greater discrepancies, however, were anticipated between these
activists on such recent issues as civil rights, law and order, and, of
course, Vietnam.

The expectation of a slighter variation in economic liberalism
than in other policy areas is related to the historical development
of certain issues. The New Deal period was sundered by a series of
programs that divided people over the degree to which government
should provide and expand social and economic services and goods.
The New Deal-Fair Deal era was characterized not only by government intervention in the economy, but also in international
affairs. Democrats supported this positive view of government,
while Republicans feared the development of a centralized state.
Yet these divisions were not as deep as one might expect from
reading Dewey. For while Dewey proposed such radical involvement of government, he was not part of Franklin Delano Roosevelt's "brain trust." These apologists emphasized incremental
pragmatism, in which one small step at a time would be taken to
solve a problem.[20] No five-year plan, but rather immediate reactions to particularly salient emergencies were the rule of the
day. In fact, Thurman Arnold, a participant and philosopher of
the New Deal, warned that all doctrine was dangerous and should
be rejected in favor of meeting practical needs.[21] Thus the solutions of the New Deal did not involve massive reconstruction of
American society and basically shored up a slightly wobbly status
quo. Thus it is no wonder that those partisan divisions waned in
importance over time. World War II and prosperity managed to
convince Republicans that government provision of services was
not the danger first anticipated. Also, the viability of such in-

volvement became clear to pragmatic Republicans interested in winning a national election. Thus, when Eisenhower became the first Republican president since the New Deal, these older economic issues had — more or less — been resolved. In fact, so much accord appeared visible to social scientists that a spate of books declared the "end-of-ideology" replaced by technical solutions for the best methods to regulate such a complex postindustrial society.[22] More of this approach will be discussed in the following chapter.

Thus, it seems rather likely that if most Republicans were willing to accept some governmental solutions in employment, education, and housing, that Democrats would be agreed such programs were fine ideas. These policies were not only philosophically pleasing, but had also shown their electoral worth at the polls. Democrats had promoted such programs and were associated in congress through the presidency with their support. In the study of McClosky, et al. of party elites, they too found Democratic support for these New Deal issues.[23] Thus, these regular Democrats proved their liberalism and were more often identified with such programs by voters. Recent surveys of the American electorate show it to be increasingly issue oriented and increasingly capable of perceiving party-policy differences.[24] This finding suggests certain weaknesses in the end-of-ideology argument, to be analyzed later.

With certain issues clearly identified with the Democratic Party, most Democrats, whether reformers or regulars, are expected to support these more traditional liberal issues of the New Deal. Not so, however, with the still unresolved questions of race, law and order, and civil liberties. Here the distinctions between kinds of Democrats may be intensely divisive. For this reason, I have anticipated variations in the degrees of liberalism evident in the two groups.

B. Three Components of Liberalism

After this rather long series of introductory explanations and clarifications, let me turn to the findings for the three components of liberalism: status quo versus an orientation toward change, substantive and procedural liberalism. Following this rather straightforward presentation, I shall deal with the question of intensity. Then, the effects of a self-ranking liberal continuum will be explored in relation to other issue areas. This will lead very easily into the analysis of ideology.

It is possible to state rather emphatically that reformers overwhelmingly accept innovation. One discovers, in fact, a strongly negative correlation of support for the status quo and reform membership (gamma = -.60). While both types of Democrats disagree with the statement that change is bad, the reformers disagree strongly with this statement 61 percent of the time, compared with 13.5 percent of the regulars.

On the whole, reformers and regulars do not agree that change is dangerous. Yet the pattern of intense response for reformers indicates that they are much more likely to disagree strongly with such support for the status quo. One might conclude from these data that the N.D.C. members are strongly antiestablishment — not unlike their liberal ancestors. Both groups can be categorized as "liberals" on the basis of this response. And yet the distinctions within the degrees of liberalism provide rather strong correlations. Substantive and procedural liberalism follow this pattern very much.

Certain substantive issues have already been distinguished from others. An individual who takes a liberal stand on substantive issues that derive from the New Deal but not on the more recent developing divisions such as Vietnam, civil rights, and law and order might well be only an economic liberal. This same individual may also be diametrically opposed to procedural civil liberties.

Much of the literature, in fact, emphasizes the lack of coherence between liberals in one issue area and similar positions on others. Ideologues are few and far between in America.[25] Examining political activists, however, most researchers discover much more constraint between issues.[26] Even within these informed and involved groups, the strength of interrelationship is not overwhelming.[27] This constraint between liberalism on many issues, however, will be explored further in the discussion on ideology.

Even for the reformers studied in the 1950s, liberal stands on substantive issues were not thought to be essential ingredients of their most important characteristics. Instead, what Wilson found to be the major issue-oriented distinction between regulars and reformers was a concern with procedural or reform issues.[28]

The Stevenson reformer emphasized procedural reform, the means by which political decisions were made, rather than the end or policy that was espoused. In their concentration upon democracy, these 1950s amateurs stressed the process of policy formulation. Out of this dedication to total democracy and involvement of all in each and every part of the decision came a confusion that is well illustrated by Robert Michels in his disillusioned account of the "oligarchic tendency" of even leftist-socialists parties.[29] Leadership for such amateurs became the antithesis of democracy.

Michels derided those parties' lack of democracy in the need for electoral compromises. Not procedures for their own sake, but rather for the means they provided to substantive goals were important. The same could be said for the more recent reformers. Procedures do not seem as important for the N.D.C. as Wilson claims they were for the Stevenson amateurs.[30] The purposive motivations of such activists are rather distinct from their participatory motives, as was detailed earlier. Not merely participatory benefits accrue to reformers, but rather — and far more essential — the rewards that are derived from substantive issue orientation are eagerly sought.

It is easy to forget that control by a small elite was more than a paranoid obsession of the reformers. How could they influence the path of policy formulation in a liberal direction, when the insurgents could not even control the party structures that made such a direction possible? The emphasis upon party democracy was a way to demand entré into a self-perpetuating group of limited size.

Most of the literature obscures the rather pragmatic reason for this emphasis upon procedural democracy by post-World War II amateurs. Yet the tactic for the stress on procedural over substantive democracy was relatively clear. The parties of the 1950s and 1960s were relatively closed to outside control of reform-oriented participants. As the McGovern Commission had pointed out, after the 1968 Democratic debacle, few regulations required any party to make clear its methods of selecting officers or candidates, let alone advertising and holding open meetings that such decisions would be made.[31]

Since reforming the decision-making process for substantive ends was the goal of the reformer, it is essential not to obscure this point. Part of the confusion may arise over the "liberal" nature of both reform and regular Democrats.

For both Michels's activists and mine, one is drawing a distinction between degrees of liberalism or left-wing philosophies. In comparison with Republicans, both the N.D.C. and the regular Democrats would appear liberal.[32] Thus the samples in this study are composed of the comparatively more and less liberal strata of two "objectively" liberal Democratic groups.

Yet lumping all liberals together and ignoring the degrees of liberalism can be a mistake that this study will try to avoid. McClosky's questions provide simple "agree-disagree" responses.[33]

TABLE 24

LIBERALISM OF REFORMERS AND REGULARS
(ONE-WAY ANALYSIS OF VARIANCE)

Issue	F*	N
Subjective liberalism		
Self-perception as a liberal	830.6	(1,311)
New Deal-economic liberalism		
Government involvement in employment	141.88	(1,317)
Government involvement in education	93.71	(1,337)
Government involvement in housing	137.93	(1,330)
Great Society: Welfare and racial issues		
Law and order	473.15	(1,302)
Government solve job inequities of blacks	308.34	(1,295)
Perception blacks' status mobility	146.01	(1,383)
College open-admissions	421.21	(1,327)
Great Society: Southeast Asian involvement		
Vietnam withdrawal	335.51	(1,301)
Shipment of military supplies to S.E.A.	286.84	(1.305)
Further troop intervention in S.E.A.	182.63	(1,032)
Procedural issues		
Rights of peaceful demonstrators	576.15	(1,363)
Freedom of speech	617.68	(1,331)

*All findings significant.

P ≤ .001.

Later researchers, using five-point scales, still combined categories of liberals who "agreed" and "agreed strongly."[34] Thus, for Soule and Clarke, no differences in liberalism are evident between reformers and regulars.[35] I have tried to distinguish between degrees of liberalism, since these degrees appeared to be so essential in describing the reformer's purposive goals.

This study does illustrate the qualitative aspects of liberalism. In fact, it is rather amazing to note the differences that exist between regulars and reformers on all issues.

A one-way analysis of variance indicates that these great deviations between the responses of regulars and reformers can not be attributed to chance. Table 24 clearly demonstrates the great variation between the two groups of activists on all issues.[36] I note this statistical procedure merely in passing. These tests of significance are especially influenced by the size of the sample. Since this survey consists of approximately 1,300 respondents, the size alone makes it very unlikely that a statistical test of significance will discount discoveries as caused by chance alone. A more important question revolves around the strength of relationships between reform membership and liberalism, as well as the amount of variance explained by these two sets of variables.

The strength of the relationship is only partially illustrated by the gamma. Yet contrary to expectations of wide variations between regulars and reformers on Great Society issues, but not the older New Deal policies, one discovers very strong gamma correlations on all issues. Procedural as well as substantive policy areas provide impressive correlations. Table 25 displays the relevant issues, according to descending order of strength.

It would appear that regardless of my contention that older policies have been resolved, reformers are noticeably more liberal than regulars on every issue. The New Deal conflicts over economic liberalism seem to be as potent a series of distinguishing variables as the procedural civil-liberties issues of free speech and the right to demonstrate peacefully.

Since these policy divisions provide the highest correlations discovered during the analyses, one can not help but question the past description of the reformer, which hastily brushes aside his liberalism as a rather unessential trademark.[37]

These strong correlations only paint a partial picture of the relative liberalism of reformers and regulars. Another aspect of this orientation can be illustrated by examining the amount of variance in liberalism explained by reform or regular membership. The eta squared (η^2) is especially useful for determining

TABLE 25

LIBERALISM OF REFORMERS AND REGULARS
(GAMMA CORRELATIONS)

Issues	Gamma*	N
1. Government involvement in housing	.93	(1,330)
2. Further Southeast Asian troop intervention	.91	(1,032)
3. Government solve job inequities of blacks	.90	(1,295)
4. Self-perception as liberal	.87	(1,311)
5. Vietnam withdrawal	.87	(1,301)
6. Rights of peaceful demonstrators	.83	(1,363)
7. Government involved in employment	.79	(1,317)
8. Freedom of speech	.75	(1,331)
9. Government involvement in education	.73	(1,337)
10. Shipment of military supplies to S.E.A.	.72	(1,305)
11. Law and order	.70	(1,327)
12. College open-admissions	.70	(1,327)
13. Perception of blacks' status mobility	.52	(1,383)

*Percentages can be found in Table 28.

the explanatory power of variables. Gamma is rather strongly influenced by clustering of data. As I shall indicate, this clustering is especially prominent in the liberalism of the N.D.C.

TABLE 26

VARIANCE IN LIBERALISM EXPLAINED BY REFORM MEMBERSHIP (ETA^2)

Issue	Eta^2	N
Subjective liberalism		
1. Self-perception as a liberal	.39	(1,311)
New Deal-economic liberalism		
2. Government involvement in employment	.10	(1,317)
3. Government involvement in education	.07	(1,337)
4. Government involvement in housing	.09	(1,330)
Welfare and racial issues		
5. Law and order	.27	(1,302)
6. Government solutions to job inequities of blacks	.19	(1,295)
7. Perception of blacks' status mobility	.10	(1,383)
8. College open-admissions	.24	(1,327)
Southeast Asian conflict		
9. Vietnam withdrawal	.21	(1,301)
10. Shipment of military supplies to S.E.A.	.18	(1,305)
11. Troop intervention in S.E.A.	.15	(1,032)
Procedural issues		
12. Rights of peaceful demonstrators	.30	(1,363)
13. Freedom of speech	.32	(1,331)

A slightly modified picture is presented by the amount of variance in liberalism explained by N.D.C. membership in Table 26. The economic liberal issues provide fewer distinctions than do the procedural civil-liberty issues, just as hypothesized. Even more important is the self-perception that the reformer has of himself as a liberal. His subjective liberalism produces greater differences between himself and the professional than do any of the objective issues.

Where racial issues, such as black job inequities or perceptions of black status mobility, are described in the traditional liberal language, reformers and regulars do not differ that much from each other, according to the amount of variance explained. Yet in the more recent racial issues implicit in law and order or college open-admissions, knowledge of N.D.C. membership is quite helpful in understanding these differences.

It is interesting to note that by 1970, when this study was completed, Vietnam, while explaining twenty percent of the variance between regulars and reformers, seems to have created a relatively similar reaction among both groups. It is obviously not the divisive force the Southeast Asian issue may have been when members of the N.D.C. first began their activities in the 1968 presidential primaries. Substantial nubmers of regulars also rejected that policy, according to this correlation. The percentages might clarify this picture further.

In this discussion of liberalism one might overlook the fact that while regulars may not be strong liberals, they are by no means all conservatives. On the self-perception ranking only seven percent of them claim to be much more conservative than the mainstream of the Democratic Party, while 25.6 percent admit to being slightly more conservative than other Democrats. Similar evidence is reflected in objective liberalism, except for the New Deal issues. Only 8.3 percent sought increased military intervention in Vietnam, 24.6 percent approved of all available force to resolve problems created by riots, 20.7 percent strongly disapproved of open admissions, and 9.5 percent strongly disapproved of peaceful demonstrators. These examples help illustrate the regulars' issue orientation. It surely is not conservative.

C. Intensity

After the analysis above, which made use of questions exactly as they were answered in the questionnaire, the responses were then dichotomized and coded to compare extreme liberals — those

TABLE 27

REFORMERS AND REGULARS SELECTING
MOST LIBERAL ISSUE RESPONSES

Issue	Regular %	Differences between reg. and ref. %	Reformer %	N
Subjective liberalism				
1. Degree of self-perceived liberalism	14.2	58.1	72.3	(1,311)
New Deal-economic issues				
2. Government involvement in housing	76.8	22.2	99.0	(1,330)
3. Government involvement in employment	70.3	25.1	95.4	(1,317)
4. Government involvement in education	77.1	18.5	95.6	(1,337)
Great Society: Welfare and racial issues				
5. Law and order	28.8	37.9	66.7	(1,302)
6. Government solve job inequities of blacks	54.2	42.1	96.3	(1,295)
7. Perception of blacks' status mobility	7.4	12.3	19.7	(1,383)
8. College open-admissions	11.9	33.4	45.3	(1,327)
Southeast Asian conflict				
9. Vietnam withdrawal	37.7	53.4	91.1	(1,301)
10. Further S.E.A. troop intervention	67.6	30.3	97.9	(1,032)
11. Shipment of military supplies to S.E.A.	38.5	46.2	84.7	(1,305)
Procedural issues				
12. Rights of peaceful demonstrators	24.8	55.6	80.4	(1,363)
13. Freedom of speech	10.4	35.7	46.1	(1,331)

who selected the most liberal response possible — with all others. In this redefinition of the issue variables, one must be extremely liberal to "count" as a liberal. The evidence of percentages helps to describe the range and concentration of liberal responses that may not have been visible through the gamma and eta correlations. These percentages are not completely comparable, since some questions permitted a choice between three answers, while others offered a selection among five or seven. In any case, Table 27 indicates a remarkable difference between strength or intensity of liberal attitudes for regulars compared with reformers. Not only does the distribution of liberalism vary, but it is also concentrated in the most strongly liberal cells for the N.D.C.

The first detailed conclusion that can be drawn from Table 27 is that, except for the "red flag" offered by the Vietnam War issue, both regulars and reformers are most liberal on the issues that pertain to federal involvement in the economy. While reformers are more liberal than regulars on the New Deal-economic issues, the percentage differences between the groups on liberal responses is not noticeably less than on any other, except for the general unwillingness to commit further military troops to Southeast Asia and a belief that mobility of blacks has occurred. Reformers might be more liberal than regulars on traditional as well as contemporary issues, but in these areas, the differences between the groups appear to be less, thus supporting the eta statistic, which dealt with the responses in their unrevised form.

An interesting issue that seems to indicate less intense distinctions between regulars and reformers is the question of military intervention as a future American policy in Southeast Asia. Strong differences between the groups of activists exist over immediate withdrawal, much in keeping with all expectations. Yet even the regulars think that the lesson learned from the present venture should lead to cautious behavior in the future. This prudence applies only to the commitment of troops, however, because clear conflict exists between these Democrats on the decision to ship military supplies to that area. Almost all the reformers endorse immediate withdrawal as well as reject any form of military supplies or troop support for Southeast Asia. Compare this with a little over one-third of the regulars who endorse such positions and one's awareness of the chasm on issues that exists between the two groups is further reinforced. The correlation ratio masked the importance of Vietnam as a continuing issue.

Great schisms also exist between the two groups on racial issues, whether on overt programs such as the government insuring job equality or on covert ones in the case of law and order and open admissions. Once again, almost all the reformers, 96.3 percent, endorse federal government resolution of job inequities, compared with 54.2 percent of the regulars. While the open racial issues illustrate greater discrepancies between those who espouse the most liberal point of view, in each group, law and order indicates almost as much of a division, with about one-fourth of the regulars compared with two-thirds of the reformers selecting the most liberal choice. Reformers may be less universally liberal on the issue of law and order than they are on federal involvement to solve job inequities due to race, but these activists are still remarkably far apart from the regulars.

When one examines the question of college open-admissions, which hits closer to home, the education of one's children, the reformers seem less willing to espouse the most liberal possibility (only 45.3 percent did). But if one, once again, compares the two groups of Democrats, the differences between these activists remain marked with a spread between the groups of 33.4 percent.

Even controlling for age makes no difference for reformers, while it does for regulars. Thus older professionals, who are likely to have college-age children, are even less likely to support open admission than are younger regulars. Reformers remain liberal, even when self-interest may be involved.

Since procedural questions involving civil liberties are expected to be primary for the reformer, but rather unimportant for the regulars, it is certainly in keeping with this hypothesis that only 24.8 percent of the regulars check the most liberal attitude in support of legal and peaceful demonstrators. Notice, on the other hand, the remarkably large percentage of reformers (80.4 percent) who agree strongly with the rights of these activists.

The second question involving civil liberties, freedom of speech, tapped the rights of militants to be heard in the public schools. Here, as in the other question about schools (open-admission programs), reformers are considerably less liberal than they are on any other issue. This decrease in liberalism, however, is accompanied by considerable variation between both regulars and reformers. While only 46.1 percent of the N.D.C. strongly support the right of free speech for unpopular groups in the public schools, this percentage is still 35.7 percent above the regulars.

Another question that deals with procedural liberalism indirectly should be introduced as evidence for this extraordinary liberal orientation of the reformer. While these newcomers are often seen in terms of the support they verbalize for participatory politics with a vengeance, they are also characterized as elitists.[38] This is to say they idealize participatory democracy, but they rather look down upon the values and interests espoused by the "lower orders." My findings do not sustain this contention. In fact, one should recall that the regular is more likely to agree with the statement that few people know what is in their own best interest than is the reformer (gamma = -.32). The reformer praises mass participation in theory as well as in practice.

In concluding the examination of the individual issues for both groups, it is important to emphasize that all issues illustrate vast and fundamental variations between regulars and reformers. Whether one looks at the gamma or eta or at the recorded percentages for those who espouse only the most liberal position, one must conclude that reformers are much more liberal than regulars. This is not to imply that regulars are conservatives, since the data would not support such a claim for most of the issues, but rather that the distinctions within the categories of liberalism are very great, just as proposed earlier.

Nothing points this up more directly than the question that deals with self-perceived liberalism. The responses here illustrate the greatest percentage difference between these activists of any of the issues. Seventy-two percent of the reformers claim to be much more liberal than the mainstream of the Democratic Party, while only fourteen percent of the regulars do. The contrast between them, fifty-eight percent, is greater than any of the other issue differences. Not only are reformers much more liberal than regulars on the policies they support, but they also *think* they are more liberal than they may, in fact, be when one looks at their actual opinions.

This, of course, raises the question of how regulars and reformers define their liberalism. It is only possible to speculate about the perceptions of each group. While reformers seem to be intensely liberal on a whole range of policies, perhaps some issues are less important than others. And for the professional politician one wonders whether his moderate liberalism is more likely to be described through — and only through — such older issues as government intervention in the economy. One way to approach this possibility might be to understand the issues (objective liberalism) that correlate most effectively with the question of self-perceived liberalism (subjective liberalism). This correlation provides some interesting results, apparent in Table 28.

There is some support for the previous contention that regulars represent a more traditional liberalism. While the correlations

TABLE 28

REFORMERS AND REGULARS SELECTING MOST-LIBERAL RESPONSES FOR BOTH OBJECTIVE AND SUBJECTIVE LIBERALSM (GAMMA CORRELATIONS)

| Issue | Percent both objective and subjective liberals | | | |
| | Reformers (N = 633) | | Regulars (N = 770) | |
	Percent	Gamma	Percent	Gamma
New Deal Issues				
1. Government involvement in housing	71.5	.46	13.7	.45
2. Government involvement in employment	70.3	.51	12.7	.38
3. Government involvement in education	69.7	.39	13.5	.47
Welfare and racial issues				
4. Law and order	54.9	.58	8.5	.43
5. Government solve job inequities of blacks	71.1	.45	12.1	.40
6. Perception of blacks' status mobility	17.1	.39	1.7	.24
7. College open-admissions	37.7	.45	4.7	.37
Southeast Asian conflict				
8. Vietnam withdrawal	69.0	.68	11.9	.43
9. Further S.E.A. troop intervention	70.5	.54	13.7	.36
10. Shipment of military supplies to S.E.A.	65.8	.62	10.4	.32
Procedural issues				
11. Rights of peaceful demonstrators	62.9	.52	9.3	.42
12. Freedom of speech	38.2	.34	4.5	.42

are not high between subjective liberalism and specific issues, the strongest relationship exists between self-perception and the New Deal issues of government involvement in housing and education. Since the correlations are not very different between self-defined liberalism and immediate withdrawal from Vietnam or law and order or civil libertarian issues, it would be difficult to conclude that liberalism has one specific connotation for regular Democrats. The percentages support this conclusion.

Reformers, on the other hand, indicate that their liberalism may be defined more strongly and clearly in terms of recent issues. Vietnam and law and order stand out through the gamma as important, but to a lesser extent so do the rights of demonstrators and the need for federal solutions to unemployment. In fact, the percentages could support the same conclusion for insurgents as for regulars. It would be difficult to conclude that liberalism has one specific connotation for the reform Democrat. Yet the subjective liberalism of the reformer is related to a wide variety of issues, and while the liberalism of the regular also has no one issue equivalent, this orientation for the professional appears less closely tied to the strong commitments for the N.D.C. activist. Liberalism has no one definition according to individual perceptions in either group. Yet strength of liberalism related to subjective orientations does vary tremendously between reformers and regulars.

The intensity with which the regular defines his liberalism in actual issues correlated with this self-perception is much weaker than the same relationship for the reformer. The highest correlation is .47 for the regular and .68 for the reformer. Whether or not this intense liberalism on many issues is part of the picture of a constrained liberal will have to wait until the analysis of ideology is presented. Certainly the higher correlations indicate a greater self-consciousness of the N.D.C. member as to his own political philosophy.

While intensity of political philosophy does not prove strong issue-oriented politics, there is some indirect support for the relative lack of issue salience among professional politicians whose moderation is evident. One can find a higher proportion of regulars compared to reformers who did not answer the questions related to issues or selected the neutral position,[39] "depends on circumstances," where it was offered. On the question relating to law and order, about eleven percent of the regulars, compared with three percent of the reformers, chose not to answer. A similar pattern is evident in relation to Vietnam. Since the percentages are so much alike, one can simply note that the issue of government involvement in employment, while relating a similar picture (approximately eight percent nonresponse for regulars, five percent for the reformers) might also support the historical resolution of different issues. Regulars are less likely to avoid questions about traditional issues to which they may be more strongly tied — and perhaps knowledgeable — than they are about the more recent proposals, which may be less salient and rather confusing to them. These fresher issues, such as procedural ones, plus open admissions permitted a neutral response in the questionnaire and did evoke it rather distinctly.

The regular's neutral answers are much more apparent on two of the three issues where they were possible, although on the third, free speech, the difference between the groups is minimal. Table 29 presents the information. While these findings are only suggestive, they are related to previously confirmed hypotheses about the issue-oriented motives of the reformer. Where issues are salient, opinions are evident also — especially in political organizations.

TABLE 29

NEUTRAL RESPONSES FOR REFORMERS AND REGULARS ON THREE ISSUES

	Neutral response	Reformers	N	Regulars	N
		%		%	
1.	Open admission	25.8	(158)	41.3	(295)
2.	Right to demonstrate	5.4	(34)	34.6	(256)
3.	Free speech	25.3	(157)	27.8	(198)

In analyzing the findings on liberalism, one might suggest that the intense and almost universal liberalism of the reformer sheds some light on the qualitative aspects of his purposive incentives. This quality is summarized by creating an intense liberalism scale.[46] Summing together each liberal response for eleven of the issues, one can describe only 15.5 percent of the regulars as intense liberals on eight or more of the questions. In sharp contrast, 72.9 percent of the N.D.C. can meet such stringent criteria. Intense liberalism on such a wide range of issues might help to explain why the purposive orientation of the reformer has been maintained over time. Such extreme opinions would have very different implications for an individual who claims that his motivations are purposive than for one whose issues arouse moderate feelings.

It might be early to draw this conclusion from the data presented, since I have separated motivations from the qualitative aspects of the purposive incentives in the presentation so far. Yet it is useful to remember that the relationship between motivations and both liberalism and ideology is an important facet of any discussion of purposive reformers. I shall return to this point later.

To draw together the analyses of this chapter is also to disprove some of the hypotheses in a direction that only reinforces the general argument of this study. The extreme liberalism of the reformer does not disappear when one examines the older substantive issues of the New Deal. It remains as a distinction between the insurgent and the regular (although to a lesser degree) on all procedural and substantive issues, whether domestic or foreign policy. Perceiving himself as liberal, the N.D.C. member confirms not only that hypothesis, but the one that ties liberalism to progress and change.

All these findings are simplified by the discovery of such intense and overwhelming liberalism that one wonders if this is not exactly what is meant by the concept *ideology*.

It might be that the liberal dynamic that developed and was reinterpreted represents an ideological commitment for those whose lives are dedicated to its possibilities. The N.D.C. activist's liberalism is one of fundamentals as well as specific interpretations. Open to change, dedicated to the expansion of opportunity for greater numbers — this would be the bond to the liberalism of Locke. Not merely accepting, but rather anticipating positive government programs — this would be the tie to the liberalism of Dewey. The N.D.C. took certain aspects of that varied and complex tradition, coordinating Locke and Dewey, but avoiding Sumner.

Notes to Chapter 7

1. Bowman and Boynton, "Activities and Role Definitions," p. 126.
2. Marvick and Nixon, "Recruitment Contrasts," in Marvick, p. 211.

3. Eldersveld, *Political Parties*, p. 179.

4. Ibid., pp. 183-90.

5. Converse, "Nature of Belief Systems," in Apter, p. 207.

6. Ibid., p. 225.

7. Hofstetter, "Organizational Activists," p. 249.

8. Conway and Feigert, "Motivation, Incentive Systems," p. 1,165.

9. Apter, "Introduction: Ideology and Discontent," in Apter, pp. 16-17.

10. Louis Hartz, *The Liberal Tradition in America: An Interpretation of American Political Thought Since the Revolution*, (New York: Harvest Book, Harcourt, Brace & World, Inc., 1955).

11. John Locke, *The Second Treatise of Government*, ed. with an Introduction by Thomas P. Peardon (New York: Liberal Arts Press, 1952).

12. Kenneth R. Minogue, *The Liberal Mind* (New York: Vintage Books, Random House, 1963), p. 65.

13. Alan Pendleton Grimes, *American Political Thought*, rev. ed. (New York: Holt, Rinehart and Winston, Inc., 1960), pp. 302-309.

14. Thomas Hill Green, *Lectures on the Principles of Political Obilgation,* in *Works of Thomas Hill Green*, vol. 2: *Philosophical Works*, ed. R. L. Nettleship (London: Longmans, Green, and Co., 1906); John Dewey, *Characters and Events*, vol. 2 (New York: Henry Holt and Company, 1929).

15. Green, *"Lectures,"* in Green, *Works*, p. 349.

16. John Dewey, "The Future of Liberalism," in *New Deal Thought*, ed. Howard Zinn, American Heritage Series (Indianapolis: Bobbs-Merrill Company, Inc., 1966), p. 31.

17. Grimes, *American Political Thought*, chap. 17.

18. Wilson, *Amateur Democrat*, p. 133.

19. This distinction between subjective and objective liberal classifications has been used rather widely. For one of the more recent applications, *see* Jeff Fishel, *Party and Opposition: Congressional Challengers in American Politics* (New York: David McKay Company, Inc., 1973), pp. 66-72.

20. Zinn, Introduction, *New Deal Thought*, p. 18.

21. Thurman W. Arnold, *The Folklore of Capitalism* (New Haven, Conn.: Yale University Press, 1937), p. 87.

22. Daniel Bell, *The End of Ideology: On the Exhaustion of Political Ideas in the Fifties* (Glencoe, Ill.: Free Press, 1960), and Lipset, *Political Man*, pp. 339-456, are probably the best known. *See also* Rober E. Lane, "The Decline of Politics and Ideology in a Knoweldgeable Society," *American Sociological Review*, 31 (October 1966): 649-62.

23. McClosky, et al., "Issue Conflict and Consensus," pp. 406-427.

24. Gerald M. Pomper, "From Confusion to Clarity: Issues and American Voters, 1956-1968," *American Political Science Review* 66 (June 1972): 415-28. *See also* other articles and comments in the same issue by Richard W. Boyd, Richard A. Brody and Benjamin I. Page, John Kessel, Gerald Pomper, and Richard Boyd.

25. Campbell, et al., *The American Voter*, chap. 10. *See also* V. O. Key, Jr., *Public Opinion and American Democracy* (New York: Alfred A. Knopf, 1961). pp. 153-81.

26. Converse, "Nature of Belief Systems," in Apter, p. 213; McClosky, "Consensus and Ideology," pp. 372-73.

27. Converse, "Nature of Belief Systems," in Apter, p. 213.

28. Wilson, *Amateur Democrat*, pp. 180-88.

29. Michels, *Political Parties*, pp. 22, 35.

30. Wilson, *Amateur Democrat*, pp. 180-88.

31. *Mandate for Reform: A Report of the Commission on Party Structure and*

Delegate Selection to the Democratic National Committee, George McGovern, chairman (Washington, D.C.: The Commission on Party Structure and Delegate Selection, Democratic National Committee, 1970).

32. McClosky, et al., "Issue Conflict and Consensus," pp. 406-427.

33. Ibid.; *see also* Lloyd A. Free and Hadley Cantril, *The Political Beliefs of Americans: A Study of Public Opinion* (New York: Clarion Books, Simon and Schuster, 1968).

34. Soule and Clarke, "Amateurs and Professionals," pp. 894-95; Survey Research Center, University of Michigan, cited in Flanigan, *Political Behavior of the American Electorate*, p. 87.

35. Soule and Clarke, "Amateurs and Professionals," p. 895.

36. For exact wording, *see* Appendix A, questions 40, 43-51.

37. Wilson, *Amateur Democrat*, p. 2.

38. Wilson, *Amateur Democrat*, pp. 9, 269, 273.

39. Refer to Appendix A, questions 40, 43-51, to understand how the possible nonresponse or neutral responses varied in the policy questions.

40. In creating the scale, I omitted the questions on subjective liberalism and perception of black mobility, because they seemed less descriptive of specific policies and programs.

8

Ideology:
Constrained Issues
and Restrained Parties

The conclusions reached in the previous chapter on liberalism might lead one to infer that reformers are so liberal they are ideologues. In distinguishing between these two traits, I have not argued that "never the twain shall meet." Yet the focus upon direction and intensity of political attitudes, through the examination of liberalism, is still separated from ideology, which concerns not the direction, but rather the coherence and interrelationships between various issues. This constraint can be either liberal, moderate, or conservative. The only requirement for issue constraint is that an individual's position on one issue be predicted from his stand on another. [1]

This very specific definition of ideology does not require intensity of opinion, only consistency. Why then should one expect intense liberals to be ideologues? Such a likelihood is probable merely from the large percentage of liberals found. So few reformers espouse any other positions that the coherence of their attitudes is predictable from the information gathered so far.

But this expectation is also predicated upon another aspect of ideology that is not articulated in the operational definitions of this study. Intensity connotes passion. The intensity of the reformers' liberalism leads one to expect emotional investment in political activity. Such an explanation relates to the previous findings about purposive incentives. The committed reformer is fulfilled by the political vocation. At the time it seemed a bit unclear as to why purposive motivations might lead to increased activity in the N.D.C. but not the regular organization. I directed my attention to the effects of organizational socialization. But now such explanations can be complemented by the discovery of intensity or "passion" in the reform group. This very description of emotion, in fact, is often used in the discussion of ideology.[2] While that epithet is usually pejorative, the quality of psychological commitment attached to ideological orientations seems quite clear.

The emotional dedication to a set of principles is neither in itself praiseworthy nor reprehensible. Nor, as Clifford Geertz and Joseph LaPalombara point out, can such intensity be judged as nonscientific, mere distortions, or sheer dogmatism without careful analysis.[3] Thus ideology imputes a world view, which not only describes present reality, but proffers future interpretations and remedies for social ills as well. This broad description of ideology as a "weltanschauung" seems to apply to widely diverse conceptions of reality. The end-of-ideology school tends to relate such concepts of ideology only to Marxist and socialist revisionism, which they declare dead and buried by technology and affluence.[4] Yet Apter has indicated that science is itself an ideology, since it provides its adherents with underlying assumptions about society, as well as norms for leading the good scientific life.[5]

While "ideology and outrage"[6] have clear affinities, the concept of constraint may be unable to deal directly with this aspect of ideology. Only because the strength and clustering of liberalism is so obvious in the N.D.C. can one suggest the homogeneity of both facets of ideology in this analysis. Thus not only constraint, but also intensity of issue preferences contribute to the suggestion that the N.D.C. member is an ideologue in this broader sense. The intensity of programmatic supports along a coherent liberal dimension is coordinated with another factor in ideological orientations: "commitment to action."[7] Since this study is of activists, their reason and emotions are incorporated in a dedication to implement policies. Harnessing the liberal tradition of reason to a deep concern about social and economic injustice, the N.D.C. politico may produce an ideological portrait of the modern reformer.

The rhetoric of the N.D.C. is quite indicative of this approach:

> We seek to transform the Democratic Party into a means of basic change by adopting the tactic of creative independence of the organization and its candidates.

We will formulate criteria by which to test Democratic aspirants for office. Does the candidate oppose the foul, brutalizing, pointless war in Vietnam? Does he seek dramatic remedies for the foul, brutalizing, pointless institutions of racism and economic deprevations. . . . Does he favor thoroughgoing party reform? Does he favor reordering national priorities, relentless scrutiny and paring of Pentagon demands? Is his record proof of the integrity of his rhetoric? And so on.

Suppose a candidate fails these tests, . . . we will not shy from painful, divisive decisions. . . . We will not be locked into a strategy of loyalty to a party that betrays our deepest moral commitments.

Our power lies in our potential ability to coalesce a massive constituency of the oppressed with a massive constituency of conscience. America's poor, its racial minorities, its very young and very old have always suffered tokenism. By joining their strength to that growing segment of mainstream Americans who are sick of being manipulated and abused because they dare to demand redemption of the promise of American life, we can build a force capable of effectively moving the country toward a dramatically different and better future.[8]

This emotional attachment may be obscured by the approach taken in this study, but it does underlie the belief system of the reformer. Thus in opting for Converse's description of ideology as a belief system in which the various elements are bound together, that is, constrained,[9] it is important to understand that this emotional aspect of ideology is ignored.

Aware that one slights the passion of the reformer, another problem involves possible distortions for the regular. In constructing this measure of ideology, one assumes that anyone who is an ideologue relates his ideas to each other in some consistently conservative or liberal fashion. It is conceivable, however, that an ideologue compartmentalizes certain issues as more salient than others in his belief system. Another potential conflict might be in an individual's self-defined brand of ideology, in which he mixes supposedly liberal and conservative elements together in a way that makes complete sense to him.

Converse's research is reassuring on these points. He did not find any other methods of evaluating political objects and realities, even when respondents were offered open-ended questions: "We did not require that this dimension be the liberal-conservative continuum itself [in order to qualify a respondent as ideologue], but it was almost the only dimension of the sort that occurred empirically."[10]

This issue-ideology must be translated into strategies and tactics in the politician's world. After all, an activist is forced to use his conception of reality in his attempts to make it come closer to his ideal. The strategy and tactic chosen are related to his belief in the best way to achieve these reforms.

Thus it is conceivable that even an intense liberal may see the political universe in rather pragmatic electoral terms. Concerned about issues, he may not necessarily view the party as a mechanism for ideological positions. "After all," he might reason, "in order to implement these policy commitments, I've got to win elections. This might require me to make certain compromises. Yet without this acceptance of reality, I'll never implement any of the issues about which I care so deeply." This possibility will be examined in the context of party ideology.

The reformer gives some evidence for this possible combination of motivations, liberalism, and ideology. The chapters on motivation illustrated this point for the N.D.C. member who sought only nondivisible, tangible benefits. To this activist, electoral roles were even more important than to the nonissue-oriented reformer, while the reverse finding was evident for the regular. One found, in fact, that the professional's purposive orientation was negatively linked to electoral role perceptions.

With these findings in mind, one should approach the series of variables that tap ideology with some care. This analysis involves two distinct components. One is the extent to which an activist holds ideological expectations of the party system, that is, his normative party orientation. The other accepts Converse's notion of issue constraint. The ideologue's political field is expected to exhibit marked interrelatedness of similar positions within an issue area.

I go beyond even this for my reformers and expect there to be strong correlations between issue areas, as well as within certain general topics. This anticipation for reformers is unlike the pattern of constraint expected for the regulars, who may illustrate linkages within categories, especially in the New Deal-economic programs. Yet the professionals are unlikely to illustrate important interarea correlations.

These two different aspects of ideology are both essential. In examining only issue positions, one might obscure an individual's perception of issues as important or irrelevant political variables. As stressed above, it seemed a somewhat tenuous assumption that internal constraint automatically combines with an intense concern for issues. A "constrained liberal" or a "constrained conservative" might hypothetically still rank issues rather low in terms of his own political motivations. And a "nonconstrained liberal," that is, a pragmatist whose position on one issue can not be predicted from a knowledge of his position on any other, might evaluate certain issues as immensely salient in his rationale for political participation. The strength or weakness of an individual's ideological views are not self-evident from the fact that all his positions seem to cohere in a certain direction. In fact, these are two distinct aspects of my operational concepts of ideology. For this reason, constraint must be supplemented by an ideological view of the party system to develop a more accurate reading of ideology. It is to this party ideology, as opposed to individual ideology as measured by constraint among issues, that I now turn.

This analysis is derived from a scale that distributes regulars and reformers according to their ideological expectations about political parties.[11] The scale, described as one tapping ideological or pragmatic orientations, has been discussed in an earlier chapter.

Such words and phrases as *compromise, reconciliation of differing interests,* should be anathemas to the ideologue who will emphasize *sticking to principles* above all else. As previous hypotheses suggested, one anticipates that reformers will emphasize ideological responses, while regulars will lean toward the pragmatic end of the scale.

The responses to these questions about pragmatic orientation toward party did not reveal as much variation between regulars and reformers as suggested. Forty-one percent of the regulars and 46 percent of the reformers agreed strongly that a party "should stand fast to its goals and principles" even if this meant losing votes (gamma = .08). Thirty-eight percent of the professionals agreed (but not strongly), compared with similar proportions for reformers, 36.3 percent. It would seem that this question might have been too general to do more than elicit the symbolic rhetoric about high principles that have become de rigueur for all politicians.

When asked about compromise through such statements as: "politics . . . is more a matter of getting the best possible out of a given situation . . . ," almost 15 percent of the regulars but 7.4 percent of the reformers agreed strongly (gamma = -.24). Equal percentages, slightly more than 28 percent in both groups, admitted that they agreed with the question, although moderately.

The findings are in the expected direction, for willingness to compromise is inversely related to reform-group membership.

A good ideologue is one who is less willing to settle for getting the best possible in any circumstances. While N.D.C. members do not appear to be inherently ideological from this question, they certainly are distinct from regulars.

Probably the most crucial question deals with the pluralist approach to interest-group bargaining versus the ideological position of taking clear stands on issues. Here, 31.6 percent of the reformers disagree strongly that the party should reconcile interests. Only 14.6 percent of the professionals disagree strongly with this position (gamma = -.38). Even more interesting, only 18.8 percent of the reformers, compared with 35 percent of the regulars, could agree with the statement to any degree. The reformer perceives the party as a normative vehicle for issues, while the regular leans more toward the interest-group bargaining model in which process and accommodation reign supreme.

Purity of motivation — supporting the right policy for the right reason, not merely for electoral expediency — is associated with ideological politics. Reformers are more likely to concur that "it is not important to agree with a person's reasons for supporting policies, as long as he supports the right policies." But since 16.9 percent of the regulars, compared with 8.2 percent of the reformers, agree strongly with this statement (and almost 35 percent of both groups agree moderately), the differences between the groups do not seem impressive (gamma = -.24).

The process of determining outcomes and the accommodation of interests predominate for the regular, while the most perfect solution, based upon rational decision making and efficient goals, is more important to the reformer. This distinction is so reminiscent of the contrast between locals and cosmopolitans, presented in the chapters on demographic variables, that it is useful to point out the similarities. An activist whose orientation toward politics has a cosmopolitan flare would, of course, reflect this in his political opinions. Thus party ideology may reflect some of the discoveries made earlier about the socialization experiences of the regular and reformer. In applying their cosmopolitanism, the reformer may project a different view of the appropriate role of the political party, compared to the local regular.

A simple measure combining three of the four items was designed to create a party-ideology scale.[12] With the responses to the three questions averaged together, I discovered a moderate relationship between support for ideological parties and N.D.C.

membership (gamma = .38). In this analysis 23.5 percent of the regulars, compared with 40.5 percent of the reformers, can be considered ideologues.

While the differences between regulars and reformers do not come near the strength evident in the liberal-policy commitments of each group, there does appear to be a distinction in the values each organization holds toward political compromise and accommodation of varying points of view. Yet, one could not conclude that these 1968 reformers represent a strongly dogmatic view of the political party's role.

The intensity of the reformer's liberalism far outweighs his expectations of ideological purity from his party. One can only speculate on the reasons for this discovery. Perhaps the pervasiveness of pluralist values as an ideal for American parties even influences reformers. There are other possibilities.

While these questions have been used with success in Germany and Israel, they may be culturally inapplicable to a political system that idealizes compromise of disparate interests to the degree found in the United States.[13]

Another possibility is that while the rhetoric of compromise might influence the reformer, a similar emphasis upon "ideals" and "principles" might bias the responses of pragmatic politicians. In this context, a political actor might describe his actions in terms of high principles, while an outside observer might note the tremendous amount of compromise and log-rolling that actually ensues.

There is another reason why the questions may have elicited symbolic rhetoric from the regular. Since issues seemed to be of much less relevance to him as a motivating force, his support for a party of principles might be to the rather vague and general principles that any program or proposal could easily acommodate.

While all these explanations for the relative weakness of party ideologies in distinguishing reformers from regulars may be relevant, another explanation seems to dominate many of the earlier findings. The reformer who has turned to the ballot, as he so evidently has in both his role perceptions and tasks performed, is rather unlikely to take rigid positions in electoral politics. Compromise, bargaining, trading-off advantages may be as much a part of the insurgent's political repertoire as it is of the professional.

This manipulation of electoral activity also conforms to what was suggested about the technical proficiency of the cosmopolitan activist. Seeing his world in terms of skills that can be applied to control and regulate his society, contesting primaries may provide the very arena for application of his techniques. Not only does this explanation of the rather weak party ideology discovered in the N.D.C. add to one's understanding of both socialization and motivational discoveries, but it also contributes to an expansion of his philosophical roots in the liberal tradition. The cosmopolitan technician with a strong attachment to progress and reform of social institutions through the application of reason also reflects the pragmatic liberalism of John Dewey. Thus, rather than the disappointment lack of party ideology might have produced, it seems instead to draw many of the findings into greater coherence.

Before downgrading the ideological-party orientation of the reformer too completely, one might still note that 40 percent of them can be characterized as party ideologues, compared with only 23 percent of the professionals. In keeping with this ideological purity, the reformer is much more likely to vote outside the Democratic Party structure than is the regular. In higher-level elected offices, 31.1 percent of the regulars admit to voting against their party, compared with 63 percent of the reformers (gama = .58, illustrating a negative relationship between reformed membership and party cohesion).

Party primaries might not be the place to describe ideological fervor, but certainly general elections, when all good Democrats support their candidate, are more proof of the pragmatic bent of the loyal party activist. This behavior is evident in the 1968 presidential election, also. While 64.1 percent of the N.D.C. supported Eugene McCarthy in the primary, compared with 10.4 percent of the regulars, 14.1 percent of the N.D.C. registered protest votes outside the two main contenders, Hubert Humphrey and Richard Nixon, in the general election.[14]

The protest vote is probably a much more issue-oriented act. One would expect such behavior of more ideologically motivated activists, who could not merely stay home from the polls. Still, in keeping with the rather modest ideology found in reformers, 73.9 percent of the N.D.C. did vote for Humphrey in 1968, while 91.1 percent of the regulars did so.

Party perceptions and voting actions illustrate the ways ideology can be implemented. If these differences were the only proof one could muster as to the ideological orientations of the reformer, one would have to conclude that he is a liberal, but not an ideologue. Yet there is the second component of ideology that I have proposed to examine: that of constrained liberalism. This concept does not deal with normative expectations of party behavior, but rather with individual orientations toward a wide-ranging liberalism.

These patterns are expected to illustrate much interrelationship both within and across issue areas. Regulars might exhibit this intraissue area constraint, but reformers will prove themselves constrained liberals also between issue clusters. Thus substantive and procedural issues will be correlated for reformers, compared with regulars. Within substantive subdivisions, moreover, foreign affairs and domestic issues will also be related for insurgents but not for professionals. Dissecting domestic policies further, one expects much constraint between New Deal-economic issues and racial questions for reformers, quite unlike regulars.

Previously, several relevant questions about ideology were analyzed. In the prior chapter, the liberalism of regulars and reformers contrasted quite strongly. The differences in intensity between the groups illustrated a clear and present dichotomy between the types of activists. Reformers were characterized as intensely liberal, while regulars were only moderately liberal in their positions.

In Table 27, the percentages who selected the most liberal replies to illustrate the range of responses were enumerated. Looking at that table again from the perspective of ideology, one notes that in eight of thirteen items over eighty percent of the reformers fall into the most liberal category. None of the regulars can meet this criterion, although for governmental solutions to housing and education problems, they do come close.

These percentages are so high for the reformers that the low variation (illustrated in Table 30) on many of the responses influences the correlational analyses. One might even raise the question of whether such issues as government involvement in housing, unemployment, education and job inequities for blacks, as well as solutions to the Southest Asian war and the rights of demonstrators are actually variables. Variables by definition vary. With the N.D.C., on the other hand, such overwhelmingly and universally liberal responses appear, that in certain issue areas the results may not be variables, but rather constants.

The data on constraint may support the likelihood that among reformers, issues are not variables, but rather constants. In separating N.D.C. members from regulars and correlating the issues, two at a time, one discovers support for my hypotheses. Table 31 examines constraint within issue areas. A further operational requirement will be the necessity for fifty percent of each group to maintain the most extreme liberal position on both issues compared in

TABLE 30

Standard Deviation In Liberal-Issue Responses For Reformers And Regulars

Issue	Reformers		Regulars	
	S.D.	N	S.D.	N
1. Subjective liberalism	.60	(600)	1.16	(711)
New Deal-economic issues				
2. Government involvement in housing	.28	(610)	1.12	(720)
3. Government involvement in employment	.49	(603)	1.22	(714)
4. Government involvement in education	.48	(612)	1.13	(725)
Great Society: Welfare and racial issues				
5. Law and order	.91	(615)	2.34	(687)
6. Government solve job inequities of blacks	.27	(589)	.90	(706)
7. Perception of blacks' status mobility	1.32	(628)	1.26	(758)
8. College open-admissions	.98	(612)	1.31	(715)
Southeast Asian conflict				
9. Vietnam withdrawal	.66	(606)	1.38	(695)
10. Further S.E.A. troop intervention	.72	(510)	2.68	(516)
11. Shipment of military supplies to S.E.A.	1.90	(608)	2.44	(697)
Procedural issues				
12. Rights of peaceful demonstrators	.62	(624)	1.22	(739)
13. Freedom of speech	.98	(620)	1.31	(711)

TABLE 31

INTRAISSUE-AREA CONSTRAINT FOR
REFORMERS AND REGULARS

Within issue areas	Percentage most liberal on both issues	
	Reformers	Regulars
New Deal-economic issues		
Government employment by government education	92.4*	60.8*
Government employment by government housing	94.5*	64.0*
Government education by government housing	95.2*	68.6*
Great Society: Welfare and racial issues		
Law and order by job inequities of blacks	65.5*	24.0
Law and order by open admissions	37.5	6.8
Job inequities of blacks by open admission	44.6	10.5
Southeast Asian conflict		
Vietnam withdrawal by S.E.A. military supplies	81.8*	27.1
Vietnam withdrawal by S.E.A. troops	89.3*	36.9
S.E.A. military supplies by S.E.A. troops	82.9*	33.4
Procedural issues		
Rights of demonstrators by free speech	42.7	8.9

*Those interrelationships where fifty percent of the group are extreme liberals on both issues.

order to be classified as a "constrained relationship." With this limiting criterion, the professional can be considered a constrained liberal only on New Deal issues, much as expected. Over sixty percent of them are most liberal on interrelationships within this category. Reformers, however, are not only constrained economic liberals, but exhibit another feature. Almost none of the N.D.C. present a nonideological picture on these New Deal issues, since over ninety percent exhibit such relationships here.

After this one category, New Deal economics, the regular falls by the wayside in other issue areas quite remarkably. Reformers, on the other hand, remain strongly constrained on all issues that involve the Southest Asian conflict. Certain racial issues are also related to each other. The law-and-order issue, a seven-point scale, required one to determine whether riots should be solved with either police solutions or through eliminating poverty. The "liberal" answer here would have included at least three points on that scale. Yet I have counted only the extreme liberal reply. Still, one discovers that 65.5 percent of all reformers support the most extreme response on both this question as well as the one on government programs to reform job inequities of blacks.

Compared to other responses, the N.D.C. was noticeably less liberal on the two questions that dealt with education: open admissions and free speech for militants to talk in the public schools. Thus, one finds little constraint between categories wherever these questions appear. Questions relating to schools, whether racial or civil liberties, seem to arouse distinctly different orientations from what one might expect.

Yet with these discrepancies, and leaving aside the New Deal-economic issues, the lowest percentage of reformers who are liberal on both issues within any area (37.5 percent for law and order and open admissions) is still higher than the highest percentages of regulars (36.9 percent support both immediate withdrawal from Vietnam and refusal to commit further troops to Southeast Asia).

With such low constraint for the regular within issue domains, it seems unlikely that he will illustrate constraint between issue areas. The orignal hypothesis that regulars would exhibit constraint within issue areas has not even been supported to any strong degree. Quite distinct from the pattern was that found for the reformer. Whether constraint across policy areas can be established for the N.D.C. member is yet to be explored.

Converse found among his elites the strongest yet only moderate ties within the New Deal areas of government intervention in employment, education, and housing. Federal support for an antidiscriminatory commission was less closely related to these other domestic policies. Foreign military aid was unrelated to these domestic issues, but foreign economic aid did seem to touch similar orientations toward education, housing, and fair employment to some degree.[14] Table 32 presents the interissue area relationships for reformers and regulars in this study.

TABLE 32

INTRAISSUE-AREA CONSTRAINT FOR REFORMERS AND REGULARS

Between issue areas	Percentages most liberal on both issues	
	Reformers	Regulars
New Deal and racial issues		
Employment by law and order	65.4*	26.5
Employment by jobs for blacks	92.4*	45.1
Employment by open admission	44.3	10.7
Education by law and order	65.6*	26.6
Education by jobs for blacks	92.4*	48.0
Education by open admission	43.7	11.4
Housing by law and order	66.9*	27.2
Housing by jobs for blacks	95.7*	48.6
Housing by open admission	44.9	11.0
Racial issues and Southeast Asian conflict		
Law and order by Vietnam	62.9*	17.8
Law and order by military supplies	59.7*	16.9
Law and order by troops	64.2*	23.9
Jobs for blacks by Vietnam	88.6*	26.9
Jobs for blacks by military supplies	82.4*	25.2
Jobs for blacks by troops	94.6*	42.2
Open admission by Vietnam	42.6	8.7
Open admission by military supplies	40.5	7.3
Open admission by troops	43.7	9.8

continued

TABLE 32 (continued)
INTRAISSUE-AREA CONSTRAINT FOR REFORMERS AND REGULARS

Between issue areas	Percentages most liberal on both issues	
	Reformers	Regulars
New Deal and Southeast Asian conflict		
Employment by Vietnam	87.2*	33.4
Employment by military supplies	81.5*	32.0
Employment by troops	93.6*	51.5*
Education by Vietnam	87.1*	33.8
Education by military supplies	81.1*	33.1
Education by troops	93.9*	56.3*
Housing by Vietnam	90.1*	34.9
Housing by military supplies	83.7*	33.2
Housing by troops	97.0*	56.6*
Procedural issues and New Deal		
Demonstrators by employment	78.0*	22.2
Demonstrators by education	77.5*	23.2
Demonstrators by housing	80.4*	23.4
Free speech by employment	45.0	9.6
Free speech by education	43.9	9.8
Free speech by housing	46.5	9.6
Procedural issues and racial issues		
Demonstrators by law and order	58.6*	14.5
Demonstrators by jobs for blacks	78.8*	22.5
Demonstrators by open admissions	41.9	8.0
Free speech by law and order	36.6	6.5
Free speech by jobs for blacks	45.4	9.3
Free speech by open admissions	27.4	3.5
Procedural issues and Southeast Asian conflict		
Demonstrators by Vietnam	75.4*	17.5
Demonstrators by military supplies	70.5*	15.8
Demonstrators by troops	79.5*	22.9
Free speech by Vietnam	43.7	8.5
Free speech by military supplies	41.2	7.2
Free speech by troops	47.5	9.7

*Those interrelationships where fifty percent of the group are extreme liberals.

Setting the same standards, that is, that a constrained relationship must place at least fifty percent of the activists in the most liberal category, one can find only three such pairs for the professionals. All relate economic issues to refusal to commit further troops to Vietnam. Thus for regulars, out of forty-five possible pairs of issues between issue areas, only three meet these standards. The reverse picture is highlighted by the data on the reformer . For these activists, twenty-nine out of forty-five possible pairs illustrate constraint between issue areas. This discovery is remarkably high. In describing Table 32, one can notice that the only pairs that do not illustrate constraint are those in which free speech or open admissions are involved. The regular can certainly be categorized as a pragmatist on the basis of this component of ideology. He does not relate his issue positions to each other in any systematic way. In fact, on the more recent issues, he exhibits even greater lack of constraint than on the traditional economic issues.

Not so for the reformer, who more aptly fits the picture of an ideological liberal. Not only the number of issues that interrelate make this obvious, but also the widely diverse kinds of issues that are correlated detail this picture. Foreign affairs, concerning the conflict in Southeast Asia, are completely integrated with domestic issues, whether of traditional New Deal or recent orientation. This finding is quite unique, for even the studies of political elites stress the segregation of foreign and domestic opinions — to some extent.[16]

There does seem to be a dilemma in this finding of ideological liberalism for the N.D.C. member. One must conclude that one of the original hypotheses is invalid. Intensely liberal and constrained across and within issue areas, the reformer does not approve an ideological version of party politics. If anything, the N.D.C. member appears to be a liberal ideologue, but not a party ideologue. Yet he will use his vote to express dissatisfaction with his party more often than the regular. These two components of ideology are rather distinct and provide quite different aspects of the portrait of the reformer.

This suggestion is confirmed by comparing ideologues and pragmatics on party orientation to constrained liberals for each group. While ideologues are more likely to be extremely liberal than are pragmatic politicos, the differences are remarkably slight. For regulars, being an ideologue makes one approximately ten percent more liberal on support for demonstrators and about seven percent more liberal in supporting government involvement in education. These are the highest variations evident for regulars. For reformers, ideological orientations make one approximately eleven percent more likely to be extremely liberal on law and order, approximately ten percent more liberal on open admission, and seven percent more liberal on subjective liberalism. Quite obviously, the effects of ideological party beliefs are weakly related to ideological issue constraint for both groups.

Perhaps this schism in ideological orientations for the reformer helps one understand my previous contention that the reformer, as evident in the N.D.C., seems quite different from his historical brethren. The validity of considering the N.D.C. activist an insurgent or reformer — and refusing to call him an amateur — is strengthened by the growing evidence of his electoral concerns.

These electoral orientations, exhibited in tasks performed, roles interpreted, and now through party ideology, lend further credence to the suggestion that a political shrewdness characterizes the new-style reformer, capable of directing his strong ideological liberalism into rather pragmatic channels.

The liberalism and constrained ideology of the reformer are the most outstanding findings of this study. The data available on this intense and constrained liberalism of the reformer are so distinct that they overwhelm all other demographic and motivational discoveries. If one were to stop here, it would be necessary to conclude that liberalism explains the difference between reformers and regulars. Certainly motivations, purposive though they might be, do not seem as important in this light. Surely demographic descriptions, cosmopolitan though they might appear, pale in significance, compared with such intense liberalism. Only content quality of these issue-oriented purposive incentives, that is, the liberal and ideological components, remain paramount. Yet I have not illustrated that status or cosmopolitan or purposive incentives are actually secondary to this ideological explanation. Perhaps demographic and motivational variables do explain intense and constrained liberalism. Perhaps these programmatic variables are merely a reflection of middle-class status or purposive incentives. In order to answer these questions, the next chapter will attempt to explore the relative weight of intense liberalism in exploring the differences between reformers and regulars.

Notes to Chapter 8

1. Converse, "Nature of Belief Systems," in Apter, p. 207.

2. Bell, *End of Ideology,* pp. 370-71; *see also* Clifford Geertz, "Ideology as a Cultural System," in *Ideology and Discontent,* ed. Apter, pp. 49-52.

3. Ibid., pp. 57-60; Joseph LaPalombara, "Decline of Ideology: A Dissent and an Interpretation," *American Political Science Review,* 60 (March 1966): 5-18.

4. Bell, *End of Ideology,* pp. 369-75; Lipset, *Political Man,* pp. 339-456.

5. David E. Apter, "Ideology and Discontent," in *Ideology and Discontent,* ed. Apter, pp. 30-34.

6. Ibid., p. 16.

7. James P. Young, *The Politics of Affluence: Ideology in the United States, Since World War II* (San Francisco: Chandler Publishing Company, 1968), p. 204.

8. Arnold Kaufman, "N.D.C. Statement of Political Purpose," in *National N.D.C. Newsletter,* November 1971, p. 5.

9. Converse, "Nature of Belief Systems," in Apter, p. 207.

10. Ibid., p. 126.

11. Wright, "Ideological-Pragmatic Orientations," pp. 381-402. For the specific wording, *see* Appendix A, questions 32-35.

12. The first question, 32, was removed, since it seemed to evoke rather rhetorical responses that almost all respondents supported.

13. Wright, "Ideological-Pragmatic Orientations," pp. 381-402; Gerald M. Pomper, "Ambition in Israel: A Comparative Extension of Theory and Data," *Western Political Quarterly* 27 (December 1975): 712-32.

14. Wallace received only one vote from the N.D.C. members and fourteen from regular Democrats.

15. Converse, "Nature of Belief Systems," in Apter, p. 228.

16. McClosky, et al., "Issues, Conflict and Consensus," pp. 406-427, Key, *Public Opinion and American Democracy,* pp. 153-81; Converse, "Nature of Belief Systems," in Apter, p. 228.

9

The Relative Importance of Demographic, Motivational, Liberal, and Ideological Factors

The characteristics of the reformers are important in assessing how and why he behaves as he does. Essentially, however, his behavior is the variable upon which one tends to focus. And yet here the reformer in role perception and tasks performed does not seem that different from the professional politician. Of course his political activity is directed toward different kinds of candidates, but this effort itself is rather surprising. Throughout past studies there have been expectations that reform orientation would lead to quite different electoral efforts. If the only distinction is in the kinds of candidates and issues found attractive, then it is important to delve back into those demographic, motivational, liberal, and ideological factors to describe what forces produce similar overt results. Is it the Catholic religion of the regular that explains his behavior? Is it the cosmopolitan or liberal leanings of the reformer that explain his actions? Neither a morning glory nor one repelled by electoral politics, the reformer more and more seems to copy the political chores of the regular.

Yet just as the description of past reformers does not quite fit my findings about the N.D.C., so does my research on the regular seem slightly out of joint with what one might expect. True, the regular illustrates lower status, local orientation, less liberal ideo-

logy, and less purposive motivation — compared to the N.D.C. activist — but he is surely not the activist rewarded by divisible benefits, whether of the tangible or intangible sort. Solidary goals
motivate him more easily than the reformer, but he also claims a
purposive incentive as initial and even continuing motivation.

His activism may outweigh that of the reformer in terms of
sheer continuity, but the chores he is willing to perform for his
party are no different. In fact, the reformer even more eagerly
accepts campaign-oriented tasks. Furthermore, unlike the patronage recipient, the present-day professional had few jobs to maintain his continuous activity for the party. His attachment sustained itself through an inherent party loyalty, which was influential as an initial motivating force. Yet, few divisible benefits
come his way, according to my findings. This is a far cry from the
regular strongly motivated and rewarded by his party.

In drawing conclusions from the preceding study, it would be
difficult to claim that the reformer has changed, without also
noting the variations apparent for the professional as well. The
trends noted in the first few chapters may explain the sources of
certain developments. Higher status of the electorate turn the ever-
shrinking patronage into a less and less attractive benefit of political participation. Increasing numbers of independent voters,
whose party loyalty can no longer be tapped automatically,[1]
help to clarify many of the patterns found among party regulars.

How does this contention of few patronage positions match
other data available?

The information on public employment in New Jersey is rather
scanty. It makes difficult a comparison of state data with my
findings. Yet it is noticeable that in 1966 48.4 percent of all full-
time state and local government employees were involved in
education.[2] Such occupations require skills. A job that results
in teaching can hardly be considered a patronage appointment.
Not only does education involve such a large slice of government
employment, but it is the most rapidly increasing of all the
functional areas, when compared to such divisions as police, sani-
tation, and public welfare.[3] One can not judge how many of
the jobs in public welfare might be patronage appointments from
this information. A case worker whose training in social work
makes him or her a professional might be quite different from the
clerk who works in the local welfare office. Yet even that clerk
may be a civil service appointee. These figures make any comparison inconclusive.

My study, though, indicates that few people hold government

jobs. If this reflects broader patterns in the state and nation, it is no wonder the reformer as activist is on the rise and the regular on the wane. The reformer had never sought divisible benefits. His energies were directed to the "cause." Participation for a worthy goal provided reward enough for him. The nondivisible benefit of policy promulgation satisfied the insurgent, because of the intensity with which he sought that goal. Thus, one could claim that it was not the purposive motivation that was primary to the reformer, but rather the way he defined these purposive incentives, that is, his liberalism and ideology.

It hardly seems any wonder, if patronage is dissipating, as I have found, that professional politicians should claim so few divisible rewards as incentives for continuing participation. Solidary rewards increase in importance, but can they encourage the same dedication and activity that divisible rewards had? Without the benefits of jobs or status, the fun of the game might not be enough to encourage massive efforts for the party.

These findings involve two distinct components that need further elaboration. The first question is: why does the extreme liberalism of the reformer now stand out in relation to the N.D.C? Where philosophy was once a relatively unessential aspect of the insurgent's make-up, it has become central. The second question concerns the continuous political involvement of the reformer in campaigns. What explains these shifts in behavior? In attempting to answer these queries, I shall return to my data and try to expand upon some of the information available.

My first interest will be to dissect the liberalism of the reformer. Is it merely a function of class, cosmopolitanism, religion, or purposive motivations? I have claimed that demographics would not be important. Yet the findings also indicate the vast differences between the groups in terms of status, cosmopolitanism, and certainly religion. While these demographic characteristics would precede liberalism in any causal explanation, I would still claim that they will not describe reform or regular membership as well as will liberalism. Furthermore, I also suggest that initial-purposive incentives will be unimportant in explaining reform identification.

These motivations can best be interpreted through strength of liberalism and do not add much to an understanding of what makes an insurgent "tick." To weigh the relative importance of these various factors in predicting N.D.C. membership, I shall make use of multiple regression, in which the variables will be

employed as interval measures, where appropriate, or dichotomized, dummy variables,[4] where necessary, as it is in the case of
religion, cosmopolitanism, and motivations. Stepwise regression
provides a useful tool to help one assess the potency of a whole
range of independent variables in predicting a dependent variable,
such as N.D.C. membership, while also accounting for interrelationships between independent variables.[5]

While this approach may appear to avoid theorizing, the reason
is rather the opposite. It is because liberalism may explain most of
the variation between reformers and regulars that one can permit
demographic and motivational variables to contend with liberalism
to prove their relative strength in the stepwise regression. Carrying
the analysis one step further, I shall then decompose liberalism
within the two groups to discover how much of this important
component can be explained by other factors.

Before presenting these findings, it is necessary to describe a
few of the variable transformations created for this analysis. Cosmopolitans were operationalized as each respondent who read
nationally oriented newspapers, whether the *New York Times,
Wall Street Journal, Washington Post,* and the like.

The concern in the earlier discussions of cosmopolitanism was
the national focus of the cosmopolitan. Furthermore, his national
interests would be developed through media habits, since information was perceived as a status-sustaining commodity. An activist,
whose position in the community depends upon purveying facts
to his constituents, will make continuous use of the media. The
particular newspaper he selects will describe his orientation quite
well.

Since mobility was also an important aspect of cosmopolitan
orientations, how long one resided in a particular county was
used. It did not correlate highly with cosmopolitan media habits,
and so could be considered a distinct aspect of cosmopolitanism.
Liberalism was measured by the liberalism scale analyzed in the
preceding chapter. Initial motivations remained the dichotomized
variables discussed in chapters 5 and 6. The party-ideology scale
was also employed as the composite of three questions on party
orientation, which dealt with perceptions and norms for "correct"
party behavior.

Demographic variables, initial motivations, liberalism, and ideology were all the independent variables, while N.D.C. membership
was to be predicted from their strength. That is to say: N.D.C.
membership was the dependent variable to be explained by the

four main categories of variables, according to the relative potency of demographics, motivations, liberalism, and ideology.[6]

TABLE 33

REFORM MEMBERSHIP EXPLAINED BY THE MOST
POWERFUL VARIABLES IN A STEP-WISE
MULTIPLE-REGRESSION EQUATION*

Independent variable	Variance explained in N.D.C. membership (R^2) (N = 699)	Beta
Liberalism	.423	.461
Cosmopolitanism	.027	.124
Professional occupation	.016	.100
Total	.466	

*Only variables that explained at least one percent of the variance were included.

The results of this regression procedure, illustrated in table 33, clearly reconfirm the strength of liberalism in predicting N.D.C. membership. Knowing an individual's degree of liberalism, in fact, explains 42.3 percent of the variance between reform and regular membership. All other variables add practically nothing as explanatory factors. Thus while media cosmopolitanism, professional occupations, and, to a much lesser extent, Catholicism and age do rank higher than the other demographic and initial-motivation variables in explaining membership in the different organizations, one would not cite them as important findings. Even Catholic religion and age each contribute less than 1 percent of the variance toward understanding N.D.C. membership, although they are the next powerful explanatory variables. Furthermore, the additional explanatory power of 2.7 percent for cosmopolitanism or even 1.6 percent for professional occupation makes one wonder if anything but liberalism is operating here. Such a finding is rather anticlimatic after the chapter on liberalism and ideology, but it does lay to rest the contention that membership in the N.D.C. is anything but liberalism. Another way to confirm this finding is by exploring the percentage of liberalism explained by other factors.

To do this, one can examine liberalism as a dependent variable for N.D.C. members apart from professionals. In this way, one can see what influences the liberalism of the reformer and, separately, what contributes to the liberalism of the regular. Concomitantly, one can also assess the percent of variance in liberalism explained by these factors apart from N.D.C. membership. The rationale for this process should be clear. If both sets of politicians do the same tasks, the next question is: "Are the same influences operating in each group?"

As is shown in table 34, more liberalism can be explained by these other factors for the regular than for the reformer. Catholicism provides the strongest explanation for liberalism — or in this case conservatism, since it is inversely related to this philosophy — for both groups. Within the reform group, knowing a person's religion, whether Catholic or Jewish, provides a fair amount of the variance explained in liberalism. Remarkably enough, Jewish as well as Catholic reformers are both less liberal in orientation than are Protestant or agnostic insurgents.[7] Since, as one recalls, agnostics, much more liberal than believers, make up almost 28 percent of the N.D.C. group, this finding only reinforces the extraordinary liberalism of the N.D.C. Jewish religion is associated positively with liberalism in the regular organization (r = .162), but is overwhelmed by the large numbers of agnostics in the N.D.C.

Another interesting finding is that within the reform group, knowing one's initial purposive motivations helps to explain 3.5 percent of the variation in degrees of liberalism. The other variables provide so little explanatory power that only a few of the total are presented to illustrate the point that liberalism for the N.D.C. can not be understood simply through demographic or motivational factors.

While this is true for both the reformer and regular, one should note that demographic variables "explain" liberalism for the regular much more accurately than they do for the N.D.C. member. For him, purposive motivations and antiparty motivations are also relevant. Furthermore, the total explanation available through these variables is much less for the reformer than the regular. The insurgent's liberalism is not reducible to other factors as easily as that philosophy is for the professional politician.

TABLE 34

LIBERALISM EXPLAINED BY THE MOST POWERFUL VARIABLES IN A STEP-WISE MULTIPLE-REGRESSION EQUATION*

Independent variable	Variance explained in liberalism (R^2)	Beta
Reformers (N = 338)		
Catholic religion	.065	−.265
Initial motivation purposive	.035	.195
Initial motivation party loyalty	.025	−.163
Jewish religion	.015	−.137
Total	.140	
Regulars (N = 358)		
Catholic religion	.127	−.230
Cosmopolitanism	.053	.187
Years resident in county	.034	−.165
Income	.017	.142
Total	.231	

*Only variables that explained at least one percent of the variance were included.

Another question is raised by the relationship between motivations and liberalism. Do motivations, such as issue-oriented rewards, lead one to clarify and accentuate his liberal policy concerns? Or do deep commitments to liberal principles precipitate a purposive motivation to implement these policy goals through a reform organization?

Another alternative (and one for which I opt) would explain motivations as separate and distinct from liberalism. While liberalism might shape the purposive reward that an activist anticipates, on the whole, my findings would argue the separation of the two factors, with liberalism outranking purposive motivations in strength. There is some indication of the distinction between motivation and liberalism. Purposive continuing rewards were claimed by 62.1 percent of the regulars, as well as 90.1 percent of the reformers. Yet only 15.5 percent of the regulars, compared with 72.9 percent of the reformers, could be considered intense liberals in at least eight out of eleven issues. Purposive motivations do not explain the attraction of reform politics as much as liberalism does.

TABLE 35

REFORM MEMBERSHIP EXPLAINED BY THE MOST
POWERFUL VARIABLES WHEN LIBERALISM IS
HELD UNTIL THE LAST STEP IN THE
MULTIPLE-REGRESSION EQUATION*

Independent variable	Variance explained in N.D.C. membership (R^2) (N = 699)	Beta
Cosmopolitanism	.190	.124
Catholic religion	.087	−.115
Age	.047	−.105
Professional occupation	.023	.100
Initial motivation sociability	.011	−.079
Total	.358	

*Only variables that explained at least one percent of the variance were included.

One can also support this contention through the multiple-regression technique. Holding back liberalism until all other variables have been permitted to exert their full strength in explaining reform membership, as one may do in stepwise regression, purposive motivations do not appear to be very important.[8] In fact, table 35 indicates that cosmopolitan orientation, Catholicism, age, and professional occupation all seem more important in understanding membership patterns than do initial motivations. In one instance only can such a motivation qualify for inclusion in the table — and this is barely possible, since it explains only 1 percent of the variance. And after all the variables that explain at least 1 percent of the variance have been included in the equation, liberalism still adds 13.1 percent to predicting N.D.C. membership.

The prominence of cosmopolitan media habits has to be accepted warily for the regular. While all nationally oriented newspapers were coded for this variable, the percent who read the *New York Times* predominated (approximately 81 percent for reformers and about 38 percent for regulars). The liberal positions of the *New York Times* might repel the more conservative regular. But, one must then ask, "Is this variation in media consumption a reflection of cosmopolitanism or of liberalism?" There is some indication of the latter possibility for the regular. The simple R between this media variable and liberalism for professional politicians is .326, while for reformers it is only .049.

Also, if one recalls table 33, after liberalism has explained all it could of reform membership, cosmopolitan media habits (moderately strong as a simple R, .436, correlating media and membership) can only contribute 2.6 percent more in understanding the dependent variable. Thus, in holding back liberalism, I may not have been controlling for the effects of this philosophy as it manifests itself in other variables. In any case, some aspect of liberalism outweighs purposive incentives no matter what one does.

I conclude from these findings that initial motivations are relatively useless in describing reform membership — and perhaps even useless in characterizing party activists in general. In the chapter on motivations, I hypothesized that it was not so much the incentive, but its qualitative interpretation through a specific issue orientation that would be important in distinguishing types of activists. These findings further support this contention by the very weakness that motivations exhibit in explaining reform or regular membership or in elucidating liberalism when membership is controlled.

Catholicism for both groups contributes much more to the dependent variable, whether it is reform membership or liberalism.

The meaning of this combined effect is clear. While Catholicism varies between groups and has a distinct and similar effect on liberal attitudes within groups, Catholic reformers are still remarkably more liberal than are Catholic regulars. The percentages will suffice to make this point through one example.

Non-Catholics are more likely to support immediate withdrawal from Vietnam than are Catholics within both groups. For reformers, only 77.7 percent of the Catholics would support this policy, compared with 93.7 percent who were not Catholic. The similar percentages for regulars are 28.3 percent to 49.5 percent. While the variation within the groups is obvious, the variation between groups over the issue is immense. Comparing only non-Catholics, a gamma = .87 related N.D.C. membership and withdrawal from Vietnam. When one examines Catholics, a rather strong gamma = .72 expresses the same relationship. Thus, Catholicism is important within and between groups, although stressing the great variation between reformers and regulars, whether they are Catholic or not, seems more essential. Thus religion can not answer all of my questions about the liberalism of the reformer.

In trying to interpret the N.D.C. insurgent as anything but a liberal, I find much weaker explanations, whether one examines demographic or motivational factors. In other words, one can not reduce the liberalism of the reformer to either Catholicism or purposive incentives. In this respect, the increasing importance of liberalism to the insurgent (compared with what older studies found), may reflect similar shifts in the electorate. Increasingly, voters identify Democrats and Republicans with distinct programs.[9] One could argue that this change in the electorate merely copies the developments in parties from the nonissue-oriented 1950s to the more deeply policy conscious 1960s and 1970s. In any case, the choices and evidence important to the electorate, whether offered by the parties or discovered by the voter, illustrate this issue-oriented concern, so important in any characterization of the reformer. The reformer's ideological leanings may echo the directions that the voter would select, if given a choice. This is not to say that the reformer's liberalism copies a similar necessarily liberal bent in the electorate, but rather that this interest in policies may represent a trend increasing in importance. Where philosophy was once a relatively unessential aspect of both the insurgent's and the electorate's make-up, it has become a central concern for both.

In answering this question about the liberalism of the reformer before I faced the second query about continuous political involvement of this alleged "morning glory," I am actually contending that this higher level of participation, compared to past amateur movements, is related to intense liberalism. Motivations need not be divisible to sustain activity. Ideology firmly and deeply felt can provide enough rewards to maintain continuous involvement under the proper conditions. If this were true, the intense as well as purposive liberal would not reflect a decreased nor more recent level of involvement compared to his nonintense comrades. Where nondivisible tangible benefits were seen as detractions from continuous activity, I would claim that such goals, if intensely sought and rewarded, would provide and sustain motivation.

I also stated that this would occur "under the proper conditions." By this I am reintroducing the discussion about organizations with which I began chapter 5. The intensely liberal and purposive activist — I shall call him the *purposive liberal* — within a nurturing environment, for example, the N.D.C., should find his needs met much more readily than a similar activist within a regular organization. To prove this hypothesis within the structure of my data would only be possible indirectly. The effect of an organization can be surmised, if under one set of circumstances the same type of politician is more active than the other members of his group and under different circumstances that same type is less involved.

Percentages are more useful for this analysis. In order to test this hypothesis, I have created a new variable by examining only those who represent — at one and the same time — intense liberalism (at least eight out of eleven most liberal responses) and a continuing purposive incentive. I shall call this group *purposive liberals*. One should find no differences between these activists in terms of party activity, if the "morning glory" syndrome no longer operates for the reformer.

Length of political activism is slightly related to purposive liberalism for the N.D.C. (gamma = .10). The professional, however, who has been involved for a longer period of time, is less likely to be a purposive liberal (gamma = -.41). Table 36 illustrates this interesting distinction, which supports my hypothesis. The regular conforms to the stereotype of the activist who becomes more pragmatic and less issue oriented the longer he remains involved: 25.7 percent of those who became active within the last four years are purposive liberals, compared with 11.3 percent who became active before 1964.

TABLE 36

RELATIONSHIP BETWEEN LENGTH OF POLITICAL
PARTICIPATION AND PURPOSIVE LIBERALISM
WITHIN REFORM AND REGULAR GROUPS
(GAMMA CORRELATIONS)

| Year of first participation | Percent purposive liberals | | | |
| | Reformers | | Regulars | |
	Percent	N	Percent	N
1968-71	62.8	(207)	25.7	(38)
1964-67	67.6	(102)	22.8	(437)
Prior to 1964	68.9	(289)	11.3	(278)
Gamma	.10	.10	-.41	

The political socialization of the insurgent, however, dedicated as he might be and now involved in a reform organization, illustrates a reverse pattern. Of those active more recently, 62.8 percent can be categorized as purposive liberals, compared with 68.9 percent of those involved prior to 1964. Involvement leads the reformer toward more intense liberalism, supporting his issue orientation and sustaining the motives he has developed.

In terms of tasks performed, the purposive liberal in both groups does more election-oriented chores than the nonpurposive liberal. In the reform organization, purposive liberals are even more likely to contact voters than are such nonpurposive liberals within their groups (gamma for the reform group is .32, compared with .23 for the regulars). Furthermore, while there are no major distinctions in other tasks performed within each organization, the purposive liberal reformer is slightly more likely to accommplish these chores every year (gamma = .08) than is the same type in the regular organization. For the regulars, in fact, purposive liberals are less likely to be involved yearly than are other professionals (gamma = -.29).

These findings about purposive liberals within a reform organization are only suggestive. Yet I think they can point to some possible developments in American politics. Thus, while the N.D.C. member may be representative of a new breed of reformer, maintaining his purposive incentives through the rewards that intense liberalism offers, it is where he exaggerates certain general trends within the electorate that he is most interesting.

Before pursuing this point in the final chapter, let me sum up the results of the regression analysis. In this procedure — which permitted one to calculate the relative importance of demographic, motivational, liberal, and ideological factors in "producing" a reformer or regular politician — one is forced to conclude that the difference is related mainly to a liberal dimension. The N.D.C. member is overwhelmingly liberal and his concern with these issues segregates him from the regular of the same political party. This philosophy is also bound to a cosmopolitan viewpoint, that explains some of the variation between the groups, as does religious identification. Yet one must question Wilson's perception of the reformer as "stylistically" distinct from the regular. My findings indicate that much more than "style" is involved. In fact, substantive issues divide the groups so completely that perhaps this is more the value conflict that characterized the Populist-anti-Populist battle[10] than it is the stylistic variations that one might anticipate in an age allegedly typified by the "end of ideology."

Notes to Chapter 9

1. Survey Research Center, University of Michigan, in Flanigan, *Political Behavior of the American Electorate*, pp. 44-48.

2. Harold M. Klein, *Patterns of Public Employment in New Jersey* (New Brunswick, N.J.: Rutgers — The State University, Bureau of Government Research and University Extension Division, 1968), p. 11.

3. Ibid.

4. Jacob Cohen, "Multiple Regression as a General Data-Analytic System," in *Contemporary Problems in Statistics: A Book of Readings for the Behavioral Sciences,* ed. Bernhardt Lieberman (New York: Oxford University Press, 1971), pp. 421-40. The widespread use of dichotomous variables in multiple regression is firmly supported by Cohen.

5. Norman H. Nie, Dale H. Bent, and C. Hadlai Hull, *Statistical Package for the Social Sciences (S.P.S.S.)* (New York: McGraw-Hill Book Company, 1970), pp. 175-80.

6. Using a dichotomous variable as the dependent variable creates certain problems in multiple regression, which requires the assumption of a normal distribution. Since this would be a fallacy in a dichotomous variable, such as N.D.C. membership, it must be clear that I am relaxing certain basic assumptions by employing this technique with my data. Since the findings, however, are so much what one would predict from the preceding analysis, this possible bias does not seem to have materialized. Another point concerns the large size of the sample, which diminishes the need for a normally distributed population. For details on this, *see* John C. Blydenburgh, "Probit Analysis: A Method for Coping with Dichotomous Dependent Variables," *Social Science Quarterly,* 1 (March 1971): 889-99, esp. footnote 2, p. 889: "For large samples the estimates may have the same asymptotic properties even if the dependent variable is not normally distributed.

Therefore the violation of this assumption may be inconsequential for large samples."

This warning is useful and thus directs one to examine the outcome of this procedure through a general comparison of one variable to another, rather than any great concentration upon the exact coefficients in the predictability of N.D.C. membership.

7. While agnostic religious identification does not appear directly as a variable in the analysis, it is incorporated through the process of creating dummy variables from religion, a nonordinal variable. The exclusion of one category in the dummy-variable transformation prevents redundant information from being introduced into the analysis. Multiple regression requires that no variable be a linear combination of any one or any set of variables. Including all categories of religion would introduce just this problem. For further details, refer to Cohen's article, "Multiple Regressions as a General Data-Analytic System," in Lieberman, pp. 421-40.

8. The stepwise method selects the independent variables most potent in explanatory power by constructing all possible combinations of variables as predictors of the dependent variable in a linear equation. As each new variable is brought into the explanation of what predicts N.D.C. membership, it is, then, the next most valuable in explaining the dependent variable. This method also permits one to construct inclusion levels at which point some variables are considered for the equation, while others are held for a later stage. In not entering liberalism at the first step in the procedure, all other variables are permitted to contribute as much weight as they can to the explanation of N.D.C. membership. Just such a process is illustrated by table 35.

9. Pomper, "From Confusion to Clarity," pp. 415-28.

10. Kleppner, *Cross of Culture,* p. 4.

10
Conclusions

This analysis of the reform politician produces a rather straightforward and simple conclusion: the N.D.C. activist is a liberal — by any measure, by any definition. Yet such a political philosophy is not unique in American politics, where coalitions of diverse interests have been able to shelve their philosophical animosities in order to collect the spoils of electoral victories. Thus a suspicion survives that one has not explained much by claiming that liberalism accounts for 42.3 percent of the variance in N.D.C. membership. The question remains unanswered as to why liberalism has surfaced in importance at this point and why it is so relevant for the insurgent. If it is the intensity and salience of the reformer's liberalism that accounts for these distinctions between the N.D.C. member and the regular Democrat, then what does the reform movement tell scholars about American society at this juncture in history?

In a concern for clarification, it seems that this study moves from a description of mere stylistic differences between reformers and regulars to one of intense value conflicts, suggested in the previous chapter. If one regards purposive liberalism as a value, held as deeply as the pietistic protestant values of the Populists,[1] then some of the conflicts between my two types of Democrats may be highlighted. In effect, the intensity of liberalism is equal to the pietistic religion in the qualitative effects it produces upon political behavior. Politics and religion, where moral fervor intertwines them, may not be very far apart.

Thus, in concluding this portrait of the reformer, these unanswered questions leave several tasks to be performed. The first involves retracing one's footsteps back to chapter 2 where the hypotheses were first presented, to review which ones were confirmed and disconfirmed. The second requirement would be to draw these findings together by speculating about the effects of reform values upon the alterations in American parties. In this latter analysis there will be some discussion of what such groups as the N.D.C. reflect about the present state of politics, as well as the effects of reformers upon the future of party organizations. In other words, in this concluding section, the N.D.C. will be examined first as a dependent variable and then as an independent influence upon the course of future electoral arrangements.

In reviewing these hypotheses, one can then lay the foundation for tracing the possible directions of American parties. Tables 37 and 38 list the hypotheses that were confirmed and disconfirmed.

TABLE 37

CONFIRMED HYPOTHESES

Strongly confirmed

Hypothesis 1 — There will be a significant difference between reformers and regulars in their cosmopolitan orientations.

Hypothesis 2 —There will be a significant difference in the class status of reformers and regulars.

Hypothesis 3 — There will be a significant difference in the upward-mobility patterns of reformers and regulars.

Hypothesis 4 — There will be a significant difference in the ethnic and religious backgrounds of reformers and regulars.

Hypothesis 6 — Reformers will be significantly younger than regulars.

Hypothesis 13 — There will be a significant difference between the liberalism of reformers and regulars.
a. Regulars will be significantly more supportive of the status quo than reformers.
c. Reformers will be significantly more likely to perceive themselves as liberals than will regulars.

Hypothesis 14 — Reformers will be significantly more constrained in their issue concerns than regulars.

Moderately confirmed

Hypothesis 5 — There will be a significant difference in the socialization experiences of reformers and regulars.

Hypothesis 7 — Reformers will be significantly more suburban in life-style than regulars.

Hypothesis 8 — Entrance Motivation: There will be no significant difference between reformers and regulars in purposive motivation.

Hypothesis 9 — Continuing Motivation: Amateurs will be significantly more purposive than regulars.

Hypothesis 15 — Reformers will be significantly more ideological about party activity than regulars.

TABLE 38

DISCONFIRMED HYPOTHESES

Strongly disconfirmed

Hypothesis 13b — There will be a proportionately greater difference between reformers and regulars on procedural rather than substantive issues.

Moderately disconfirmed

Hypothesis 10 — Role Perceptions: There will be a significant difference in the ways reformers and regulars perceive their roles.

Hypothesis 11 — Career Patterns: Reformers will be significantly less likely than regulars to hold high-party positions.

Hypothesis 12 — Political Tasks: Reformers will be significantly less likely to perform election-oriented tasks than regulars.

The most strongly confirmed propositions were those for demographics and liberalism. In fact, while the supposition that reformers would vary on procedural versus substantive issues was disconfirmed, the actual finding only adds more heavily to the strength of issue-oriented liberalism for understanding the reformer. The only other hypotheses that were disconfirmed, those that dealt with tasks performed, role perceptions, and career patterns, are also useful for what they contribute to my contention that the reformer is a new hybrid, quite different from his past relations. The fact that the N.D.C. member does not describe his role differently nor perform diverse chores from that of the regular sustains my argument that the reformer has become a pragmatist in his use of the

the ballot. The limited ideological expectations of parties — only weakly confirmed — also underlies the probability that the reformer represents a new species of political activist. Strongly constrained in his liberalism, he does not hold inflexible attitudes toward the proper role of the party. While the insurgent is working more diligently than ever before in electoral efforts, the regular seems less sustained by his traditional rewards. This is also evident through the disconfirmation of the hypothesis about career patterns. Reformers may be unlikely to hold higher party or public positions, but so too are the grass roots Democratic committeemen in the study.

These apparent developments among insurgents and professional politicians might lead one to expect a growing similarity and greater cooperation between these supposedly distinct organizations. Agreeing on tasks, not that distinct in motivation, objective criteria would make one anticipate greater unity between the groups. While this might sound reasonable, such an interpretation seems to overlook the real and fundamental opposition each group has to the other's perceptions of politics, reflected in intense versus moderate liberalism and — even more essential — the values that these orientations mirror.

In effect, I suggest that the reformer and the regular believe two rather opposing and valued myths about American politics: one, that it consists of conflicting heterogeneity derived from diverse and immigrant heritage,[2] the other, that political relations are subsumed under a general liberal consensus[3] in which the rules of the pluralist game are sustained by an elite — if not mass — that agrees on civility above any substantive arguments.[4].

The myth to which the regular seems tied can be described through a variety of distinct explanations that do share a common belief in politics as consensual arrangements, rather than either class or value conflicts, evident through issue-oriented politics.

One strand of this argument derives from the end-of-ideology school. Daniel Bell and Seymour Lipset describe the termination of class conflict due to increasing affluence.[5] The antagonisms between working and middle class, proletariat and bourgeoisie are destroyed by industrial success. Under these conditions, ideology dissipates, since it is only the expression of the class conflict. In place of class warfare, one discovers a politics reduced to technical decisions over how best to distribute governmental goods. These trends move the society beyond class conflict and toward consensus in values.

If class antagonisms are perceived as absent — or at least not relevant to political behavior — the regular's moderate liberalism may sustain an entirely opposing set of norms or myths about political relations from the reformer who views such conflicts as real.

This end of ideology and growth of consensus also rests upon the pluralist view that all groups are represented in the political arena.[6] If essential interests are part of the bargaining process, it seems unlikely that class-based divisions of the "ins" versus the "outs" would be salient. After all, this myth supposes that everyone who chooses to be involved is part of the "ins."

Conflict can be restrained, since there also exists procedural consensus. Furthermore, according to this view, the valuables are in plentiful supply and hence become a question of distribution from base of plenty, not redistribution from a base of scarcity.[7] Resources are plentiful; pressure groups are equally balanced and representative. Thus no rigid program for social priorities is necessary. This political laissez-faire doctrine permits government to be merely one of the coequal contenders or at most a mediator between groups by developing administrative mechanisms to implement policies derived from "interest-group liberalism."[8] This rather optimistic view allows the regular to regard politics as one of "interests" and "compromise," where any outcome is sanctified through the process by which it is reached.

Not only the less constrained liberalism of the regular, but also his local orientations fit the values of consensus pluralism. Where one perceives politics as the balance of separate interests, whose claims are all valid, there would be weak foundation for discriminating between various demands. What better criteria for decisions, under such ambiguous conditions, than personal loyalty, group attachments, or other interpersonal relationships? Who one knows and with whom one interacts might influence decisions and one's status greatly. This would be especially true since no philosophical set of priorities is available to guide the local's behavior through a maze of contradictory problems and solutions.

Motivated somewhat by purposive goals (for he would probably give lip service to such aims, in any case), the local would respond to material rewards — if available — but more likely to the benefits that derive from social, for example, solidary, rewards. The data support this possibility for the regular politician.

If one accepts this picture of the professional politican as well as the speculations about his political value system, what contradictory perceptions might the reformer express through his political involvement? And also, what does this value orientation indicate about the direction of party politics?

I suggest that in resorting to a strongly issue-oriented politics, the reformer rejects the view that the goal of political activity is the distribution of goods to divergent interests, in order to hold the electoral coalition together. Of greater concern for the N.D.C. member is the output end of politics. In this he seems to have moved from past amateur-based movements, in which the major focus was upon implementing democratic procedures to open up party politics. These procedural reformers were much in evidence from the Populists and civil service associations to the Progressives and municipal reformers. Even the club movement was more characterized by this approach than any overt emphasis upon substantive policy. The N.D.C. member, however, appears somewhat different, since all arenas of public policy are touched by his liberal orientation.

These liberal values may lead to a perception of politics as conflict. In this respect, the reformer refutes the argument for the "end of ideology" through his very existence. The N.D.C. as a group of cosmopolitan professionals, whose educational skills admit them to the elite, does not perceive politics only as a realm for technical decisions about the best way to operate a government. While these skills are important, the foundations of N.D.C. politics rest, instead, on conflict over the substantive policies of government. These are strongly held values and, in themselves, represent a kind of ideology.

This orientation diverges from the school that claims the end of class-based conflict, and, hence, of all deeply ideological antagonisms. The strength of feeling of the N.D.C. member illustrates that politics does not have to reflect one brand of class politics or any class antagonism in order to provoke deep and fundamental disagreements.

One source for such stresses might be very different perceptions of how important and salient liberal issues should be in political decisions. If one values — and not merely holds — a liberal philosophy of government, that view might create an unresolvable conflict in relation to a politician who values liberal issues in the most general and ephemeral way.

The values of the reformer can be tied to a certain class status as well as to a constrained liberal philosoply. The definition of class, however, differs from that of Bell and Lipset. Birnbaum analyzes the transformation of occupational class status in advanced technological societies. He rejects Bell's and Lipset's notion of ending ideology and argues that class conflict has been restructured rather than destroyed in industrial countries.[9] The description does not differ in essentials from Apter's dissection of American society as composed of the "technologically competent," the "technologically obsolete," and the "technologically superfluous."[10]

The scientifically competent category would certainly include the reformer: professional and cosmopolitan in status. This relationship to the economic order influences the insurgent's political perceptions. Thus while he, the reformer, derives from the elite, he also does not merely apply his technical skills without purpose to governmental programs. Bound to a liberal philosophy, he develops priorities and only then decides which tasks deserve the application of his skills.

These priorities in turn, derived from his liberal philosophy, both direct his motivations in a purposive direction and also help him structure his political universe in rather specific ways. Since his liberalism is so essential, he has a perceptual map for defining and categorizing political events. This detailed map of liberalism is quite different from the rather vague outline of which the issue-oriented map of the regular consists.[11]

Not only liberalism but the effects of constrained liberalism also give the insurgent standards by which to judge suggestions for reform. Thus this activist, who is also a cosmopolitan, evaluates politics through objective standards, rather than personal obligations.

In describing these possible variations in the political interpretations of reformers and regulars, I believe that the conflict between the groups is deeper than a categorizing of liberalism or cosmopolitan orientations might suggest. The values that the philosophical and demographic components reflect might make accommodation difficult.

One might, in fact, paraphrase Kleppner, who stated that the division between the ritualists and the pietists in the 1850s "was a conflict rooted in divergent and conflicting religious perspectives."[12] In place of "religious perspectives," read "political perspectives" and one might have the source of reform and regular antagonisms. More than style or rhetoric, these orientations direct the perceptions and political lives of these activists as they attempt to realize their values through political participation. But this value suggestion is also to be pursued into the discussion of how and why the reformer suddenly appears in all his liberal glory. For I do suggest that he is not a freak of nature, but rather the harbinger of the kinds of changes evident in the electorate, quite different from the historical amateur. I now turn to some information on how this value orientation of the reformer is reflective of certain shifts in American politics — for example, the reformer as dependent variable.

The first development in electoral characteristics that one must note is that strong ties to political parties are diminishing for many voters. The increasing numbers of Independents attest to this fact.[13] In contrast to this development, the strength of party loyalty as an initial incentive certainly stood out for the regular in contrast to the reformer. Thus, in his lessening ties to the political party, the reformer depicts certain trends evident among voters. Furthermore, the kind of Independent voter the reformer represents is also significant.

In the classic works of voting behavior from the 1950s, the Independent voter as personification of the good citizen was rejected:

> The ideal of the Independent citizen, attentive to politics, concerned with the course of government, who weighs the rival appeals of a campaign and reaches a judgment that is unswayed by partisan prejudice . . . fits poorly the characteristics of the Independents in our samples. Far from being more attentive, interested, and informed, Independents tend, as a group, to be somewhat less involved in politics. They have somewhat poorer knowledge of the issues, their image of the candidates is fainter, their interest in the campaign is less, their concern over the outcome is relatively slight, and their choice between competing candidates, although it is indeed made later in the campaign, seems much less to spring from the discoverable evaluations of the elements of national politics.[14]

New times, new analyses of those data[15] have provided a rather contradictory view of the Independent, much in keeping with my knowledge of the N.D.C. activist. Information and interest do not necessarily vary between Independents and partisans.[16]

The Independents are now more bimodal in composition. Independents are both the apolitical lower-status individual, who fits this picture of *The American Voter,* but also a more educated, active, and knowledgeable type,[17] who seems attuned to the characteristics of the N.D.C. member.

This increase in proportion of Independents is accompanied by an increase in split-ticket voting in each election, as well as movement between parties in successive contests.[18] V. O. Key proposed that the voter who "floats" moves from party to party in accord with his policy preferences. Awareness and interest permit such flexibility of voting patterns — not apathy.[19] Surely the reformer who has no qualms about voting across party lines reflects this development.

In an even more salient way the insurgent mirrors patterns of electoral behavior. With a public that has become more Independent, another trait is its increasing issue orientation. Compared with the 1950s voter, the electorate in 1968 was more capable of differentiating between the Democrats and the Republicans on specific issues and then of aligning its party identification in accord with chosen policy preferences — or vice versa.[20] This alteration in perceptions (whether due to shifts and clarifications in a party's position or to the voter's accretion of better information) certainly makes it probable that the reformer derives from a population sharing many of his most obvious traits.

This issue orientation, furthermore, is characterized by a national focus for the reformer. Similarly in the electorate, a decline in sectionalism and expansion of the mass media encourage less local preoccupations.[21] The "six o'clock" or "seven o'clock" news provides most television viewers with identical country-wide information to shape their political worlds.

These similar patterns, in fact, have led several analysts to make an argument for the appropriateness of the "responsible-party model" of issue-oriented politics, very much based on the nationalizing tendencies of the economy and the political system traced in the above discussion.[22]

An added factor, and one that characterizes the reformer, par excellence, is the resurgence of participatory politics to which the insurgent is strongly oriented.[23] All these trends not only illustrate the reformer's characteristics, but also point to the potential influence that the insurgent may wield in American parties. Now the discussion shifts to the reformer as an independent force and his possible effectiveness.

Issue-oriented, the reformer has a responsive audience for his approach to politics. Seeking attention to programs, he contacts voters, speaks to them about policies, discovers their interests, and, hence, receives the very reward he may not have received in the past. This reward, convincing people about his policy commitments, can provide a benefit that continuously motivates him toward additional work for the cause. At the same time the reformer can prod the system toward more issue-oriented politics. It might well be that the insurgent would know how to make the most appropriate appeals to this very important group in the electorate, since he shares many of the same perspectives.

Not only his motivations but also his opportunities for influence have expanded. The "new politics" develops techniques with which the cosmopolitan professional is supremely confident. The importance of the reformer as a "wave of the future" is emphasized by this relationship between party politics in its "new" form and the cosmopolitan and professional occupations of the reformers. The "new politics" represents a technical involvement of media specialists, campaign consultants, computer technicians, and public relations men.[24] Elections have become the domain of scientific polling and application of efficient methods for locating and activating votes. This approach ties in much more easily with the cosmopolitan orientation of the reformer. The N.D.C. member is likely to be more effective in this political environment.

As campaigning moves from the intimate face-to-face contact of loyal partisans to the impersonal arousal of the inert masses by Madison Avenue specialists, the high-status professional, represented by the N.D.C. will be at home in politics more than the regular whose political crafts involve personal relationships and local orientations.

The reformer's comfort with the new techniques does not guarantee that his skills will be sought. One possible development, however, the Democratic Party-McGovern reforms, provides access points at all levels of party organization from internal decisions to nominations.[25] These guidelines, even in the early months after adoption, changed the entire shape of the Democratic Party's 1972 presidential selection process.

That participation—with a vengeance—of thousands of reformers illustrates another potential impact of the insurgent. If one recalls the section on career patterns, it is obvious that reformers and regulars alike are eager to accept government appointments. The primary campaigns of 1972 prove that they are also willing to run for party positions. Perhaps this kind of activity can be converted into more electoral contests for all levels of public office. Striking a meaningful response in the electorate, the reformer-candidate might infiltrate the governmental structures about which he only complained in the past.

This possibility is exhibited in the New Jersey gubernatorial campaign of Judge Brendan Byrne. His amazingly successful victory for the Democrats was the result of multiple factors, such as the corruption issue, the fragmentation of the Republican Party, as well as the conservative stance of the Republican candidate, Charles Sandman. The main point, however, is that many reformers worked assiduously for the election of Byrne, although he ran a rather issueless campaign. The pragmatic use of the ballot, which is now beginning to filter these old reformers into government appointments, was a suggestion of this study that is being confirmed by recent events. How these cosmopolitan liberals behave in positions of authority is yet to be seen, but their integration into the works of government may be quite probable in New Jersey.

All these developments, whether they continue to grow or remain the same, do reflect some major revisions in party politics. Echoing and influencing these changes are reformers who once could be described as a small, ineffectual elite. It is with slightly exaggerated prose that I suggest the insurgent's cosmopolitan, motivational, and constrained liberal characteristics may represent the vanguard of the electorate in its movement toward the long-awaited ideal of issue-oriented reform politics.

Furthermore, these new patterns not only elucidate the path of the reformer, but also may help to explain his increasing involvement as a source of direction in party affairs. The rewards — nondivisible and derived from intensely liberal motivations — may be the only foundation for political participation that the changing party system is capable of supporting. Far from the divisible tangible rewards expected for the regular politician, I found their notorious absence. Undercutting the bases of a traditional party politics, this revision of benefits available makes one wonder if the regular's sustained efforts are at all predictable. In a period of transition, I think the reformer is a prototype of the kinds of motivations likely to reward any party activist, as the Goldwater, McCarthy, and McGovern campaigns illustrate.

If this pattern illuminates the future of American politics, a final question wonders whether it describes a regeneration and flowering of the American party system or the malignant growth of a dangerous mutant. To be more specific: "What does the reformer portend about the 'end-of-consensus' politics?"

Many of the fears that issue-oriented politics raise in the hearts of many political analysts derive from the regular's myths about American parties. The rejection of "responsible parties" in the 1950s was surely shaped by that epoch of nonissue-oriented politics, epitomized by the overwhelming adoration of President Eisenhower. Social scientists raised in that era described the electorate as if the picture, snapped in *The American Voter* and by the "end-of-ideology" school, was a continuous full-length movie, rather than a still photograph. Time bound in descriptive relevance, as well as usefulness in resolving conflict, it is perhaps a testament to the failure of the consensus approach that confrontation politics has replaced it today.

Thus consensus might merely have been successful exclusion of certain grups from society's benefits, rather than any strong commitment to interest-group pluralism. In his awareness of the truly divisive issues and his willingness to assess racial and international questions, then, the reformer displays a more timely and relevant political attitude. These issues emphasize the traumatic tensions of the 1960s and 1970s. They appear now very much as a result of the "solutions" developed by the New Deal, Fair Deal, New Frontier, and Great Society.

In retrospect, consensus politics looks more like the behavior of an ostrich, hiding his head to avoid an unpleasant reality. Such actions can be dangerous in the long run, for what one does not know *can* surely hurt him. Ignoring racial and economic inequities does not cause them to evaporate. They fester and develop into the very confrontations that consensus politics hoped to avoid. The period of unrest that faces America now derives from the unresolved problems of earlier decades, where winning elections and combining heterogeneous coalitions was an excuse for ignoring major injustices. "Muddling through" was raised to the heights of moral principle, instead of the political expediency it actually was.[26]

The reformer, in reflecting this issue orientation of the electorate as well as its substantive policy concerns, provokes conflict within the system, quite clearly, but he also gives air to the actual grievances that past approaches obscured.

The reformer's view that politics should be based upon a dialogue about issues directs one toward the quality of that dialogue in future years. Surely the insurgent has not chosen an easy row to hoe. In declaring his issues to be those of economic and social inequity, he seeks to draw together a new alliance, quite distinct from the New Deal coalition. The union of a portion of the "technologically competent," and the "technologically superfluous," to cite Apter's terms, may not be a natural arrangement, as the McGovern campaign indicates. This attempt, however, produces one result, already obvious: the erosion of Democratic loyalty from the "technologically obsolescent." The skilled worker grows more and more alienated from his traditional party, whose liberal directions are no longer his own. The hard-hat syndrome finds a home with George Wallace's appeals to perceived threat. This worker, who the reformer also thought would be magnetized by his issues, reacts instead with antipathy to such economic programs.

And this leads one back to the claim that much of the antagonism visible today is the result of value conflicts. The N.D.C. member defined his appeals on the basis of economic and liberal policies. Instead of accepting his definition, the natural constituency of the reformer turned to such "irrelevant issues" as law and order and busing. But one might claim that these issues arose because they were not irrelevant, but were an accurate reflection of the kinds of values that were salient to lower-middle-class groups: preservation of an individualistic ethic of hard work plus a strong ethnic identification.

While the reformer may not have been able to draw the worker to his version of the good life, the two share an interpretation of politics as one of value conflicts, rather than mere "interest-group liberalism."

Just as the regular's perceptions now seem to be outdated by technological and political developments, so, too, the reformer's orientations appear much more in tune with modifications in American society. The dire warnings that reform politics sound a note of doom greatly overestimates the past benefits of consensus politics.

If the reformer is illustrative of these modifications, it is not at all certain that the abandonment of the pluralist myth of consensus politics will necessarily produce a thorn that prickles with conflict and tears the fabric of society, for the reformer has changed over time. His alterations indicate both an ability to compromise in electoral goals as well as the strength to remain a strong and constrained liberal. Not an ideologue by standards of party expectations — in fact, rather pragmatic in this regard — the reformer may reflect a regeneration rather than a disintegration of American parties. These speculations are simply that and must wait the test of time. Until then the reformer's growing impact on politics gives him experience in political organizations with which he can continue to evolve as an original species of the reform politician.

Notes to Chapter 10

1. Kleppner, *Cross of Culture*.
2. *See* Michael Kammen's *People of Paradox: An Inquiry Concerning the Origins*

of American Civilization (New York: Alfred A. Knopf, 1972), for a recent updating of this approach.

3. Hartz, *Liberal Tradition in America*.

4. McClosky, "Consensus and Ideology," pp. 361-79.

5. Bell, *End of Ideology*; Lipset, *Political Man*, pp. 399-456.

6. One of the best-known apologists for this theory is Robert A. Dahl. *See Who Governs?* (New Haven, Conn.: Yale University Press, 1961), and *Pluralist Democracy in the United States: Conflict and Consent* (Chicago: Rand McNally & Co., 1967).

7. Theodore J. Lowi, "American Business, Public Policy, Case Studies, and Political Theory," *World Politics* 16 (July 1964): 677-715.

8. Theodore J. Lowi, *The End of Liberalism: Ideology, Policy, and the Crisis of Public Authority* (New York: W. W. Norton & Company, Inc., 1969).

9. Norman Birnbaum, *The Crisis of Industrial Society* (New York: Oxford University Press, 1969), *see* especially pp. 3-40, for a detailed analysis of the continuing occupational definition of class, based upon differing occupations as industrial society becomes "postmodern."

10. Apter, "Ideology and Discontent," in Apter, pp. 15-43.

11. Harry R. Wilker and Lester W. Milbrath, "Political Belief Systems and Political Behavior," *Social Science Quarterly* 1 (December 1970): 477-93.

12. Kleppner, *Cross of Culture*, p. 370.

13. Survey Research Center, University of Michigan in Flanigan, *Political Behavior of the American Electorate*, p. 42.

14. Campbell et al., *The American Voter: An Abridgement*, p. 83; *also see* Bernard Berelson, "Democratic Theory and Public Opinion," *Public Opinion Quarterly* 16 (Fall 1952): 313-30.

15. *See* V.O. Key, Jr. (with the help of Milton C. Cummings, Jr.), *The Responsible Electorate: Rationality in Presidential Voting, 1936-1960* (Cambridge, Mass.: The Belknap Press of Harvard University Press, 1966); David E. RePass, "Issue Salience and Party Choice," *American Political Science Review* 65 (June 1971): 389-400.

16. Flanigan, *Political Behavior of the American Electorate*, pp. 45-48.

17. Walter Dean Burnham, *Critical Elections and the Mainsprings of American Politics* (New York: W. W. Norton & Company, 1970), p. 125.

18. John S. Saloma, III, and Frederick H. Sontag, *Parties: The Real Opportunity for Effective Citizen Politics*, with an Introduction by James MacGregor Burns (New York: Alfred A. Knopf, 1972), p. 328.

19. Key, *Responsible Electorate*.

20. Gerald M. Pomper, "Toward a More Responsible Two-Party System? What, Again?", *Journal of Politics* 33 (November 1971): 924-33.

21. Ibid., pp. 938-39.

22. Ibid.; Saloma and Sontag, *Parties*. The original call for responsible parties grew out of a committee of the American Political Science Association and was greeted with a less than enthusiastic response. *See* Committee on Political Parties of the American Political Science Association, *Toward a More Responsible Two-Party System* (New York: Rinehart & Company, Inc., 1950). For one typical response, *see* Austin Ranney, "Toward a More Responsible Two-Party System: A Commentary," *American Political Science Review* 45 (June 1951): 488-99.

23. Saloma and Sontag, *Parties*. In fact, the subtitle of their book is: "The Real Opportunity for Effective Citizen Politics."

24. There is much literature on the new campaign techniques. *See* Dan Nimmo, *The Political Persuaders: The Techniques of Modern Election Campaigns* (Englewood Cliffs, N. J.: Prentice-Hall, Inc., 1970); Ithiel de Sola Pool, Robert Abelson, and Samuel

Popkin, *Candidates, Issues, and Strategies* (Cambridge, Mass.: M.I.T. Press, 1964); Ray Hiebert, et al., eds., *The Political Image Merchants: Strategies in the New Politics* (Washington, D.C.: Acropolis Books, Ltd., 1971).

25. *Mandate for Reform.*

26. For more details on this contention, *see*: Burnham, *Critical Elections*, chaps. 5 and 6; Lowi, *End of Liberalism*.

Appendix A
The Questionnaire

1970 Political Leadership Survey

Confidential

(If you have received 2 questionnaires by mistake, please fill one out, but mail both of them back together. Thank you.)

We would like to begin with some questions about your development as a political leader.

1. How did you first become interested in politics?
   ( ) Family;   ( ) Friends;   ( ) Job;   ( ) School, reading;
   ( ) Candidate;   ( ) Issue;   ( ) Other _____.
   (specify)

2. When was this?   ( ) Childhood;   ( ) Adolescence;   ( ) Adulthood.

3. Were your parents born in the United States?
   Father ( ) yes ( ) no; Mother ( ) yes ( ) no;
   You ( ) yes ( ) no. If yes for you, what state? _____ .

4. How long have you lived in your present county? _____ .

5. What were your parents' occupations when you were growing up?
   Mother: _____ ; Father: _____ .

6. When you were growing up did your parents belong to the same political party to which you belong?
   Father: ( ) yes ( ) no; Mother: ( ) yes ( ) no.

7. Did your parents ever hold party or public office?
   Mother: Party ( ) no ( ) yes
           Public ( ) no ( ) yes
   Father: Party ( ) no ( ) yes
           Public ( ) no ( ) yes

8. When you first started working in politics, how important were each of the following reasons for your initial participation? Mark every choice.

253

	Very important	Slightly important	Unimportant
Desire to serve community ..	( )	( )	( )
Friends urged me	( )	( )	( )
Possibility of business or political contacts	( )	( )	( )
Family was always active ...	( )	( )	( )
My job experience	( )	( )	( )
Concern with policy matters	( )	( )	( )
Particularly interesting candidate	( )	( )	( )
Attachment to a political party	( )	( )	( )
Community recognition	( )	( )	( )
Excitement of campaigns ...	( )	( )	( )
Duties of citizenship	( )	( )	( )
Enjoyment of working with others in important jobs..	( )	( )	( )
Other (specify)	( )	( )	( )

9. When was the first campaign in which you worked: Year_____.
   Candidate for what office? _____

10. How active have you been in campaigns since then?
    Active: ( ) Every year;   ( ) Every 2 years;   ( ) Every 3 years;
    ( ) Every 4 years or less.

11. In what kinds of campaigns have you worked?
    ( ) Mostly municipality and/or county; ( ) mostly state,
    ( ) mostly national; ( ) all kinds.

12. Were you active in the gubernatorial campaign of 1969? ( ) yes ( ) no.

13. Do you expect to be active this year? ( ) yes ( ) no. If no, why?

_____

14. Which of the following party positions have you held?

		No. of years
County committeeman.............	( )	_____
Ward leader	( )	_____
Delegate to state convention	( )	_____
Municipal chairman	( )	_____
State committee	( )	_____
County chairman................	( )	_____
Alternate or delegate to national convention..................	( )	_____
Other	( )	_____

15. What public-elected offices have you held?

Elected offices held	Number of years

16. What jobs (full-time and part-time) have you held working for municipal, county, sate, or federal government?

Job held	Number of years

17. In how many primary elections have you appeared as a candidate? _____ . Number of victories?_____

18. Would you be willing to accept an appointment to either state, county, or municipal office?

State ( ) no   County or municipal ( ) no
     ( ) yes.   ( ) yes.

19. Which activities have you performed for your party?
( ) Contacted voters; ( ) Distributed literature; ( ) Gave speeches; ( ) Helped people get jobs; ( ) Made finiancial contributions; ( ) Managed campaigns; ( ) Made policy decisions; ( ) Candidate selection; ( ) Showed people how to get their due rights; ( ) Other _____

20. What do you see as your most important political job?
_____
_____
_____

21. Number 1 and 2 what you would miss most if you had to stop your political work tomorrow: A. ( ) Community recognition; B. ( ) Business and political contacts;   C. ( ) Supporting important issues and ideals; D. ( ) Working with friends in the party; E. ( ) Knowing what is happening in the community; F. ( ) Nothing;
( ) Other:_____

22. What do you think most party activists would miss? Choose the letter from question #21 that would be most appropriate. Letter _____

23. Is there anything you dislike about party work?
( ) no ( ) yes. If yes, what? _____

24. Have you ever voted against your party in a Presidential or Congressional election? ( ) yes ( ) no.
If yes, for what candidates? _____
_____
_____

25. Before the 1968 Presidential convention, who was your personal choice for the Democratic nomination?
( ) Humphrey;   ( ) Johnson;   ( ) Robert Kennedy;   ( ) McCarthy; ( ) Wallace;   ( ) Other _____

26. Who did you vote for in the Presidential election, 1968?
( ) Humphrey; ( ) Nixon; ( ) Wallace; ( ) Did not vote;
( ) Other _____

27. Who did you support in the 1969 Gubernatorial Primary?
( ) Helstoski;   ( ) Kelly;   ( ) Meyner;   ( ) Parsekian;   ( ) Tonti;
( ) Other _____

28. Have you heard of the New Democratic Coalition, N.D.C.? ( ) yes ( ) no.
If you answered no to question #28, please skip to question #32.

29. Have you been a member of the N.D.C.?   ( ) yes   ( ) no.

30. What do you think the N.D.C. is trying to accomplish in state politics?
_____
_____

31. By what method should qualified people be chosen to fill administrative or patronage positions? Check one. By: ( ) Civil Service; ( ) Length of party service;   ( ) Party leadership groups;   ( ) Party rank and file; ( ) No opinion.

We would like to know if you agree with the following statements about parties and politics. (Check only one answer in each statement in questions 32-39.)

32. My party should always stand fast to its goals and principles even if this should lead to a loss of votes. ( ) Agree strongly; ( ) Agree; ( ) Disagree; ( ) Disagree strongly; ( ) No opinion.

33. Politics for me is more a matter of getting the best possible out of a given situation rather than firmly sticking to principles. ( ) Agree strongly; ( ) Agree; ( ) Disagree; ( ) Disagree strongly; ( ) No opinion.

34. The job of the party is to reconcile different interests rather than to take clear stands on issues. ( ) Agree strongly; ( ) Agree; ( ) Disagree ( ) Disagree strongly; ( ) No opinion.

35. It is not important to agree with a person's reasons for supporting policies, as long as he supports the right policies. ( ) Agree strongly; ( ) Agree; ( ) Disagree; ( ) Disagree strongly; ( ) No opinion.

36. Few people really know what is in their own best interest in the long run. ( ) Agree strongly; ( ) Agree; ( ) Disagree; ( ) Disagree strongly; No opinion.

37. Almost all the people running the government are capable people who usually know what they are doing. ( ) Agree strongly; ( ) Agree; ( ) Disagree; ( ) Disagree strongly; ( ) No opinion.

38. Nothing I do seems to have any effect upon what happens in politics.
   ( ) Agree strongly;   ( ) Agree;   ( ) Disagree;   ( ) Disagree strongly;
   ( ) No opinion.

39. If you start to change things very much you usually make them worse.
   ( ) Agree strongly;   ( ) Agree;   ( ) Disagree;   ( ) Disagree strongly;
   ( ) No opinion.

Now we would like to turn to your opinions on several issues.

40. How do you rank yourself in comparison to most other Northern
   Democrats? ( ) In the mainstream of the Democratic Party; ( ) Slightly
   more conservative than the mainstream; ( ) Much more conservative
   than the mainstream; ( ) Slightly more liberal than the mainstream;
   ( ) Much more liberal than the mainstream.

41. In the coming year will you devote most of your political reading and
   listening to local, state, or national issues? ( ) Mainly local; ( ) Mainly
   state; ( ) Mainly national; ( ) Equal mixture of all; ( ) Don't know;
   ( ) Other: _____

42. What newpapers and magazines do you read regularly? _____

43. On Vietnam, which statement is most in accord with your point of
   view? ( ) Immediate withdrawal from Vietnam; ( ) Continued neg-
   otiations prove fruitful; ( ) Increased military offensive; ( ) No opinion.

44. Should the U.S. respond to requests for military supplies, advisers, and
   troops in Cambodia and Laos? Military supplies and/or advisers: ( ) no
   ( ) yes ( ) don't know. Military troops: ( ) no ( ) yes ( ) don't
   know.

45. Some people think the national government should do more in trying to
   deal with such problems as unemployment, education, and housing.
   Others think the government already does too much. On the whole,
   would you say the government does in:

   Unemployment: ( ) too much   ( ) about enough
                     ( ) not enough   ( ) no opinion.
   Education   :   ( ) too much   ( ) about enough
                     ( ) not enough   ( ) no opinion.
   Housing   :   ( ) too much   ( ) about enough
                     ( ) not enough   ( ) no opinion.

46. Some people say it is more important to correct the problems of poverty
   and unemployment that produce rioting. On the other hand are those
   who say it is more important to use all available force to maintain law
   and order, and, of course, there are those who fall in between these two
   positions. If we give a score of 1 to those whose first concern is to
   correct all the problems of poverty and unemployment, and a score of 7

to those whose first concern is to use all available force to maintain law and order, how would you score yourself? (Circle appropriate number): 1. Solve problems of poverty   2.   3.   4.   5.   6.   7.   Use all available force.

47. Some people feel that if Negroes are not getting fair treatment in jobs, the national government should see to it that they do. Others feel that this is not the federal government's business. How do you feel? ( ) Federal government should see to it; ( ) Leave matters to state and local government; ( ) Leave it to private initiative; ( ) No opinion.

48. We have heard a lot about civil rights groups working to improve the position of the Negro in this country. How much real change do you think there has been in the position of the Negro in the past few years? ( ) A lot; ( ) Some; ( ) Not much at all.

49. Do you approve of open-admission policy at Rutgers for disadvantaged groups? ( ) Strongly approve; ( ) Approve; ( ) Depends on circumstances; ( ) Disapprove; ( ) Strongly disapprove; ( ) No opinion.

50. Would you approve of people taking part in protest meetings or marches that are permitted by the local authorities? ( ) Strongly approve; ( ) Approve; ( ) Depends on circumstances; ( ) Disapprove; ( ) Strongly disapprove; ( ) No opinion.

51. Would you agree that left-wing groups like the S.D.S. or right-wing groups like the Minutemen should be permitted to speak in our public schools? ( ) Agree strongly; ( ) Agree; ( ) Depends on circumstances; ( ) Disagree; ( ) Disagree strongly; ( ) No opinion.

Now a few background questions:

52. What is your major occupation? (Please state) _____

53. Sex: ( ) Male ( ) Female.

54. Are you employed by: ( ) Government; ( ) Institution; ( ) Private Business; ( ) Self; Other

55. Check your age: ( ) 21-29; ( ) 30-39; ( ) 40-49; ( ) 50-59; ( ) 60-69; ( ) 70 or over.

56. What municipality do you live in? _____

57. Indicate how many years of formal education you have completed? Check only one: ( ) No formal education; ( ) Elementary school only; High School only: ( ) 1-3 years; ( ) 4 years; College only: ( ) 1-3 years;   ( ) 4 years.   ( ) Graduate School: state advanced degree _____

58. If you are a member of any of the following minority groups, please check one: ( ) Italo-American; ( ) Afro-American; ( ) Irish-America; Puerto-Rican; ( ) Eastern European; ( ) Other_____

59. What is your approximate annual family income: ( ) Less than $4,999;
( ) $5,000-9,999;   ( ) $10,000-14,999;   ( ) $15,000-19,999;
( ) $20,000-24,999; ( ) $25,000 and over.

60. What is your religious preference? ( ) Catholic; ( ) Jewish; ( ) Protestant; ( ) None; ( ) Other _____

61. How frequently do you attend religious services? ( ) Once a week or more; ( ) 1 to 2 times a month; ( ) A few times a year; ( ) Never.

62. To which of the following kinds of voluntary organizations do you belong and in which are you an officer?

	Officer
( ) Business and Civic	_____
( ) Political (other than party)	_____
( ) Religious	_____
( ) Professional	_____
( ) Charitable	_____
( ) Labor Union	_____
( ) Veteran's	_____
( ) Social or fraternal	_____
( ) Ethnic	_____
( ) Other _____	_____

Thank you very much for your time and effort. Please know that it is appreciated.

Appendix B
Cover Letters

First Mailing

A. To all N.D.C. Members, Except Those from Union County

RUTGERS UNIVERSITY The State University of New Jersey

THE EAGLETON INSTITUTE OF POLITICS
Wood Lawn, Neilson Campus
New Brunswick, New Jersey 08903

Dear N.D.C. Delegate:

In this time of national change you represent a style of politics with fresh ideas and programs. The National Science Foundation and Eagleton Institute at Rutgers University have sponsored a study of this new leadership that you epitomize. The purpose of the research is to provide for others a better understanding of how this new group of national leaders differs from the old.

Many of your fellow New Democratic Coalition delegates and leaders are quite interested in the study. This list includes the following who urge your full and immediate cooperation:

George Callas	Estelle Greenberg
Pete Curtin	Irving Halperin
John Doyle	Chris Hill
Don Edwards	Joel Jacobson
Ron Eisele	Nate Johnson
Dorothy Eldridge	Jay Spigler
Milton Filker	Stuart Spiegler
Dan Gaby	Harvey Turner
	Ken Wooden

Only if we get enough responses can any analysis give insight into the new politics and its potential.

Please take 20 minutes now to complete the questionnaire. In return for your cooperation, N. S. F. and Eagleton promise total confidentiality, as well as the availability of any findings.

Yours truly,

(Mrs.) Vicki Semel,
Director, 1970 Political
Leadership Survey

B. To all N.D.C. Members from Union County

1230 Lake Avenue
Clark, New Jersey 07066
May 6, 1970

Dear N.D.C. Delegate:

In this time of national change, you represent a style of politics with fresh ideas and programs. Under Mrs. Vicki Semel, the National Science Foundation and Eagleton Institute of Rutgers University have undertaken a study of this new leadership that you epitomize. I would appreciate your full and immediate cooperation with the project.

The purpose of this research is to provide for others a better understanding of how this new group of national leaders differs from the old. Please take time now to complete the questionnaire. In return for your participation, N.S.F. and Eagleton promise total confidentiality as well as the availability of any findings.

Sincerely yours,

Michael Diamond, Chairman
Union County New Democratic
Coalition

C. To all Regular Democratic County Committee Members

DEMOCRATIC STATE COMMITTEE   NEW JERSEY

31-33 North Willow Street   Telephone 392-3471
Trenton, New Jersey 08608   Area Code 609

Dear County Committee Member:

During this period of national census taking, the National Science Foundation and the Eagleton Institute of Politics at Rutgers has sponsored a research project under Mrs. Vicki Semel. This study adds to the census material on the whole population with a look at the opinions of a sample of the nation's important political leaders.

We urge full cooperation with this study that should produce interesting findings contributing to our understanding of the ideas and interests of our country's leaders. While the questions asked represent the work of Mrs. Semel, we in the State Committee look forward to and will be guided by your answers. Recently we polled you on the Thompson Commission Report and your responsiveness was most encouraging.

Of course, the project promises total confidentiality for each individual, plus the availability of the findings for those who would like to see them. Please, we urge you, fill out and return this questionnaire today.

                              Very truly yours,

                              John T. Connor, Jr.
                              Executive Director
                              Democratic State Committee

Encl.

Second Mailing

A. Postcard to Everyone

RUTGERS UNIVERSITY The State University of New Jersey

THE EAGLETON INSTITUTE OF POLITICS
Wood Lawn, Neilson Campus
New Brunswick, New Jersey 08903

A few days ago we sent you a questionnaire as part of our Political Leadership Survey. If you have already returned it, consider this a special thank you. If you put it aside to finish later, please fill it out and return it right away. There will probably never be a better time. If we do not hear from you in the next week, we will contact you to see if there is any problem with the questionnaire we can solve.

Thank you for your cooperation.

Yours truly,

(Mrs.) Vicki Semel
Director, 1970 Leadership Survey

Third Mailing

A. To all N.D.C. Members

RUTGERS UNIVERSITY The State University of New Jersey

THE EAGLETON INSTITUTE OF POLITICS
Wood Lawn, Neilson Campus
New Brunswick, New Jersey 08903

Dear N.D.C. Delegate:

We were disappointed not to receive your questionnaire from our survey. On the whole, the N.D.C. has answered fully and rapidly. Since our study is statistical, however, we must receive your form to make it valid.

If you are reluctant to reply because of the code number, please delete it. Let us also explain that the sole intent of the number is to permit us to know who has not returned the questionnaire. Thus we can undertake further mailings without inconveniencing N.D.C. members who have already responded. Once the sample is gathered, the list matching names and numbers is discarded.

Since our purpose is to provide understanding of the new national leadership that you represent, your immediate participation could not be more relevant to you.

If you have already mailed in your questionnaire, accept our gratitude; if you have put it aside, we wish you would reconsider. A second form is enclosed for your convenience.

Thank you for your time.

Sincerely yours,

(Mrs.) Vicki Semel, Director,
Political Leadership Survey

B. To all Regular Democratic County Committee Members

RUTGERS UNIVERSITY The State University of New Jersey

THE EAGLETON INSTITUTE OF POLITICS
Wood Lawn, Neilson Campus
New Brunswick, New Jersey 08903

Dear County Committee Member:

The summer months probably find you free from political work for a time. Several weeks ago we sent you a form as part of our Political Leadership Survey. You might have been too busy then, or perhaps you misplaced it. (We have enclosed another copy for your convenience.)

As the responsible leaders of your communities, we are sure you will realize the importance of your cooperation in this study of grass roots activists who were committee members in 1969.

One further word: due to a typing error, some are told to skip question 31. This is a mistake. *All* should answer question 31.

Sincerely yours,

Vicki Semel, Director,
Political Leadership Survey

Bibliography

Books

Abrams, Richard M., and Levine, Lawrence W., eds. *The Shaping of Twentieth-Century America: Interpretive Articles*. Boston: Little, Brown & Company, 1965.

Adler, Renata. *Toward a Radical Middle*. New York: Random House, 1969.

Almond, Gabriel A., and Verba, Sidney. *The Civic Culture*. Princeton, New Jersey: Princeton Unversity Press, 1963.

Apter, David E., ed. *Ideology and Discontent*. New York: Free Press of Glencoe, 1964.

Argyris, Chris. *Interpersonal Competence and Organizational Effectiveness*. The Irwin-Dorsey Series in Behavioral Science in Business. Homewood, Illinois: The Dorsey Press, Inc., and Richard D. Irwin, Inc., 1962.

Arnold, Thurman W. *The Folklore of Capitalism*. New Haven, Connecticut: Yale University Press, 1937.

Banfield, Edward C., and Wilson, James Q. *City Politics*. New York: Vintage Books, Random House, 1963.

Barber, James Alden, Jr. *Social Mobility and Voting Behavior*. Chicago: Rand McNally & Co., 1970.

Bell, Daniel. *The End of Ideology: On the Exhaustion of Politcal Ideas in the Fifties*. Glencoe, Illinois: Free Press of Glencoe, 1960.

Benson, Lee. *The Concept of Jacksonian Democracy: New York as a Test Case*. New York: Atheneum Press, 1961.

Berry, David. *The Sociology of Grass Roots Politics: A Study of Party Membership*. London: Macmillan Company, 1970.

Birnbaum, Norman. *The Crisis of Industrial Society*. New York: Oxford Unversity Press, 1969.

Blaisdell, Donald C. *The Riverside Democrats*. Cases in Practical Politics, Case 18. New Brunswick, New Jersey: Eagleton Institute, 1960.

Blalock, Hubert M., Jr. *Social Statistics*. New York: McGraw-Hill Book Company, 1960.

Blau, Peter M. *Bureaucracy in Modern Society*. New York: Random House, 1956.

Burnham, Walter Dean. *Critical Elections and the Mainsprings of American Politics*. New York: W. W. Norton & Company, Inc., 1970.

——. *Presidential Ballots, 1836-1892*. Baltimore: Johns Hopkins Press, 1955.

Burns, James MacGregor, *Uncommon Sense*. New York: Harper & Row Publishers, Inc., 1972.

Callow, Alexander B., Jr. *The Tweed Ring*. New York: Oxford University Press, 1966.

Campbell, Angus; Converse, Philip E.; Miller, Warren E.; and Stokes, Donald. *The American Voter*. New York: John Wiley & Sons, Inc., 1960.

——; Converse, Philip E.; Miller, Warren E.; and Stokes, Donald E. *The American Voter: An Abridgement*. New York: John Wiley & Sons, Inc., 1964.

——; Converse, Philip E.; Miller, Warren E.; and Stokes, Donald E., eds. *Elections and the Political Order*. New York: John Wiley & Sons, Inc., 1966.

Carney, Francis. *The Rise of the Democratic Clubs in California*. New York: Henry Holt and Co., Inc., 1958;

Carpenter, William Seal. *The Unfinished Business of Civil Service Reform*. Princeton, New Jersey: Princeton University Press, 1952.

Chambers, William Nisbet, and Burnham, Walter Dean, eds. *The American Party Systems: Stages of Political Development*. New York: Oxford University Press, 1967.

Chester, Lewis; Hodgson, Godfrey; and Page, Bruce. *An American Melodrama: The Presidential Campaign of 1968*. New York: The Viking Press, 1969.

Childs, Richard S. *Civic Victories: The Story of an Unfinished Revolution*. New York: Harper & Brothers Publishers, 1952.

Comfort, George O. *Professional Politicians: A Study of British Party Agents*. Washington, D.C.: Public Affairs Press, 1958.

Committee on Political Parties of the American Political Science Association. *Toward a More Responsible Two-Party System*. New York: Rinehart & Company, Inc., 1950.

Connors, Richard J. *A Cycle of Power: The Career of Jersey City Mayor Frank Hague*. Metuchen, New Jersey: The Scarecrow Press, Inc., 1971.

Costikyan, Edward N. *Behind Closed Doors: Politics in the Public Interest*. New York: Harcourt, Brace and World, Inc., 1966.

Croly, Herbert. *The Promise of American Life*. Edited by Arthur M. Schlesinger, Jr. Cambridge, Massachusetts: The Belknap Press of Harvard University Press, 1965.

Crotty, William J., ed. *Approaches to the Study of Party Organization*. Boston: Allyn and Bacon, Inc., 1968.

——. Freeman, Donald M.; and Gatlin, Douglas S., eds. *Political Parties and Political Behavior*. Boston: Allyn and Bacon, Inc., 1971.

Dahl, Robert A. *Pluralist Democracy in the United States: Conflict and Consent*. Chicago: Rand McNally & Co., 1967.

——. *Who Governs?* New Haven, Connecticut: Yale University, Press, 1961.

David, Paul T.; Goldman, Ralph M.; and Bain, Richard C. *The Politics of National Party Conventions*. Edited by Kathleen Sproul. Washington, D.C.: Brookings Institution, 1960.

Davis, Allen F. *Spearheads for Reform: The Social Settlement and the*

Progressive Movement, 1890-1914. New York: Oxford University Press, 1967.

Dawson, Richard E., and Prewitt, Kenneth. *Political Socialization.* Boston: Little, Brown & Company, 1969.

Dewey, John. *Characters and Events.* Vol. 2. New York: Henry Holt and Company, 1929.

Dobriner, William M., ed. *The Suburban Community.* New York: G. P. Putnam's Sons, 1958.

Dorsett, Lyle W. *The Pendergast Machine.* New York: Oxford University Press, 1968.

Downs, Anthony. *An Economic Theory of Democracy.* New York: Harper & Row, 1957.

Duverger, Maurice, *Political Parties.* New York: John Wiley & Sons, Inc., 1954.

Edinger, Lewis J., ed. *Political Leadership in Industrialized Societies: Studies in Comparative Analysis.* New York: John Wiley & Sons, Inc., 1967.

Eldersveld, Samuel J. *Political Parties: A Behavioral Analysis.* Chicago: Rand McNally & Co., 1964.

Epstein, Leon D. *Politics in Wisconsin.* Madison, Wisconsin: University of Wisconsin Press, 1958.

Etzioni, Amitai, ed. *A Sociological Reader on Complex Organizations.* New York: Holt, Rinehart and Winston, Inc., 1969.

Eulau, Heinz; Eldersveld, Samuel J.; and Janowitz, Morris. *Political Behavior: A Reader in Theory and Research.* Glencoe, Illinois: Free Press of Glencoe, 1956.

Faulkner, Harold Underwood. *American Political and Social History.* 5th ed. New York: Appleton-Century-Crofts, Inc., 1948.

——. *Politics, Reform, and Expansion, 1890-1900.* The New American Nation Series. Edited by Henry Steele Commager and Richard B. Morris. New York: Harper & Brothers, 1959.

Festinger, Leon. *A Theory of Cognitive Dissonance.* Stanford, California: Stanford University Press, 1957.

Fishel, Jeff. *Party and Opposition: Congressional Challengers in American Politics.* New York: David McKay Company, Inc., 1973.

Flanigan, William H. *Political Behavior of the American Electorate.* 2nd ed. Boston: Allyn and Bacon, Inc., 1972.

Flynn, Edward J. *You're the Boss.* New York: The Viking Press, 1947.

Forthal, Sonya. *Cogwheels of Democracy: A Study of the Precinct Captain.* New York: The William-Frederick Press, 1946.

Fowler, Dorothy Ganfield. *The Cabinet Politician: The Postmasters General, 1829-1909.* New York: Columbia University Press, 1943.

Free, Lloyd A., and Cantril, Hadley. *The Political Beliefs of Americans: A Study of Public Opinion.* New York: Clarion Books, Simon and Schuster, 1968.

Freeman, Linton C. *Elementary Applied Statistics: For Students in Behavioral Science.* New York: John Wiley & Sons, Inc., 1965.

Frost, Richard T., ed. *Cases in State and Local Government.* Englewood Cliffs, New Jersey: Prentice-Hall, Inc., 1961.

Garrett, Charles. *The LaGuardia Years: Machine and Reform Politics in New York City.* New Brunswick, New Jersey: Rutgers University Press, 1961.

Glazer, Nathan, and Moynihan, Daniel Patrick. *Beyond the Melting Pot: The Negroes, Puerto Ricans, Jews, Italians, and Irish of New York City.* Cambridge, Massachusetts: M. I. T. Press and Harvard University Press, 1963.

Goldman, Eric. *Rendezvous with Destiny: A History of Modern American Reform.* New York: Alfred A. Knopf, 1952.

Golembiewski, Robert T. *Behavior and Organization: O. & M. and the Small Group.* Chicago: Rand McNally & Co., 1962.

——. *The Small Group: An Analysis of Research Concepts and Operations.* Chicago: University of Chicago Press, 1962.

——. Welsh, William A.; and Crotty, William J. *A Methodological Primer for Political Scientists.* Chicago: Rand McNally & Co., 1969.

Gosnell, Harold F. *Machine Politics: Chicago Model.* Foreword by Theodore J. Lowi. 2nd ed. Chicago: University of Chicago Press, 1968.

Gouldner, Alvin W. *Patterns of Industrial Bureaucracy.* Glencoe, Illinois: Free Press of Glencoe, 1954.

Green, Thomas Hill. *Works of Thomas Hill Green.* Vol 2: *Philosophical Works.* Edited by R. L. Nettleship. London: Longmans, Green, and Co., 1906.

Grimes, Alan Pendleton. *American Political Thought.* Rev. ed. New York: Holt, Rinehart & Winston, 1960.

Halberstam, David. *The Unfinished Odyssey of Robert Kennedy.* New York: Random House, 1968.

Hartz, Louis. *The Liberal Tradition in America: An Interpretation of American Political Thought Since the Revolution.* New York: Harvest Books, Harcourt, Brace & World, Inc., 1955.

Hays, Samuel P. *Conservatism and the Gospel of Efficiency: The Progressive Conservation Movement, 1890-1920.* Cambridge, Massachusetts: Harvard University Press, 1959.

Herzog, Arthur. *McCarthy for President.* New York: Viking Press, 1969.

Hess, Robert D., and Torney, Judith. *The Development of Political Attitudes in Children.* Chicago: Aldine Publishing Co., 1967.

Hiebert, Ray; Jones, Robert; Lorenz, John; and Lotito, Ernest, eds. *The Political Image Merchants: Strategies in the New Politics.* Washington, D.C.: Acropolis Books, Ltd., 1971.

Hinderaker, Ivan, ed. *American Government Annual, 1962-63.* New York: Holt, Rinehart & Winston, 1962.

Hofstadter, Richard. *The Age of Reform: From Bryan to F. D. R.* New York: Alfred A. Knopf, 1955.

——. ed. *The Progressive Movement, 1900-1915.* Englewood Cliffs, New Jersey: Prentice-Hall, Inc., 1963.

Holli, Melvin G. *Reform in Detroit: Hazen S. Pingree and Urban Politics.* New York: Oxford University Press, 1969.

Hoogenboom, Ari. *Outlawing the Spoils: A History of the Civil Service Reform Movement, 1865-1883.* Urbana, Illinois: University of Illinois Press, 1961.

Ions, Edmund, ed. *Political and Social Thought in America, 1870-1970.* London: Weidenfeld and Nicolson, 1970.

Irish, Marian D., ed. *Continuing Crisis in American Politics.* Englewood Cliffs, New Jersey: Prentice-Hall, Inc., 1963.

James, Dorothy B. *Poverty, Politics, and Change.* Englewood Cliffs, New Jersey: Prentice-Hall, Inc., 1972.

James, Judson L. *American Political Parties: Potential and Performance.* New York: Pegasus, 1969.

Janowitz, Morris, ed. *Community Political Systems.* Glencoe, Illinois: Free Press of Glencoe, 1961.

Josephson, Matthew. *The Politicos: 1865-1896.* New York: Harcourt, Brace and Company, 1938.

Kammen, Michael. *People of Paradox: An Inquiry Concerning the Origins of American Civilization.* New York: Alfred A. Knopf, 1972.

Katz, Daniel, and Kahn, Robert L. *The Social Psychology of Organizations.* New York: John Wiley & Sons, Inc., 1969.

Kaufman, Arnold S. *The Radical Liberal: The New Politics, Theory and Practice.* Foreword by Hans J. Morgenthau. New York: Clarion Book, Simon and Schuster, 1968.

Kelley, Stanley. *Professional Public Relations and Political Power.* Baltimore: Johns Hopkins Press, 1956.

Kent, Frank R. *The Great Game of Politics.* Garden City, New York: Doubleday, Page and Co., 1923.

Key, V. O., Jr. *American State Politics: An Introduction.* New York: Alfred A. Knopf, 1956.

——. *Public Opinion and American Democracy.* New York: Alfred A. Knopf, 1961.

——. (with the help of Milton C. Cummings, Jr.). *The Responsible Electorate: Rationality in Presidential Voting, 1936-1960.* Cambridge, Massachusetts: The Belknap Press of Harvard University Press, 1966.

Klein, Harold M. *Patterns of Public Employment in New Jersey.* New Brunswick, New Jersey: Rutgers — The State University, Bureau of Government Research and University Extension Division, 1968.

Kleppner, Paul. *The Cross of Culture: A Social Analysis of Midwestern Politics, 1850-1900.* New York: Free Press, 1970.

Knorr, Klaus, and Verba, Sidney, eds. *The International System: Theoretical Essays.* Princeton, New Jersey: Princeton University Press, 1961.

Kolko, Gabriel. *The Triumph of Conservatism: A Reinterpretation of American History, 1900-1916.* New York: Free Press of Glencoe, 1963.

Lane, Robert E. *Political Life.* Glencoe, Illinois: Free Press of Glencoe, 1969.

——. *Political Thinking and Consciousness: The Private Life of the Political Mind.* Chicago: Markham Publishing Co., 1968.

Langton, Kenneth P. *Political Socialization*. New York: Oxford University Press, 1969.

Lasch, Christopher. *The New Radicalism in America, 1889-1963: The Intellectual as a Social Type*. New York: Alfred A. Knopf, 1965.

Lawson, R. Alan. *The Failure of Independent Liberalism, 1930-1941*. New York: G. P. Putnam's Sons, 1971.

League of Women Voters of New Jersey. *New Jersey: Spotlight on Government*. Chapter by Richard P. McCormick, North Plainfield, New Jersey: Twin City Press, 1969.

Lee, Eugene C. *The Politics of Nonpartisanship: A Study of California City Elections*. Los Angeles and Berkeley: University of California Press, 1960.

Lee, Robert, and Marty, Martin E., eds. *Religion and Social Conflict*. New York: Oxford University Press, 1964.

Lieberman, Bernhardt, ed. *Contemporary Problems in Statistics: A Book of Readings for the Behavioral Sciences*. New York: Oxford University Press, 1971.

Lipset, Seymour Martin. *Political Man: The Social Bases of Politics*. Garden City, New York: Anchor Books, Doubleday & Company, Inc., 1960.

Litterer, Joseph A., ed. *Organizations: Structure and Behavior*. New York: John Wiley & Sons, Inc., 1963.

Lockhard, Duane. *The New Jersey Governor: A Study in Political Power*. The New Jersey Historical Series. Vol. 14. Princeton, New Jersey: D. Van Nostrand Company, Inc., 1964.

Locke, John. *The Second Treatise of Government*. Edited with an Introduction by Thomas P. Peardon. New York: Liberal Arts Press, 1952.

Lowi, Theodore J. *At the Pleasure of the Mayor: Patronage and Power in New York City, 1898-1958*. New York: Free Press of Glencoe, 1964.

——. *The End of Liberalism: Ideology, Policy, and the Crisis of Public Authority*. New York: W. W. Norton & Company, Inc., 1969.

——. *The Politics of Disorder*. New York: Basic Books, Inc., 1971.

Lynn, Kenneth S., and Hughes, Everett C., eds. *The Professions in America*. Boston: Houghton Mifflin Company, 1965.

McCarthy, Eugene J. *The Year of the People*. Garden City, New York: Doubleday & Company, Inc., 1969.

McKean, Dayton David. *The Boss: The Hague Machine in Action*. New York: Russell and Russell, 1940.

McWilliams, Wilson Carey. *The Idea of Fraternity in America*. Berkeley, California: University of California Press, 1973.

Mandate for Reform: A Report of the Commission of Party Structure and Delegate Selection to the Democratic National Committee. George McGovern, chairman. Washington, D.C.: The Commission of Party Structure and Delegate Selection, Democratic National Committee, 1970.

Mandelbaum, Seymour J. *Boss Tweed's New York*. New York: John Wiley & Sons, Inc., 1965.

Mann, Arthur. *LaGuardia: A Fighter Against His Times, 1882-1933*. New York: J. B. Lippincott Company, 1959.

——. *LaGuardia Comes to Power: 1933*. New York: J. B. Lippincott Company, 1965.

——. *Yankee Reformers in the Urban Age*. Cambridge, Massachusetts: The Belknap Press of Harvard University Press, 1954.

March, James G., ed. *Handbook of Organizations*. Chicago: Rand McNally & Co., 1965.

Martin, Roscoe C. *Grassroots: Rural Democracy in America*. New York: Harper & Row, 1964.

Marvick, Dwaine, ed. *Political Decision Makers*. International Yearbook of Political Behavior Research. Vol. 2. Glencoe, Illinois: Free Press of Glencoe, 1961.

Maslow, A. H. *Motivation and Personality*. New York: Harper & Bros., 1954.

Mayer, George H. *The Republican Party: 1854-1964*. New York: Oxford University Press, 1964.

Mendelsohn, Harold, and Crespi, Irving. *Polls, Television, and the New Politics*. Scranton, Pennsylvania: Chandler Publishing Company, 1970.

Merton, Robert K. *Social Theory and Social Structure*. First revised and enlarged ed. London: Free Press of Glencoe, 1957.

Michels, Robert. *Political Parties: A Sociological Study of the Oligarchical Tendencies of Modern Democracy*. Translated by Eden and Cedar Paul. Glencoe, Illinois: Free Press of Glencoe, 1915.

Milbrath, Lester W. *Political Participation: How and Why Do People Get Involved in Politics?* Chicago: Rand McNally & Co., 1965.

Miller, Zane L. *Boss Cox's Cincinnati: Urban Politics in the Progressive Era*. New York: Oxford University Press, 1968.

Minogue, Kenneth R. *The Liberal Mind*. New York: Vintage Books, Random House, 1963.

Mitchell, Stephen A. *Elm Street Politics*. New York: Oceana Publications, Inc., 1959.

Mosher, Frederick C. *Democracy and the Public Service*. Public Administration and Democracy Series. Edited by Roscoe C. Martin. New York: Oxford University Press, 1968.

Mowry, George E. *The California Progressives*. Chicago: Encounter Paperbacks, Quadrangle Books, 1963.

——. *The Era of Theodore Roosevelt, 1900-1912*. The New American Nation Series. Edited by Henry Steele Commager and Richard B. Morris. New York: Harper and Row Publishers, Inc., 1958.

——. *The Urban Nation, 1920-1960*. New York: Hill & Wang, 1965.

Mueller, John H.; Schuessler, Karl F.; and Costner, Herbert L. *Statistical Reasoning in Sociology*. 2nd ed. Boston: Houghton Mifflin Company, 1970.

Nie, Norman H.; Bent, Dale H.; and Hull, C. Hadlai. *Statistical Package for the Social Sciences (SPSS)*. New York: McGraw-Hill Book Company, 1970.

Nimmo, Dan. *The Political Persuaders: The Techniques of Modern Election Campaigns*. Englewood Cliffs, New Jersey: Prentice-Hall, Inc., 1970.

Olson, Mancur, Jr. *The Logic of Collective Action: Public Goods and the Theory of Groups*. New York: Schocken Books, 1965.

Oppenheim, A. N. *Questionnaire Design and Attitude Measurement*. New York: Basic Books, Inc., 1961.

Peel, Roy W. *The Political Clubs of New York City*. New York: G. P. Putnam's Sons, 1935.

Polsby, Nelson, and Wildabsky, Aaron B. *Presidential Elections: Strategies of American Electoral Politics*. 3rd ed. New York: Charles Scribner's Sons, 1971.

——. Dentler, Robert A.; and Smith, Paul A. *Politics and Social Life: An Introduction to Political Behavior*. Boston: Houghton Mifflin Company, 1963.

Pomper, Gerald. *Nominating the President: The Politics of Convention Choice*. With a new postscript on 1964. New York: W. W. Norton & Company, Inc., 1966.

——. McWilliams, Wilson Carey; Rosenthal, Alan; Jacob, Charles E.; Sigler, Jay A.; and Foster, Badi G. *The Performance of American Government: Checks and Minuses*. New York: Free Press, 1972.

Pool, Ithiel de Sola; Abelson, Robert; and Popkin, Samuel. *Candidates, Issues, and Strategies*. Cambridge, Massachusetts: M. I. T. Press, 1964.

Richter, Melvin. *The Politics of Conscience: T. H. Green and His Age*. The Nature of Human Society Series. Edited by Julian Pitt-Rivers and Ernest Gellner. Cambridge, Massachusetts: Harvard University Press, 1964.

Riesman, David; Glazer, Nathan; and Denny, Reuel. *The Lonely Crowd*. New Haven, Connecticut: Yale University Press, 1950.

Riker, William H. *The Theory of Political Coalitions*. New Haven, Connecticut: Yale University Press, 1962.

Riordon, William L. *Plunkitt of Tammany Hall*. New York: E. P. Dutton & Co., 1963.

Roethlisberger, F. J., and Dickson, William J. *Management and the Worker*. Cambridge, Massachusetts: Harvard University Press, 1947.

Rosenberg, Morris. *The Logic of Survey Analysis*. New York: Basic Books, Inc., 1968.

Saloma, John S., III, and Sontag, Frederick H. *Parties: The Real Opportunity for Effective Citizen Politics*. With an Introduction by James MacGregor Burns. New York: Alfred A. Knopf, 1972.

Salter, John T. *Boss Rule: Portraits in City Politics*. New York: Whittlesey House, 1935.

Sarasohn, Stephen B., and Sarasohn, Vera. *Political Party Patterns in Michigan*. Wayne State University Studies. Detroit, Michigan: Wayne State University Press, 1957.

Sawyer, Robert Lee, Jr. *The Democratic State Central Committee in Michigan, 1949-1959: The Rise of the New Politics and the New Political Leadership*. Michigan Governmental Studies, no. 40. Ann Arbor, Michigan:

Institute of Public Administration, University of Michigan Press, 1960.

Scammon, Richard M., and Wattenberg, Ben J. *The Real Majority*. New York: Berkley Medallion Book, Berkley Publishing Corp., 1971.

Schattschneider, E. E. *Party Government*. New York: Holt, Rinehart & Winston, 1942.

Schlesinger, Arthur M. *The American as Reformer*. Cambridge, Massachusetts: Harvard University Press, 1950.

Schlesinger, Joseph A. *Ambition and Politics: Political Careers in the United States*. Chicago: Rand McNally & Co., 1966.

Sherif, Muzafer, ed. *Intergroup Relations and Leadership: Approaches and Research in Industrial, Ethnic, Cultural, and Political Areas*. New York: John Wiley & Sons, Inc., 1962.

Sigel, Roberta S, ed. *Learning About Politics: A Reader in Political Socialization*. New York: Random House, 1970.

Snedecor, George W., and Cochran, William G. *Statistical Methods*. 6th ed. Ames, Iowa: Iowa State University Press, 1967.

Sofer, Cyril. *Organizations in Theory and Practice*. New York: Basic Books, Inc., 1972.

Sorauf, Frank J. *Party and Representation: Legislative Politics in Pennsylvania*. New York: Atherton Press, 1963.

Stavis, Ben. *We Were the Campaign: New Hampshire to Chicago for McCarthy*. Boston: Beacon Press, 1969.

Steffens, Lincoln. *The Shame of the Cities*. New York: Hill & Wang, 1957.

Stinchcombe, Jean L. *Reform and Reaction: City Politics in Toledo*. Belmont, California: Wadsworth Publishing Co., Inc., 1968.

U.S. Department of Commerce, Bureau of Census. *Statistical Abstract of the United States, 1969*. 90th ed. Washington, D.C.: U.S. Government Printing Office, 1969.

Van Riper, Paul P. *History of the United States Civil Service*. White Plains, New York: Row, Peterson and Company, 1958.

Weber, Max. *Politics as a Vocation. Max Weber: Essays in Sociology*. Translated, edited, and with an Introduction by H. H. Gerth and C. Wright Mills. New York: Oxford University Press, 1946.

White, Theodore H. *The Making of the President, 1960*. New York: Atheneum Publishers, 1961.

——. *The Making of the President, 1964*. New York: Atheneum Publishers, 1965.

——. *The Making of the President, 1968*. New York: Atheneum Publishers, 1969.

Whyte, William Foote, ed. *Industry and Society*. New York: McGraw-Hill Book Company, 1946.

Wiebe, Robert H. *Businessmen and Reform: A Study of the Progressive Movement*. Cambridge, Massachusetts: Harvard University Press, 1962.

Williams, Oliver P., and Press, Charles, eds. *Democracy in Urban America: Readings in Government and Politics*. Chicago: Rand McNally & Co., 1961.

Wilson, James Q. *The Amateur Democrat: Club Politics in Three Cities*. Chicago: University of Chicago Press, 1966.

Wilson, James Q. *The Amateur Democrat: Club Politics in Three Cities*. Chicago: University of Chicago Press, 1966.

Wirt, Frederick M.; Walter, Benjamin; Rabinovitz, Francine; and Hensler, Deborah R. *On the City's Rim: Politics and Policy in Suburbia*. Lexington. Massachusetts: D.C. Heath and Company, 1972.

Wood, Robert C. *Suburbia: Its People and Their Politics*. Boston: Houghton Mifflin Company, 1958.

Wright, William E., ed. *A Comparative Study of Party Organization*. Merrill Political Science Series. Edited by John C. Wahlke. Columbus, Ohio: Merrill Publishing Company, 1971.

Young, James P. *The Politics of Affluence: Ideology in the United States, Since World War II*. San Francisco: Chandler Publishing Company, 1968.

——. ed. *Consensus and Conflict: Readings in American Politics*. New York: Dodd, Mead & Company, 1972.

Zink, Harold. *City Bosses in the United States: A Study of Twenty Municipal Bosses*. New York: AMS Press, 1968.

Zinn, Howard, ed. *New Deal Thought*. American Heritage Series. New York: Bobbs-Merrill Company, Inc., 1966.

Articles

Adrian, Charles R. "A Typology of Nonpartisan Elections." *Western Political Quarterly* 12 (June 1959): 449-58.

——. "Some General Characteristics of Nonpartisan Elections." *American Political Science Review* 46 (September 1952): 466-76.

Althoff, Phillip, and Patterson, Samuel C. "Political Activism in a Rural County." *Midwest Journal of Political Science* 10 (February 1966): 39-51.

Annals of the American Academy of Political and Social Sciences 353 (May 1964).

Bachrack, Stanley D., and Scoble, Harvey. "Mail Questionnaire Efficiency: Controlled Reduction of Nonresponses." *Public Opinion Quarterly* 32 (Summer 1967): 265-71.

Barnes, Samuel H. "Participation, Education, and Political Competence." *American Political Science Review* 60 (June 1966): 348-53.

Bell, Charles G., and Buchanan, William. "Reliable and Unreliable Respondents: Party Registration and Prestige Pressures." *Western Political Quarterly* 19 (March, 1966): 37-43.

Berelson, Bernard. "Democratic Theory and Public Opinion." *Public Opinion Quarterly* 16 (Fall 1952): 313-30.

Blydenburgh, John C. "Probit Analysis: A Method for Coping with Dichotomous Dependent Variables." *Social Science Quarterly* 1 (March 1971): 889-99.

Bowman, Lewis, and Boynton, G. R. "Activities and Role Definitions of Grass Roots Party Officials." *Journal of Politics* 28 (February 1966): 121-43.

——. and Boynton, G. R. "Recruitment Patterns Among Local Party Officials: A Model and Some Preliminary Findings in Selected Locales." *American Political Science Review* 60 (September 1966): 667-76.

——. Ippolito, Dennis; and Donaldson, William. "Incentive for the Maintenance of Grass Roots Political Activism." *Midwest Journal of Political Science* 13 (February 1969): 126-39.

Boynton, G. R.; Patterson, Samuel C.; and Hellend, Ronald D. "The Missing Links in Legislative Politics: Attentive Constituents." *Journal of Politics* 31 (August 1969): 700-21.

Breed, Warren. "Social Control in the Newsroom: A Functional Analysis." *Social Forces* 33 (May 1955): 326-35.

Brown, Seyom. "Fun Can be Politics." *Reporter,* 12 November 1959, pp. 27-28.

Brown, Steven R., and Ellithorp, John D. "Emotional Experiences in Political Groups: The Case of the McCarthy Phenomenon." *American Political Science Review* 64 (June 1970): 349-66.

Browning, Rufus. "The Interaction of Personality and Political System in Decisions to Run for Office: Some Data and a Simulation Technique." *Journal of Social Issues* 24 (July 1968): 93-109.

Burnham, Walter Dean. "The End of American Party Politics." *Trans-action,* December 1969, pp. 12-22.

Cahalan, Don. "Effectiveness of a Mail Questionnaire Technique in the Army." *Public Opinion Quarterly* 15 (Fall 1951): 575-78.

Clark, Peter B., and Wilson, James Q. "Incentive Systems: A Theory of Organization." *Administrative Science Journal* 6 (September 1961): 129-66.

Clausen, John A., and Ford, Robert N. "Controlling Bias in Mail Questionnaires." *Journal of the American Statistical Association* 42 (December 1947): 497-511.

Cobb, Roger W., and Elder, Charles D. "The Politics of Agenda-Building: An Alternative Perspective for Modern Democratic Theory." *Journal of Politics* 33 (November 1971): 892-915.

Constantini, Edmund, "Intraparty Attitude Conflict: Democratic Party Leadership in California." *Western Political Quarterly* 16 (December 1963): 956-72.

——. and Craik, Kenneth H. "Competing Elites Within a Political Party: A Study of Republican Leadership." *Western Political Quarterly* 22 (December 1969): 879-903.

Converse, Philip; Clausen, Aage; and Miller, Warren E. "Electoral Myth and Reality: The 1964 Election." *American Political Science Review* 59 (June 1965): 321-36.

——. Miller, Warren E.; Rusk, Jerrold; and Wolfe, Arthur C. "Continuity and Change in American Politics: Parties and Issues in the 1968 Election." *American Political Science Review* 63 (December 1969): 1,083-1,105.

Conway, M. Margret, and Feigert, Frank B. "Motivation, Incentive Systems, and the Party Organization." *American Political Science Review* 62 (December 1968): 1,159-73.

Crotty, William J. "The Social Attributes of Party Organizational Activists in a Transitional Political System." *Western Political Quarterly* 20 (September 1967): 800-15.

——. "The Utilization of Mail Questionnaires and the Problem of a Representative Return Rate." *Western Political Quarterly* 19 (March 1966): 44-53.

Cutright, Phillips. "Activities of Precinct Committeemen in Partisan and Nonpartisan Communitites." *Western Political Quarterly* 17 (March 1964): 93-108.

——. "Measuring the Impact of Local Party Activity on the General Election Vote." *Public Opinion Quarterly* 27 (Fall 1963): 374-86.

——, and Rossi, Peter H. "Grass Roots Politicians and the Vote." *American Sociological Review* 23 (April 1958): 171-79.

——, and Rossi, Peter H. "Party Organization in Primary Elections." *American Journal of Sociology* 64 (November 1958): 262-69.

DeMott, Benjamin. "Party Apolitics." *American Scholar* 31 (Autumn 1962): 595-602.

Donald, Marjorie N. "Implications of Nonresponse for the Interpretation of Mail Questionnaire Data." *Public Opinion Quarterly* 24 (Spring 1960): 99-114.

Dye, Thomas R. "The Local-Cosmopolitan Dimension and the Study of Urban Politics." *Social Forces* 41 (March 1963): 239-46.

Fiellin, Alan. "Recruitment and Legislative Role Conceptual Scheme and a Case Study." *Western Political Quarterly* 20 (June 1967): 271-87.

Flinn, Thomas A., and Wirt, Frederick M. "Local Party Leaders: Groups of Like-Minded Men." *Midwest Journal of Political Science* 9 (February 1965): 77-98.

Forthal, Sonya. "The Small Fry and the Party Purse." *American Political Science Review* 34 (February 1940): 66-76.

Franzen, Raymond, and Lazarsfeld, Paul F. "Mail Questionnaires as a Research Problem." *Journal of Psychology* 20 (June 1945): 293-320.

Frost, Richard T. "Stability and Change in Local Politics." *Public Opinion Quarterly* 25 (Summer 1961): 221-35.

Gluck, Peter R. "Research Note: Incentives and the Maintenance of Political Styles in Different Locales." *Western Political Quarterly* 25 (December 1972): 753-60.

Goodall, Leonard E. "Reform Politics in the Big City: The Phoenix Experience." *Western Political Quarterly* 16 (September 1963): 20-21.

Goodman, Leo A., and Kruskal, William H. "Measures of Association for Cross Classifications." *Journal of the American Statistical Association* 49 (December 1954): 732-64.

Gouldner, Alvin W. "How People View Their Role in the Organization:

Cosmopolitans and Locals." *Administrative Science Quarterly* 2 (December 1957): 282-92.

Gullahorn, Jeanne E., and Gullahorn, John T. "An Investigation of the Effects of Three Factors on Response to Mail Questionnaires." *Public Opinion Quarterly* 27 (Summer 1963): 294-96.

Hacker, Andrew. "The McCarthy Candidacy." *Commentary*, February 1968, pp. 34-39.

Harned, Louise. "Authoritarian Attitudes and Party Activity." *Public Opinion Quarterly* 25 (Fall 1961): 393-99.

Hays, Samuel P. "The Politics of Reform in Municipal Government in the Progressive Era." *Pacific Northwest Quarterly* 55 (October 1964): 157-69.

Herson, Lawrence J. P. "The Lost World of Municipal Government." *American Political Science Review* 51 (June 1957): 330-45.

Hirschfield, Robert S.; Swanson, Bert E.; and Blank, Blanche B. "A Profile of Political Activists in Manhattan." *Western Political Quarterly* 15 (September 1962): 499-506.

Hochstein, Joseph R., and Athanasopoulos, Demetrios A. "Personal Follow-Up in Mail Survey: Its Contribution and its Cost." *Public Opinion Quarterly* 34 (Spring 1970): 69-81.

Hofstetter, C. Richard. "Organizational Activists: The Bases of Participation in Amateur and Professional Groups." *American Politics Quarterly* 1 (April 1973): 244-76.

Ippolito, Dennis S. "Motivational Reorientation and Change Among Party Activists." *Journal of Politics* 31 (November 1969): 1,098-1,101.

——. "Political Perspectives of Suburban Party Leaders." *Southwestern Social Science Quarterly* 49 (March 1968): 80-115.

——, and Bowman, Lewis. "Goals and Activities of Party Officials in a Suburban Setting." *Western Political Quarterly* 22 (Septermber 1969): 572-80.

Jackman, Robert W. "Political Elites, Mass Publics, and Support for Democratic Principles." *Journal of Politics* 34 (August 1972): 753-77.

Jacob, Herbert. Initial Recruitment of Elected Officials in the United States." *Journal of Politics* 24 (November 1962): 703-16.

Jennings, M. Kent, and Niemi, Richard G. "The Transmission of Political Values from Parent to Child." *American Political Science Review* 62 (March 1968): 169-84.

——, and Thomas, Norman. "Men and Women in Party Elites: Social Roles and Political Resources." *Midwest Journal of Political Science* 12 (November 1968): 464-92.

Katz, Daniel, and Eldersveld, Samuel J. "The Impact of Local Party Activity Upon the Electorate." *Public Opinion Quarterly* 25 (Spring 1961): 1-25.

Kephart, William M., and Bressler, Marvin. "Increasing the Responses to Mail Questionnaires: A Research Study." *Public Opinion Quarterly* 22 (Summer 1968): 123-32.

Krause, Merton S.; Houlihan, Kevin; Oberlander, Mark I.; and Carson,

Lawrence. "Some Motivational Correlates of Attitudes Toward Political Participation." *Midwest Journal of Political Science* 14 (August 1970): 383-91.

Lane, Robert E. "The Decline of Politics and Ideology in a Knowledgeable Society." *American Sociological Review* 31 (October 1966): 649-62.

LaPalombara, Joseph. "Decline of Ideology: A Dissent and an Interpretation." *American Political Science Review* 60 (March 1966): 5-18.

Larner, Jeremy. "Jess Unruh and His Moment of Truth." *Harper's Magazine*, April 1971, pp. 62-68.

——. "Nobody Knows . . . Reflections on the McCarthy Campaign — Part I." *Harper's Magazine*, April 1969, pp. 62-80.

——. "Nobody Knows . . . Reflections on the McCarthy Campaign — Part II." *Harper's Magazine*, May 1969, pp. 71-94.

Levine, Sol, and Gordon, Gerald. "Maximizing Returns on Mail Questionnaires." *Public Opinion Quarterly* 23 (Winter 1958): 568-75.

Longworth, Donald S. "Use of a Mail Questionnaire." *American Sociological Review* 18 (June 1953): 310-13.

Lowi, Theodore J. "American Business, Public Policy, Case Studies, and Political Theory." *World Politics* 16 (July 1964): 677-715.

Luttbeg, Norman R. "The Structure of Beliefs Among Leaders and the Public." *Public Opinion Quarterly* 32 (Fall 1968): 398-409.

McClosky, Herbert. "Consensus and Ideology in American Politics." *American Political Science Review* 58 (June 1964): 361-82.

——. "Conservatism and Personality." *American Political Science Review* 52 (March 1958): 44-45.

——; Hoffman, Paul J.; and O'Hara, Rosemary. "Issue Conflict and Consensus Among Party Leaders and Followers." *American Political Science Review* 54 (June 1960): 406-27.

McDonagh, Edward C., and Rosenblum, Abraham L. "A Comparison of Mailed Questionnaires and Subsequent Structured Interviews." *Public Opinion Quarterly* 29 (Spring 1965): 131-36.

Merelman, Richard M. "The Development of Political Ideology: A Framework for the Analyses of Political Socialization." *American Political Science Review* 63 (September 1969): 750-67.

Mitchell, William C. "The Ambivalent Social Status of the American Politician." *Western Political Quarterly* 12 (September 1959): 683-98.

Mosher, William E. "Party and Government Control at the Grass Roots." *National Municipal Review* 24 (January 1935): 15-18, 38.

Mowry, George E. "The California Progressive and His Rationale." *Mississippi Valley Historical Review* 36 (September 1949): 239-50.

Moynihan, Daniel Patrick, and Wilson, James Q. "Patronage in New York State: 1955-1959." *American Political Science Review* 58 (June 1964): 286-301.

Mullens, Willard A. "On the Concept of Ideology in Political Science." *American Political Science Review* 66 (June 1972): 498-510.

Munger, Frank, and Blackhurst, James. "Factionalism in the National Conventions, 1940-1964; An Analysis of Ideological Consistency in State Delegation Voting." *Journal of Politics* 27 (May 1965): 375-94.

Neustadt, Richard E. "On Patronage, Power and Politics." *Public Administration Review* 15 (Spring 1955): 108-14.

Niemi, Richard G., and Jennings, M. Kent. "Intraparty Communications and the Selection of Delegates to a National Convention." *Western Political Quarterly* 22 (March 1969): 29-46.

Parker, John D. "Classification of Candidates' Motivations for First Seeking Office." *Journal of Politics* 34 (February 1972): 268-71.

Patterson, Samuel C. "Characteristics of Party Leaders." *Western Political Quarterly* 16 (June 1963): 332-52.

Pomper, Gerald M. "Ambition in Israel: A Comparative Extension of Theory and Data." *Western Political Quarterly* 28 (December 1975): 712-32.

——. "From Confusion to Clarity: Issues and American Voters, 1956-1968." *American Political Science Review* 66 (June 1972): 415-28.

——. "New Jersey Convention Delegates of 1964." *Southwestern Social Science Quarterly* 48 (June 1967): 24-33.

——. "New Jersey County Chairman." *Western Political Quarterly* 18 (March 1965): 186-97.

——. "Toward a More Responsible Two-Party System? What, Again?" *Journal of Politics* 33 (November 1971): 916-40.

Prewitt, Kenneth. "Political Socialization and Leadership Selection." *Annals of the American Academy of Political and Social Science* 361 (September 1965): 96-111.

Protho, James W., and Grigg, Charles W. "Fundamental Principles of Democracy: Bases of Agreement and Disagreement." *Journal of Politics* 22 (May 1960): 276-94.

Ranney, Austin. "Toward a More Responsible Two-Party System: A Commentary." *American Political Science Review* 45 (June 1951): 488-99.

Reichley, James. "The Last Stand of Accommodation Politics." *Fortune,* October 1968, pp. 124-27, 227-29.

RePass, David E. "Issue Salience and Party Choice." *American Political Science Review* 65 (June 1971): 389-400.

Roeher, G. Allan. "Effective Techniques in Increasing Response to Mailed Questionnaires." *Public Opinion Quarterly* 27 (Summer 1963): 299-302.

Rosenau, James N. "Meticulousness as a Factor in the Response to Mail Questionnaires." *Public Opinion Quarterly* 28 (Summer 1964): 312-14.

Rosenzweig, Robert M. "The Politician and the Career in Politics." *Midwest Journal of Political Science* 1 (August 1957): 163-72.

St. Angelo, Douglas, and Dyson, James W. "Personality and Political Orientation." *Midwest Journal of Political Science* 12 (May 1968): 202-23.

Salisbury, Robert H. "The Urban Party Organization Member." *Public Opinion Quarterly* 29 (Winter 1965-66): 550-64.

Sartori, Giovanni. "Politics, Ideology, and Belief Systems." *American Political Science Review* 63 (June 1969): 398-411.

Sayre, Wallace S. "Personnel of the Republican and Democratic National Committees: 1928-32." *American Political Science Review* 26 (April 1932: 360-62.

Schwartz, David C. "Toward a Theory of Political Recruitment." *Western Political Quarterly* 22 (September 1969): 552-71.

Seligman, Lester G. "Political Recruitment and Party Structure: A Case Study." *American Political Science Review* 55 (March 1961): 77-86.

Shields, Curran V. "A Note on Party Organization: The Democrats in California." *Western Political Quarterly* 7 (December 1954): 673-83.

Sorauf, Frank J. "Patronage and Party." *Midwest Journal of Political Science* 3 (May 1959): 115-26.

——. "The Silent Revolution in Patronage." *Public Administration Review* 20 (Winter 1960): 28-34.

Soule, John W., and Clarke, James W. "Amateurs and Professionals: A Study of Delegates to the 1968 Democratic National Convention." *American Political Science Review* 64 (September 1970): 888-98.

Weaver, Leon. "Some Soundings in the Party System: Rural Precinct Committeemen." *American Political Science Review* 34 (February 1940): 76-84.

Wiggins, Charles W., and Turk, William L. "State Party Chairman: A Profile." *Western Political Quarterly* 23 (June 1970): 321-32.

Wildavsky, Aaron B. "The Goldwater Phenomenon: Purists, Politicians, and the Two-Party System." *Review of Politics* 27 (July 1965): 386-413.

Wilker, Harry R., and Milbrath, Lester W. "Political Belief Systems and Political Behavior." *Social Science Quarterly* 1 (December 1970): 477-93.

Wilson, James Q. "The Economy of Patronage." *Journal of Political Economy* 69 (August 1961): 369-80.

——, and Banfield, Edward C. "Political Ethos Revisited." *American Political Science Review* 65 (December 1971): 1,048-62.

Wolfinger, Raymond E. "Why Political Machines Have Not Withered Away and Other Revisionist Thoughts." *Journal of Politics* 84 (May 1972): 365-98.

Wright, William E. "Ideological-Pragmatic Orientations of West Berlin Local Party Officials." *Midwest Journal of Political Science* 11 (August 1967): 381-402.

Zikmund, Joseph. "A Comparison of Political Attitudes and Activity Patterns." *Public Opinion Quarterly* 31 (Spring 1967): 69-75.

Newspapers

New York Times. January 1968 - December 1970.

Newark Evening News. January 1968 - December 1970.

Newark Star Ledger. January 1968 - December 1970.

Trenton Evening Times. January 1968 - December 1968.

Unpublished Materials

Bone, Hugh A. "Grass Roots Party Leadership." Seattle, Washington, 1952. Mimeographed.

Eagleton Institute of Politics. "Political Background Reports, 1970." New Brunswick, New Jersey, 1970. Mimeographed.

Gaby, Dan. New Democratic Coalition files.

Goetcheus, Vernon M. "The Village Independent Democrats: A Study in the Politics of the New Reformers." Unpublished Senior Distinction thesis, Honors College, Wesleyan University (Connecticut), 1963.

Jacek, Henry J. "The Urban Political World of Black and White Party Officials." Unpublished paper presented at 65th Annual Meeting of the American Political Science Association, New York, September, 1969.

Kavesh, Ruth F. "The History, Structure, Problems, and Prospects of the Montclair Democratic Party." Paper presented at the New York University Graduate School of Public Administration, New York, 20 January 1971.

Kurtzman, David H. "Methods of Controlling Votes in Philadelphia." Ph.D. dissertation, University of Pennsylvania. Philadelphia: Privately printed, 1935.

Sternleib, George; Beaton, Patrick; Burchell, Robert W.; Hughes, James W.; James, Franklin J.; and Listokin, David. *Housing Development and Municipal Cost.* New Brunswick, New Jersey: Center for Urban Policy Research. (Forthcoming.)

Interviews

Barbaro, Fred. Private interview, Maplewood, New Jersey, 19 January 1971.

Eldridge, Dorothy. Private interview, Montclair, New Jersey, 15 January 1971.

Gaby, Daniel. Private interview, Springfield, New Jersey, 29 December 1970.

Jacobson, Joel. Private interview, South Orange, New Jersey, 11 January 1971.

Johnson, Nate. Private interview, Montclair, New Jersey, 22 January, 1971.

Lapidus, Rick. Private interview, Princeton, New Jersey, 12 January, 1971.

Parsekian, Ned. Private interview, Hackensack, New Jersey, 15 January 1971.

Plaut, John. Private interview, Summit, New Jersey, 4 January 1971.

Rappeport, Michael. Private interview, New Brunswick, New Jersey, 18 January 1971.

Salmore, Steve. Private interview. North Bergen, New Jersey, 29 December 1970.

Samuel, Richard. Private interview, Westfield, New Jersey, 16 January 1971.

Schiller, Bunny. Private interview, Teaneck, New Jersey 8 January 1971.

Spiegler, Stuart. Private interview, Glen Rock, New Jersey, 30 December 1970.

Wenk, Betty. Private telephone interview, South Orange, New Jersey 13 January 1971.

Index